Postcolonial Literature Today

Postcolonial Literature Today

Jagdish Batra
&
Alan Johnson

Prestige Books International
Delhi : Sydney

Published by
Prestige Books International
New Delhi 110 060
email: prestigebooks@gmail.com

Associate Office
P.O. Box 2250, Sydney 2001

ISBN: 978-93-82186-60-1

Printed in India

Contents

Preface

This book, as a humble contribution to the genre of postcolonial studies, is an attempt to deal with the multiple thought patterns thrown up by the colonial and postcolonial experience undergone by societies which were colonized by one European nation or the other—a phase that started around five centuries ago. The postcolonial views have indeed influenced writers all over the world who have not only re-told history and literature, but also myths, legends and cultural practices which were underrated, neglected, misrepresented and even corrupted by the colonizers.

Postcolonial theory started taking shape around the 1960s, and more seriously with the advent of Edward Said's book *Orientalism* in 1978. In the 21st century, it has now reached a point where scholars are fiddling with coinages like 'post-postcolonialism' to signify the contemporary mood. We have a new world order in which the colonized countries of yore like India have come a long way. As a result, many of the postcolonial pedagogical tools and interpretative frameworks seem to have become obsolete. There are dilemmas with regard to the contradictory claims to authenticity held out by indigenous and diasporic narratives. The fractured native discourse is still dominated by the metropolitan speaker of English in the power structures of countries like India. Therefore, canonical literature is under attack for neglecting the subaltern. Indeed, it appears to be the right time to examine what shape the poetics and practice of postcolonialism is taking.

Concerns such as these brought us together to work on this anthology. As the work progressed, we found wide support for the idea behind this venture. We are obliged to a number of scholars from India, U.S.A. and other places, who have contributed to this compilation. Our grateful thanks to Dr. R.K. Dhawan for his unflinching support to the project, to Dr. Suman Bala for, as always, patiently going through the manuscript, and last but not the least, to M/s Prestige Books for bringing out the book in a record period of forty-five days only.

Jagdish Batra
Alan Johnson

Introduction

JAGDISH BATRA & ALAN JOHNSON

The essays in this volume cover a range of topics and authors, but share the main goal of postcolonial critique, namely, to examine noted works of non-Western literature—in this case, mostly from India—to show how these works present both formal and substantive alternatives to mainstream offerings. Whether the work in question is a novel by Amitav Ghosh, a poem by Kumaran Asan, or a film by Satyajit Ray, we come away, as these critics observe, with glimpses into lives and landscapes that are meaningfully different from ours, and that prompt us to see our world in new ways. As the overview of postcolonialism in the following essay indicates, and as we can see by the variety of topics on display here, it is an exciting time for the profession of literary studies.

A common theme in these essays is societal change wrought by both modern colonialism and, in the postcolonial era, an increasingly interconnected globe. If noted nationalist figures like Gandhi, Tagore and Ambedkar managed the difficult task of combining the best Indian and European ideas to better serve their country's immediate and pressing needs, today's leaders face the difficult challenge of articulating a vision of nation in a world not only far more culturally and economically globalized, but also the one in which India and other states constitute a long overdue alternative to European grand narratives. It is not, of course, that India, Afghanistan, Egypt, Sudan or Sri Lanka (the other four countries represented in this book) are only now finding a "voice," as some Western critics pretentiously assert. India has, after all, a far deeper and richer literary history than that of Europe. Rather, India's many voices—in fiction and film, music and scholarship—are now attracting broad and receptive audiences in the marketplaces of New York, London and Mumbai.

These new developments do not, of course, mean that the effects of colonialism are merely a past concern. As several essays in this volume observe, colonialism's effects permeate the post-colonial nation-state, especially its bureaucracy, military, educational and legal institutions. Moreover, as Frantz Fanon long ago warned, forms of internal colonization can also appear, a reality infamously on view in settler societies that have usurped indigenous lands (as in North America and Australia), but also in the Indian subcontinent. More pertinent to our literary focus is the fact that nations narrate themselves into being, and that this act of narration, as Homi Bhabha and others have observed, is always caught between competing urges—the need to speak for a homogeneous civic body but acknowledge its innumerable parts; the desire to cement and mythify distant pasts but, at the same time, to recognize the fragmentary nature of the past. This obviously presents storytellers with a predicament: How to honestly describe this ambivalence? Not unlike Arjuna's dilemma as he rides to the battle against his cousins, writers today must work through the dilemmas of representation, articulating voices from both the peripheries and the centers of their worlds. In their case, there is no wise Krishna-like counsel, but there are at least communities of readers with whom these texts, as Sudipta Kaviraj puts it, enact a "narrative contract" that implicitly stipulate its audience (33).

"Communities" in the plural form is crucial here, for, despite claims to the contrary, there can never be either a monolithic "people" or readership. There are, instead, multiplicities. Anti-colonial novelists therefore, to take one example, had to consciously choose their audiences (often elite ones) in the hope that they could activate that group's imagination to productive ends, as Bankim Chandra Chattopadhyay did. But as these writers' characters show, they were always aware of the multiple lives who, through the subject of a narrative, would never read it. By the postcolonial era, however, writers began to turn to other, more disparate readerships, and as they did so, they shaped both language and genre to their uses.

Because the success of the novel as a serious genre coincides with the rise of nation-states, and because the progenitors of postcolonial critique—Said, Spivak, Bhabha—have understandably treated the modern nation-state as tainted by its European pedigree, scholars tend to be skeptical of nationhood itself, and of the novel as a disinterested representation of that nationhood. Said usefully reminds us, for example, of even Jane Austen's brilliant parlor games that were part of Britain's imperial orbit. More to the point was Dickens's infamous condemnation of Indians following the 1857 war. The paradox, of course, is that these very texts, as Gauri Viswanathan has shown, became objects of colonial education that stirred the imaginations of colonial India's urban readers and writers, who would go on to use it, along with many other tools, to rally anti-colonial sentiment. Bengali "bilingual elite[s]," for instance, drew on both "modern English and classical Sanskrit" to craft a prose they believed was best-suited to the nationalist novel (Chatterjee 8). The particular challenge we face today, as Partha Chatterjee argues (echoing Bhabha's previously mentioned point), is that the postcolonial nation is pulled in different directions at once—on one hand, mainstream efforts to consolidate "the hegemonic project of nationalist modernity, and on the other, . . . the numerous fragmented resistances to that normalizing project" (13).

This last point returns us to the subject of subalternity that informs postcolonial studies, and also many of the essays here. The irony of relatively privileged academics celebrating texts by and about subaltern individuals—for example, Dalits and tribals—has not gone unnoticed. The danger, as we know, is a romanticizing of disenfranchised societies in the name of liberalism even as we—that is, we the relatively privileged—help sustain the very systems that exacerbate this inequality. Critics like Arif Dirlik and, more recently, Vivek Chibber have provided bracing attacks on postcolonial studies that have generated some healthy self-scrutiny among its practitioners. A common charge in these attacks is that the postmodernist, poststructuralist tenor of postcolonialism undercuts its avowed "radical critique" (2). Chibber defends the Enlightenment project's ideals, and his criticism is a mirror image of Aijaz Ahmad's Marxist censure, two decades ago, of Fredric Jameson and Edward Said. Both Chibber and Ahmad believe that postcolonial studies has devolved into a purely academic and diffused set of practices that no longer produce anything of note.

The essays in this collection are in many ways emblematic of this range of positions, with some advocating a holistic "Indian" outlook, others a variety of discrete strands, and yet others a coexistence of these two extremes. In our view, this does not mean, as Chibber claims, that postcolonial critique is therefore hopelessly fragmented. To the contrary, such variances attest to a robust interpretive practice that accepts the value of literary works that strive to articulate the unavoidable contradictions of their region's colonial-era and postcolonial experiences. To that end, we believe there is much to learn from the diversity of voices represented here.

II

In the essay "Postcolonialism and Indian Literary Scenario," Jagdish Batra rues the fact that while the craze with postcolonial theory in the Western academy continues unabated, the colonial hangover has still not dissipated in India, and that even now the effects of the "postcolonial" phase have not seeped widely into the intellectual arterial network, leave alone the general societal outlook. He starts with the history of postcolonial studies, pointing out how the leading lights of the movement, notably Aime Cesaire, Frantz Fanon, Edward Said, Homi Bhabha, and Gayatri Spivak, have influenced other movements, such as feminism, Marxism, and the study of nationalism. Batra also focusses on issues like subjectivity and nationhood and registers his disbelief at the suggestion of some scholars that the nation-state will wither away as the pace of globalization speeds up. Regarding Indian diaspora scholars in the West, he cautions against accepting their representations of postcolonial reality at face value.

In the second part of his essay, Batra attacks what he considers to be the general colonial mindset of Indian society. He then reviews briefly the Indian literature produced in English, selecting mainly those works produced during colonial and postcolonial times which show how even post-independence fiction in English continues to follow the colonial model because of the diffidence of Indian authors. He would also like Indian poetics and critical concepts to be applied and enriched in the context of postcolonial interpretation. More than the language, Batra feels that a greater sensitivity to the Indian ethos ought to be reflected in Indian literature to make it truly representative of Indian reality. He argues that the approach of Indian English literature remains that of an "outsider," in part because many writers are based abroad and have secondary media-based access to information about India. Even those located in India mostly reflect an elite metropolitan outlook that owes much to Western assumptions. He therefore feels that literature produced in regional languages is more representative of India's cultural richness.

Diane Yerka, while analyzing Amitav Ghosh's novels *The Hungry Tide* and *The Calcutta Chromosome*, finds that the author attempts to give voice to the "subaltern characters that are in some way silent, either by choice or by circumstances, but who retain power to control either their own lives or the experiences of other characters." Moreover, as an author, Ghosh considers it his right to represent the subaltern, and when Yerka argues where the character is inarticulate, Ghosh faithfully represents his silence that conveys more than words. It happens in case of Alu in *The Circle of Reason.* Yerka also finds silence in the secrecy of counter-science in *The Calcutta Chromosome*, describing how Phulboni and Murugan are attempting to affirm the role of a subaltern group within scientific history whose experiments culminate with the ultimate transmigration of souls. *The Hungry Tide* is another example of Ghosh's ability to weave silences into human relationships. Fokir, the subaltern protagonist, is silenced by the narrative itself, which is focalized through Piya, even as he is silenced because of the language barrier between him and Piya. Though a subaltern, Fokir does have power; he is the one who saves Piya in the beginning when she is thrown overboard into the sea, and again towards the end when the deadly cyclone hits the region. As Yerka points out, this gives them life without usurping their voices.

Dahood El-Oqla's essay on the Sudanese writer Tayyeb Salih'*s Season of Migration to the North* locates postcolonial hybridity of representation in the merger of Arabic narrative techniques with the Western literary genre of the novel. He finds, for instance, orality and the circularity of native narrative wedded to the experience of westernized characters who are unable to strike harmony between their traditional Sudanese identity on the one hand and their Western education and lifestyle on the other. El-Oqla describes the function of Arabic literary styles in the novel, such as *hakawati* and *Maqamat*. The *Maqamat* tradition prescribes the creation of two characters, wherein the "curiosity of one pushes the other to physically and psychologically follow the other in a demand to learn about his origin, life, and adventures."Thus, the unnamed narrator in this novel, who has returned from England after studying there for seven years, is thrown into the companionship of Sa'eed, whose wife Hosna he befriends later when Sa'eed disappears. The narrator had told umpteen stories about his stay in England and Sa'eed is called upon to re-live that experience that leads to his partial westernization. While he seeks to wreak vengeance on the English women for the colonial oppression, the power structure in Sudan smacks of internal colonization, with the widespread corruption in government robbing the masses of the benefits of development. In contrast, the novelist presents assertive Sudanese women in Bint Majzoub and Bint Mahmoud, who challenge the local patriarchs. As other essays in this volume make clear, India's postcolonial experience resembles Sudan's in that even though the colonizers cleared out during decolonization, they left behind a culturally colonized people—the elites and high government officials—who still think and speak like their colonizer.

The Orientalist narrative is a differentiated one, as is pointed out by Kelly Meyer in her essay "Lady Winterbourne in the Harem: Rewriting the Fantasy in Ahdaf Soueif's *The Map of Love*." The novel deals with the romantic relationship and later marriage of the British woman Anna to the Egyptian youth Sharif whose family is involved in the nationalist struggle. In this piquant situation, while Anna is the butt of ridicule in British society for her unconventional step in marrying a native, the Egyptian nationalists, on the other hand, question Sharif's commitment to the nationalist cause.

Meyer underlines the intertextuality in the novel, noting that Anna had acquainted herself with the actual travel accounts of British women Deff Gorden (of Titanic fame) and Anne Blunt, though Anna kept her mind open on the issue of inter-cultural exchanges. Anna could imbibe the native position to the extent that she questioned the British agenda and supported nationalist cause of the Egyptian people. She also fantasizes about travelling like them "dressed as a man" and without any restriction. Knowing that the native articulates himself in his own language, she learns Arabic, too. Indeed, as Meyer rightly concludes, "By loving Sharif and partnering with him in the Egyptian anti-colonial movement—leaving behind her former life to embrace a new one—Anna performs her own political act; she makes history. She blurs the lines between the political and the domestic, between the public and the personal, between history and romance, rendering the lines themselves irrelevant in the sphere of her own life."

Postcolonialism shares with postmodernism the tendency to flout boundaries, so that whether the medium is textual or visual, the narrative remains the same. In their article on Satyajit Ray and Goutam Ghose's films, Akaitab Mukherjee and Rajni Singh explore visual media as used by the acclaimed director to express ecological concerns. As the writers point out, both these movies "encapsulate the relevance of forest in Indian culture in post-independent and globalised world" and "recapitulate the kinship between nature and human nature in pre-colonial, colonial and post-colonial times."

In Ray's film *Aranyer Din Ratri*, four young men from Kolkata make a sojourn to Palamau forest to escape the tedium of routine life. The forest provides them relaxation and the chance to discover self, and Ray shows us the forest through their eyes. There are the normal prejudices which the city folk venture among tribals whom they consider to be uncultured, but the fact is that they are nearer nature. The movie is a study in how the changes in ecosystems brought about by man have impacted the lives of tribal people.

Goutam Ghose's film shows that the political independence of the country has not led to the dismantling of colonial power structures. We continue to mimic the political, cultural and economic models of colonizers. The film focuses on the trip like a prequel, until the character Amrita reaches a tribal village, where she comes to know about the education system, daily life and rituals of the tribals. She immediately sees the differences between them and her urban life. Her endeavour to help these poor tribals financially ends in fiasco when the police abruptly appear and arrest the leader of the community. The sudden raid in the forest and arrest without reason points to the violence of the state that mocks the ideals of democracy upon which our Constitution rests. How the depredation of ecosystem forces the forest dwellers to adopt the ways of consumerist culture is brought out effectively in the movie.

The postcolonial condition seeks emancipation from all types of subjugation—racial, sexual, social, cultural, etc. During colonial times, native mode of storytelling that included fantastic or supernatural events as a part of ordinary life became the victim of colonial subjugation when the European realist mode became the norm. Now, in its attempt to emancipate native culture from colonial shackles, the use of fantasy in postcolonial fiction is staging a comeback. Its function is not to create a disconnect with reality, but to present a heightened sense of reality, as Santwana Haldar shows in her examination of the writings of Salman Rushdie and Manoj Das.

Rushdie, for example, chose a vast stage for *Midnight's Children* and grandiosely projected the macro-reality of national concerns. In this narrative, fantasy is used to trace and uncover the hidden and the mystical. One needs to be reminded of Saleem's assertion: "Reality is a question of perspective; the further you get from the past, the more concrete and plausible it seems—but as you approach the present, it inevitably seems more and more incredible" (165). The bilingual Indian author Manoj Das, on the other hand, deals with common situations, often set in rural India, and is hardly concerned with political or national issues. His use of fantasy helps him to render the happenings in life from the perspective of the believers—as the felt experiences of rural characters, or the dreams and hallucinations of urban characters. In her examination of Das's stories, including "The Crocodile's Lady," Haldar underlines the writer's view that a fairy tale has the capacity to reveal some basic truths in life through its distinct images and powerful symbols, and as such can also serve the purpose of a realistic story in a more effective way.

Priyanka Lamba, in her essay on Khaleed Hosseini's novels *The Kite Runner* and *A Thousand Splendid Suns,* proceeds from the broader definition of "subaltern" as one who is segregated on the bases of colour or ethnicity; demographic, religious and political minority status; and/or gender. In *The Kite Runner*, Lamba observes that even a male named Hassan is raped by Assef because the former belongs to the subaltern Hazara community whereas the latter comes from the dominant Pashtun community. His onlooker friend Amir, also a Pashtun, is hurt but can do little except carry the guilt for the remainder of his life. This mutilation of subaltern selfhood is conflated with the external devastation of Afghanistan under Taliban militancy, which finds a bigger focus in Hosseini's second novel *A Thousand Splendid Suns*. The never-ending civil war impacts the lives of ordinary people, most of all the women who have to bear the brunt of these hostilities. They have no rights to education, decent life, a single caring husband or social status. The writer perceives inequities with anguish and urges us all to stand up to age-old prejudices of the powerful.

Amitav Ghosh, as noted above, has distinguished himself as a writer with multifarious interests, including history, environment, and science. Pier Paolo Piciucco, in his essay on *The Calcutta Chromosome*, reads the novel as historiographic metafiction, as Linda Hutcheon would have it. Piciucco also identifies the novel's intertextual connection to A.S. Byatt's *Possession*. An interesting feature of Ghosh's novel is that whereas the action takes place in all timeframes, Piciucco places the narrating voice in the "fourth time limit," or the "future beyond" (with "future" played out on a humanized computer). The essay also describes the novel's cyclical movements, mirror images of characters, and such other stylistic features. Thus, *The Calcutta Chromosome* displays more than one postmodern strategy, and

Piciucco is able to establish the novel as a "cocktail of genres, perspectives and characters, [which] deals with a painstaking research of identity."

Sakunthala A.I.'s essay focusses on Dalit literature, with special attention to the writings of Sree Narayana Guru and Kumaran Asan. Deriving inspiration from Guru's famous stance against evil caste prejudices, Sakuntala notes that Kumaran Asan composed powerful works of literature that remind us of the equality of all human beings. The essay also touches upon other figures of Malayali literature who espoused the cause of the casteless subalterns in Kerala society and elsewhere, including Kuruppan, Kumaraguru, Changampuzha Krishna Pillai, Edassery Govindan Nair, K. Sachidanandan, and C.K. Janu.

There is no doubt that modern Dalit writings challenge literary canons and have shifted our focus to the neglected, suppressed and marginalized aspects of Indian society. These works flout the rules of linguistic propriety, balance, restraint, and so-called decency by using words which Savarna (mainstream) poetics considers uncouth and rustic. Writers like S. Joseph, Narayan, and T.K.C. Vaduthala often retrieve forgotten words and phrases seldom used in mainstream literature. This is indeed a truly postcolonial way of giving voice to the voiceless, and is in sync with the postmodern defiance of classic binaries in mainstream society and literature. What is more, most of it being in their own language, subalterns in this case can better represent themselves.

In their analysis of extracts from tribal autobiography published in G.N. Devy's anthology *Painted Words*, Parvathi V. and K. Balraj note in their essay that Devy, apart from being a literary scholar, is renowned for his activism in support of tribal welfare. They observe that this groundbreaking anthology has given voice to nomadic writers, who present us with first-hand accounts of their marginalized lives. The essay examines four such autobiographies, by Kishore Kale, Laxman Mane, Atmaram

Rathod and Laxman Gaikwad. The picture that emerges is of a section of society suppressed in every possible way—socially, psychologically, economically, politically. Nomadic tribals have neither a fair opportunity for education nor the protection of their basic human rights, with the result that the narratives reveal a high level of fear, anxiety and alienation in these communities. While they are subject to widespread discrimination in society, many of these nomadic communities continue to sustain such outdated practices as polygamy. And yet they dare not mix up with others in society because their experience has not entirely been good. The purpose behind taking up such texts is to make society aware of its neglectful attitude to these people, who deserve a better deal. Even though the literature of the marginalized lacks in literary quality, it does supplement the mainstream literature and complete the picture. In this, the true function of literature is indeed fulfilled.

Shraddha Tripathi, in her essay "Cultural Interface in Jhumpa Lahiri's *The Lowland*," undertakes an important concern of the postcolonial criticism, which is locating the points of convergence and divergence in the cultural negotiation that takes place between the native and the diasporic in the contemporary globalized world. The novelist has also dealt extensively with the life experience of the diasporic couple in their native country—India—where another postcolonial feature in the form of conflict between state apparatus and radical subversive forces is played out. As in her novel *The Namesake*, in this novel too, Lahiri traces the cultural impact on the first generation migrant Gauri, as also on her daughter Bela. Tripathi concludes that despite all our talk of globalization sought to be achieved through common trade practices, cultural conflict between two societies—India and America in this case—is a hard reality that cannot be glossed over. Economics plays its part but even at the back of it, these are the beliefs, and values which always guide actions in the materialist world.

Sushil Gupta in his essay "Shehan Karunatilaka's *Chinaman: The Legend of Pradeep Mathew*: A Critical Response" discusses the quest-centred tale which is a blend of truth and lies that defy sifting. Real personalities hobnob with phantasms. Historical milestones meld into make-believe happenings. These Pirandellian ambiguities keep the tale oscillating between what's real and what's made up. Liberally peppered with witticisms and wisecracks, the novel keeps one under the spell like the wedding guest who was held by the greybeard loon.

Postcolonial criticism is not, of course, only concerned with the degradation of the individual, society, and culture in colonial times; it also looks at colonialism's lasting damage to nature. Internal colonial structures of power continue to play the same political games, at times prompted by international entities, to rape nature, even as the dire consequences of such attempts are clearly seen on the wall. Postcolonial ecocriticism, therefore, has emerged as a viable discipline, as Jagdish Batra reflects in his examination of recent Indian English fiction that highlights ecological concerns. The works studied in-depth include, inter alia, Amitav Ghosh's *The Hungry Tide*, Arundhati Roy's *The God of Small Things*, Kiran Desai's *The Inheritance of Loss*, Suravi Sharma Kumar's *The Voices in the Valley*.

D.P. Digole, in his article on "The Idea of Indianness in Indian English Literature" opines that the heterogeneity arising from a bewildering variety of races, religions, castes, cultures, and languages has sometimes helped, and also at other times hindered, the process of literary homogenization. This has, however, enabled the Indian scholar-critics to adopt a holistic perspective for looking at the various Indian language-literatures as a single entity unified by one living and continuous tradition. He finds one basic inspiration behind all great ancient works. Digole stresses the need for cohesion and reciprocity between the *bhasha* literatures and Indian English literature, whether original or translated, that nurtures the ideals of unity in diversity, cultural synthesis and pan-Indian character of India's literary labyrinth.

This compilation concludes with Rahul Jayaram's scholarly and elaborate write-up on the love-hate relationship between Subaltern Studies and Dalit literary movements. It deals with the issue of nationalism from the perspective of Partha Chatterjee's influential work *Nationalist Thought in the Colonial World: a Derivative Discourse?* Jayaram analyzes various strands of modern Indian historiography in order to make sense of the way the Subaltern project distinguishes itself, as he examines the group's complicated relationship with established paradigms.

These included the Nationalist, Marxist and Cambridge/Imperial "schools" of Indian historiography. Regardless of their validity, richness and weight, these histories also worked to insinuate particular predispositions. Thereby, colonialism as a process and the colonized as a subject, assumed character through imposed lenses. Such frameworks left little space for historical contingency. Such histories also undermined identity issues, which did not settle easily with prevailing paradigms. The 'subaltern' was rendered devoid of self-expression and self-representation. Subaltern historians projected the 'subaltern' as possessing an agency of his/her own. And these voices did not necessarily coincide with existing discourse. These points of departure, simultaneously, became the Subalterns' point of entry. Some of these are the nature of Indian nationalism, the role of the educated bourgeoisie, peasants and workers, colonialism and secularism, and casteism.

The *Subaltern Studies* volumes went on to include more contemporary literary accounts. These blurred and questioned notions of nationalism and colonialism in a post-colonial, independent Indian context. In the process of so doing, critics of the volumes questioned the 'native' status of the 'subaltern'? Wasn't this 'subaltern' as much a western product? Didn't the poor, illiterate, exploited peasant of rural India, depend on the crutches of a handful of Indian intellectuals under the influence of contemporary Western fashions? If the Subalterns charged the existing historiography of India as "elitist" and adopted Western models of understanding like "nationalism," couldn't the same accusation be charged against them as well? Questions such as these have been taken up in this interesting article.

Works Cited

Ahmad, Aijaz. *In Theory: Nations, Classes, Literatures.* London: Verso, 1992.

Bhabha, Homi K. Introduction: Narrating the Nation. *Nation and Narration*. Ed. Homi K. Bhabha. New York: Routledge, 1990. 1-7.

Chatterjee, Partha. *The Nation and Its Fragments: Colonial and Postcolonial Histories*. Princeton: Princeton UP, 1993.

Chibber, Vivek. *Postcolonial Theory and the Specter of Capital.* New York: Verso, 2013.

Kaviraj, Sudipta. "The Imaginary Institution of India."*Subaltern Studies VII: Writings on South Asian History and Society*. Delhi: OUP, 1992. 1-39.

Viswanathan, Gauri. *Masks of Conquest: Literary Studies and British Rule in India.* New York: Columbia UP, 1989.

Postcolonialism and the Indian Literary Scenario

JAGDISH BATRA

In the contemporary critical scenario, the debate on postcolonialism in the academy (in the West, of course) seems at variance with the ground reality in the formerly colonized societies like India. While the current craze with regard to the topic of discussion is post-postcolonialism, the empirical observations indicate that the colonial hangover has still not dissipated and even the phase called 'postcolonial' has not seeped widely into the intellectual arterial network, leave alone the general societal outlook. This is despite the interventions made from time to time by the likes of Homi Bhabha and Gayatri Spivak. The dichotomy is marked in the failure of the intellectuals to practise what they teach. The aim of this paper is to deliberate on this yawning gap and explore the possibilities of bridging it.

Before taking up the main issue, it would be appropriate to go over the premises and assumptions on which the edifice of Postcolonialism stands. That the term 'postcolonial' is an utterly woolly term is borne out by a cursory glance at the history of most nations of the world. Since times immemorial, countries and societies have or been invaded, held in bondage, liberated, etc. The invaders even got assimilated in the society they attacked. Going by this truism, even England was ruled by Rome for around 400 years before they withdrew, so the ancient epic *Beowulf* and other literary works can be looked upon as postcolonial! Colonialism thus becomes a "transhistorical thing, always present and always in process of dissolution in one part of the world or another, so that everyone gets the privilege, sooner or later, at one time or another, of being colonizer, colonized and postcolonial—sometimes all at once," as Aijaz Ahmad states (Mongia 283). However, viewing it from the contemporary context, he describes it as a "*global* condition between the West and the Rest" (ibid). The term 'Rest' however, should be read as the so-called Third world. A reductive way to define the postcolonial literature is to look at it as only the literature of resistance (Arun Mukherjee qtd. Sheshadri, p. 185), so that it becomes unimportant for the text to have been written in the historically postcolonial period. It could well have been written in the colonial times.

Regarding the temporal reference in the term 'post-colonial' (with a hyphen), even though the colonization has been practised since ancient times, for the purpose of our study, I shall focus only upon the second half of the twentieth century when the countries colonized by various European nations won their freedom. Most of the countries in what is commonly called the Third World were, as we know, colonized by one European country or the other—Britain, France, Germany, Italy, Spain, Portugal, etc. After the colonized countries of Asia, Africa, Latin America and the Caribbean got freedom through long struggles, they were obliged to re-build their ravaged nations. It was natural that the Third World writers should focus on both colonialism and its impact on native cultures. Among the many challenges facing postcolonial writers are the resurrection of their cultures and correction of misconceptions about them.

Postcolonial Studies is, therefore, concerned with the analysis of history, culture and literature of the former colonies of various European countries, produced during colonial and even postcolonial periods of history. The aim of this critical discourse is to find out the undue bias, if any, in favour of the colonizer. By 'undue,' we mean the political considerations that moulded these narratives which could be literary, filmic, historical or cultural. Besides, as a metanarrative, the postcolonial studies also deals with its own origin and development over time and space. Various questions like its global appeal and confrontation with neo-imperialism are also addressed here. An additional premise is that the study of postcolonialism has correspondence with the postmodernism which manifested itself around the same time.

It is now widely accepted that during their rule, the colonial masters studied the colonized societies with the motive of culturally dominating native population so as to better exploit them economically. The British scholars in India deliberately represented the colonized territories as mysterious and exotic, but at the same time, full of potential for exploitation. This was done with the intention of inviting their reluctant compatriots back home to come along to tighten the colonial grip on the colonized. At the same time, this assessment of the native people, subsumed under the broad category of Orientalism, was meant to assure the colonizers of their own superiority in terms of self/other binary. Therefore, the native people were portrayed as ignorant, irrational and sentimental. More than anything, the inhuman racist mentality of the colonizer comes to the fore here.

Restricting the field of resistance to colonization to India only, one finds that the organized Indian resistance to the British Raj first manifested itself in the First War of Indian Independence in 1857 which was suppressed by the colonizers. Thereafter, the stirring is felt around the turn of the century when Gopal Krishna Gokhale, Bal Gangadhar Tilak, Aurobindo Ghosh and others represented the popular resentment. It was left to Mahatma Gandhi to turn that resentment into a unique mode of nonviolent mass resistance. He was no mere fighter for independence of the country; he was a practising philosopher who tried the unique model of putting politics on moral grounds. Such a tool of resistance was unheard of. Also his emphasis on truth, though revered at the individual level since ancient times, was never practised at the collective level. Therefore, the struggle waged by him can be referred to as 'theoretical events' as Gyan Prakash would say (Gandhi 18). Gandhi practised scrupulously what he preached. Living an austere life like any poor Indian peasant was not a simple thing. In this, he was following the life-style of the ancient sages who guided the kings in India. That is why even though he could have easily installed himself as the first President of India, he refused to do so. Gandhi was also against the cultural domination of India by the British. He intentionally drew upon the indigenous terminology—*Ram Rajya, Swaraj, Satyagraha*, etc. His concept of *harijan* (son of God) for the caste-based subaltern tried to underline the equality of human beings. Sadly, the deeply entrenched casteist prejudices in Indian society degraded the term itself rather than imbibing its uplifting connotation.

While Gandhi's mode of resistance was appreciated and also imitated at some places, it was the Martinique-based author-politician Aime Cesaire whose term 'negritude' was first lapped up in the postcolonial discourse as a theoretical formulation. The term highlighted the cultural achievements of the coloured people and was meant to make people of African stock proud of their identity. The racial overtone of colonial oppression was underlined by Frantz Fanon in his book *The Wretched of the Earth* (1961).Colonialism, he felt, is not satisfied merely with "holding people in its grip and emptying the native's brain of all form and content. By a kind of perverted logic, it turns to the past of the oppressed people, and distorts, disfigures and destroys it" (169). In a similar vein, Albert Memmi stated in his book *The Colonizer and the Colonized* (1965): "The most serious blow suffered by the colonized is being removed from history" (Groden 757). Clearly, it was done by the colonizers to attribute to them a superior image and to infuse an inferiority complex in the natives whom they had defeated politically.

While these voices were being raised against the Western attempt to culturally dominate the colonized nations, the Palestinian immigrant philosopher in America, Edward Said's book *Orientalism* (1978) became the Bible of the Postcolonial critical theory. According to Said, the Western colonial powers had a biased approach to the understanding of the colonized which he called 'Orientalism.' The discourse of Orientalism circulated narratives about cruelty, sensuality, despotism, laziness and so on to constitute the 'Other' against which a positive identity of the colonizer could be constructed. The colonial discourse was meant to convince the native that his race was inferior to the race of the colonizer. Said viewed the postcolonial writing as a form of resistance to Orientalism. In another book *Culture and Imperialism* (1993), Said analyzed the rise of colonial discourse through culture and narrative and noted that the process of subordinating the native uses narratives to

> dispel contradictory memories and occlude violence—the exotic replaces the impress of power with the blandishments of curiosity—with the imperial presence so dominating as to make impossible any effort to separate it from historical necessity. All these together create an amalgam of the arts of narrative and observation about the accumulated, dominated, and ruled territories whose inhabitants seem destined never to escape, to remain creatures of European will. (159)

Later studies have focused on the linkage between Orientalism and Humanism which drew inspiration from the European Enlightenment in which the basic notion of man was delimited to a rational being. This approach was inherently racist and imperialist as Leela Gandhi expounds quoting theoreticians like Derrida (26). Renaissance humanism found its apogee in the state. None of the variants of this celebrated concept, viz., humanism bestowed rights on the animal kingdom nor did they recognize life in vegetation. It failed to recognize alterity and difference—something stressed by postmodernism and poststructuralism.

The theoretical edifice continued to rise with Homi K. Bhabha's concepts of hybridity, mimicry and ambivalence located in the colonial discourse which he elaborated in his book *The Location of Culture (*1994).Before that he had dealt with the issue of construction of the colonial subject in his celebrated essay 'Of Mimicry and Man: The Ambivalence of Colonial Discourse' (1984). The essay is an exploration of the relations and attitudes of the colonizers and the colonized. On the one hand, the colonial discourse sought to humanize the third world native *a la* Kipling's 'White Man's Burden' postulate; on the other, it hesitated in humanizing him fearing loss of hegemony. Thus, it led to the creation of a native who was partially anglicized. The notion of 'hybridity' is central to Bhabha's work, according to which a state of 'in-betweenness,' haunts the one who straddles two cultures: "In the ambivalent world of the 'not quite/not white,' in the margins of metropolitan desire, the *founding objects* of the Western world become the erratic, eccentric, accidental *objects trouves* of the colonial discourse—the part-objects of presence" (92).

Another important postcolonial critic Gayatri Chakravorty Spivak in her influential essay 'Can the Subaltern Speak?' (1983), questioned whether people in subordinate, colonized positions are able to have a voice. Her argument is that the subaltern cannot speak for him/herself because the very structure of colonialism prevents the speaking. For the colonized woman, this is even more difficult because the double bind of colonialism and patriarchy represses her severely: "If, in the context of colonial production, the subaltern had no history and cannot speak, the subaltern as female is even more deeply in shadow" (Bertens 212). The female subaltern simply cannot represent herself. Spivak also cautions against homogenizing and thus 'essentializing' the subject and points out that the colonized subaltern *subject* is very heterogeneous and that there cannot be any comparison in the situation of a western woman and the one belonging to the Third World. She challenged postcolonial theory to address the silencing of women and other subaltern subjects not only by and in colonial discourses but also in postcolonial responses to those discourses.

Poststructuralist thinker Foucault's concept of 'epistemic violence' is relevant here. Violence had been the natural tool of the colonizer which he used to subjugate the native people. But more damage was done to the native culture through epistemic violence, which led to the destruction of non-western ways of knowing and resulted in dominance of western ways of understanding. There is no doubt that during the colonial rule, the colonizers foisted western epistemologies on the colonized. Postcolonialism, therefore, seeks to dislodge Eurocentric norms of literary and artistic values, or to 'provincialize Europe' as Dipesh Chakrabarty would say, and to expand the literary canon to include colonial and postcolonial writers. The writers here are not only the ones born in post-colonial era but those who question the colonial norms of creating literary canon. They ought to be included in the canon by virtue of their calibre and not excluded because of their anti-imperialist stance.

Foucault's formulation of discourse, on which Said relies, explains that it is through the control of the discourse that cultural imperialism mainly produces its malleable subjectivities. Indeed, as some postcolonial critics have pointed out in the British literature of 18th and 19th centuries, colonial exploitation exists as a steady and unobtrusive undercurrent. Later postcolonial writers have marked the colonizer-colonized matrix within the self-governed nations also, where the centre, having inherited a colonial apparatus, is likened to colonizer and those at the periphery, as for example, women and weaker sections of society being compared to the colonized. The exploitation on the basis of caste, creed, sex, race and sexuality is now condemned as 'internal colonization.' The Postcolonial theory attempts to recover the subaltern history/ literature as against those of the upper classes. In India, the focus on Dalit literature is the result of this movement.

While studying these aspects, one is bound to come across old theories and approaches being re-written under the impact of Postcolonialism; these include feminism, Marxism, nationalism, multiculturalism, etc. Feminism and Postcolonial theory started out together but differences could be evinced later between them. Whereas postcolonial theory focused on the plight of the women during colonial and postcolonial times in the decolonized societies, the feminist theory took the Western woman as its benchmark. The object of study was the impact of colonialism (read racism) on the non-white, non-Western woman in the postcolonial world where social stratum and cultural setting were and are different. In India, for example, women had been involved in all religious rituals along with men in almost equal fashion. They were highly talked of in religious scriptures but also degraded in some ancient books. At the same time, patriarchy seeped into the family system in a big way during the time India was enslaved by the Muslim invaders, and has stayed on ever since. As Partha Chatterjee and others have noted, Indians under the British rule intensified their conservative (mostly male-oriented) practices, such as purdah, as a means of ostensibly safeguarding their culture.

The feminine metaphor was also used in the postcolonial discourse as the theoreticians discovered that the colonizers assessed the native as woman-like who had to be husbanded. Ironically, critics like Ashis Nandy found Gandhian mode of peaceful resistance as effeminate even as Gandhi believed the moral overtones of it to be fit only for the brave. During the Indian freedom struggle, women took part along with men in a commendable manner which did impart a sense of equality with men to them. Several movements by social reformers like Jyotiba Phule, Dayanand Saraswati et al stressed the importance of education for the girl child and decried practices like Sati, child-marriage, etc. However, the Indian family system in which women remained mostly in self-denial mode was still upheld as the ideal one by the leaders of resistance. Patriarchy indeed is a big issue in India and postcolonialism takes on this aspect in a legitimate way. Postcolonial feminism likes to avoid talking of all women as a homogeneous group where no differences in terms of race, class, etc. exist and insists on marking the socio-cultural specificities.

The lack of concern for heterogeneity is also the motivation behind postcolonial theory as it intersects with Marxism. It finds Marxism problematic on account of the latter's lack of tolerance of difference in society which it envisions as a homogeneous working class formation. The Marxist theory explains the process of colonization as issuing out of the twin phenomena of modernization and industrialization, because these needed procurement of raw material and labour from outside Europe. The search for trade routes was also impelled by the desire to exploit resources and manpower belonging to other nations which were not militarily so strong. Colonialism by various European nations began soon after the discovery of the sea-route to India and America.

Marx viewed the entire world through the lens of economics and categorized classes without any concern for socio-cultural differences. Poststructuralism which forms the bedrock of postcolonialism is against negation of differences. It looks upon it as the zenith of capitalism and does not go into the accompanying process of political and cultural hegemony. As Frederic Jameson argues, stymying the growth of colonies is not touched upon by the Marxist theories of imperialism, and what is more "everywhere contradicted by them, where they raise the matter at all" (Deane 47). Using the yardstick applied earlier to feminism, it can also be observed that both Marxism and Postcolonialism suffer from Eurocentrism and the academics based in the West write about the people and literature of the postcolonized societies from the Western standpoint only.

Debating Nationhood

A fallout of the interface with conventional Marxism and current globalization has been the rise of belief in the immateriality of nation. There is no denying the fact that the 'nation' as a form of political unit practised today has come from the West. The Greek city states were small self-contained units which presented models of small democratic states. But the nation is a much larger unit today with heterogeneous groups of people deciding to come together as in a democratic set-up, or being forced to co-exist, as in a dictatorial dispensation, to assume the form of a political unit. The common denominators of land, culture, race, history, etc. do help but are not entirely necessary for it, as most political thinkers agree.

While the ancient civilizations like India and Egypt are believed to have had this notion[1], the feeling of loyalty to one's nation came into sharp focus in Europe during the empire building phase. This feeling was spurred by ruling elites in different European countries to score over one another in expanding empires which brought a sense of prestige or self-aggrandizement to them. Nation, seen thus, was a bye-product of the process of empire-building.

In the postmodern world today, the very concept of nation has come under fire on account of globalization and it is felt that the nation is an imaginary construct only. Benedict Anderson in his book *Imagined Communities* calls it "imagined community" because even though there are material conditions like common language or race, the notion remains substantially imaginary. Paul James dubs it as an "abstract community" (34) because of the impersonal nature of nation in which not everybody meets everybody else. The majoritarian rule is considered akin to the colonizer and the suppressed communities like Dalits, women, religious and racial minorities, etc. are identified as colonized. The advocates of the concept of nation point out that even though the differences are sacrosanct for the Postcolonialists, for any collective formation such as a nation, differences have to be reconciled to some extent and majority principle is the only tool available for the functioning of a democracy.

Globalization today is also looked upon as a euphemism for a new type of colonialism taking roots which is rightly called neocolonialism and whose sustaining base is the global consumerist culture. It would indeed be naïve to believe that what the UNO or even the loftiest of humanist movements have failed to achieve, the McDonald or Wal-Mart culture would achieve, viz., the unity of culture for all mankind. In fact, the phenomenon of globalization has meant a decentred and deterritorialized activity. There could be multiple rather than one centre structuring the multinational operations of a corporate catering to consumer demand. Also its production bases could be spread all over the globe so that the raw material procured from Mozambique could be transported to China for being turned into a finished product to be shipped to Malaysia or India for repackaging, storage and onward delivery to a distribution network in Dubai controlled by the regional office of the US-based corporate at Singapore! An important aspect of this type of functioning of the MNC's is a remarkable lack of control of host governments over its policies. By the sheer size of these corporates, they dominate governments of small nations and indeed prevail upon even the big governments in matters of fiscal policies which are sought to be distanced from political ideologies of host countries, the sole concern of the corporate being its own profit only.

In keeping with the postmodern ethos, however, the global is juxtaposed with the local, therefore the field of 'area studies' too has come up in which the sense of place is the foremost element in focus because it is felt that cultural moorings are tied to land only. This co-positioning of the global and local may not always be a happy marriage into 'glocal,' for as experience shows, there are ample grounds for conflict too between the two extremities.

It would be pertinent here to regard one of the leading post-modernists, Jurgan Habermas's views on the issue of emerging world order. Habermas talked enthusiastically of the post-national situation as he evinced it in the emergence of the European Union. He also espoused the old favourite shibboleth of 'world citizenship' the time for which had come, according to him, following the rise of the United States as the sole super power. He, of course, rooted for the European experience against the American 'imperialism' even as he found the meeting point for both parties in human rights.

Habermas looked at France, Germany and the Benelux countries (what he called 'core Europe') as setting the agenda for the broader European Union. In an essay that he wrote with Jacques Derrida, he listed the essentials: secularism in politics, role of the state in controlling the destructive power of capitalism, a "proper sense of cynicism about the possible achievements of technological progress (Europeans having a keen sense of the 'dialectic of enlightenment'), and the desire for a multilateral and legally regulated international order within the framework of a reformed United Nations" (Menon 318).

However, the experience hitherto holds little hope of growth of the envisioned model, what with internal suspicions, inequalities and dissensions within Europe. One of the founding principles of modern democratic nations is secularism as it enables the populace to transcend the religious barrier to savour the common nationalist feeling. It has been seen, however, that with the rise of the postmodern globalism, the religious sentiment too has risen in reaction and at several places across the world, religious fanaticism has taken the form of terrorism.[2]Under these circumstances, how secularism will gain ground enough to call the shots remains unpredictable.

The idea of 'core Europe' will naturally find few buyers among rest of the European nations. One has only to look at the growing number of disenchanted countries, particularly of erstwhile East Europe, which believe that the EC dispensation favours a few at their cost. Nivedita Menon remarks, "What the debate on post-nationalism in the European context alerts us to, is the fact that the assertion of a grand identity that transcends 'smaller' identities is necessarily insensitive to the powerless and the marginal, even when articulated in the best traditions of the Enlightenment—or perhaps especially then" (Boehmer& Chaudhuri 319).

The Marxist position envisioning the withering away of state has indeed few takers in the world today. It is like any other lofty ideal which is incapable of being translated into reality *in toto*. Marxism has underlined the status and importance of the working class and assured that this class will not be ill-treated, but no one can deny that nationalism, even if "theoretically 'outmoded,' still constitutes the—the albeit forgotten—revolutionary archive of contemporary postcolonialisty" (Gandhi 113). And let us not forget the colonizers of yore who preach the outdatedness of the nation were themselves fired by nationalist cause when they set out to expand and consolidate empire.

It is also a fact that the number of nation states is on the rise and not decline. The super-national organizations like the European Union have not been able to replace any nation-state or act on their behalf with a free hand. As no alternative to the idea of nation is proposed, this kind of Postcolonialist stand remains somewhat theoretical and impractical. The charge that the postcolonial state has become a replica of the colonial state is not tenable in all cases. The colonizer did not enlist the subjects as participatory force in the colonial power structure but in the contemporary democratic societies the participatory system is open to all adults. There is also the rule of law and the representative legislatures which give voice and security to the people at large. This is not to deny the problems that are faced like the use of force or allurement to get votes at the time of general elections. There is no country in the world where all sections of society feel free from the hegemony of the powerful through overt or covert means like a hegemonic discourse.

Diaspora & Globalism

The discipline of postcolonial studies encompasses the study of diaspora also. While in the colonized period, forced migration of labour was common, after the collapse of colonies, the phenomenon of migration of economically weaker people to rich countries started. Alongside, there was migration due to harassment of people who had politically antagonistic views vis-à-vis the establishment in their home countries. The postmodern times have seen the phenomenon of voluntary migration in the hope of accessing greener pastures.

As these people migrated to alien societies, the cultural integration with the host societies became a problem. For one, it was the realization that the 'home' was a mythic place. Even if they returned for a while to their native land, it was to be a temporary sojourn and they had to live with an 'imaginary homeland' as Salman Rushdie puts it. Derek Walcott's formulation of 'double consciousness' beautifully explains their state of mind. The longing for the left homeland and the resistance to being gobbled up culturally by the host society sums up the predicament of the diasporic.

Their maladjustment is traced to the inability of the host society to allow the immigrants to practise their lifestyle without let or hindrance on one hand, and the refusal of the first generation immigrants to drastically change their ways to correspond to the culture of the adopted homeland. Postcolonial literature is concerned with it seeks to suggest patterns to overcome the problem which is getting more and more in focus due to the transformation of the world into a global village. Homi Bhabha's concepts of hybridity, in-betweenness, liminality, etc. have come in handy for the discussion of the condition of the migrant. Diaspora Studies is now treated as part of the cultural studies.

For the Western academy, the so-called Third World literature originates from the diasporic writers who have migrated from different countries and scholars like Arif Dirlik hitch the beginning of Postcolonialismto the arrival of the Third World academics in Western academies. Multiculturalism, therefore, forms the main plank of this writing. Also termed as minority literature in the Western metropolitan academies, it feeds the non-canonical stream. The metropolitan attitude to this literature is one of condescension because it serves as a foil to the mainstream literature there.

The diasporic today is much different from the diasporic of yesteryears who was really a destitute and a victim of the colonizer's greed. If the diasporic intellectual situated in the Western academia projects himself as a victim, it is broadly seen as an act of opportunism only, because there are others who continue to struggle back home under a dispensation that is to some extent a pale copy of the colonial ruler.

The Indian diasporic writers who are taken to be representative of India are the metropolis-based writers, rooted at several removes from their native land in terms of time and space; their writing has been found deficient in reflecting the concerns of the native people. There are the descendants of the once migrant people who are now firmly ingratiated in the milieu of their adopted land. How can one expect from them the authentic representation of the native condition? Indeed, there are allegations of 're-Orientalism'—a new form of Orientalism shaped not by the Occident but by the Indian or South Asian diaspora in the West, as Lisa Lau and Om Prakash Dwivedi assert in *Re-Orientalism and Indian Writing in English.*

The Issue of Identity

One must agree with Homi Bhabha that perpetual migration is the general human condition, but at the same time and in contemporary setting, "only the privileged among the migrants can have a life of constant mobility and surplus pleasure" (Aijaz Ahmad qtd. in Mongia 289). Ahmad also points to the issue of identity which has gained prominence due to the celebrated notion of cultural differentialism and cultural hybridity that cultural criticism has come to underline as the consequence of Postcolonialism. This cultural identity, when stressed too far, leads to identity politics which "produces those many protofascisms that are stalking the world, from Iran to the former Yugoslavia, and from France to India" (ibid).

The pride in one's racial and national identity leads to a mindset that denigrates the other races and nationalities. If ever one were to go by reason, one would realize that the migration of people has always been there in history. Dreaming of purity of race or culture is a reverie. Then, such dreamers have a fixed notion of history from which they cull out their icons to venerate, fetishes to cherish and ideals of life to emulate. While trying to impose these on contemporary reality, they forget that history is always in a flux and when they take out these models, they do not for a moment realize the transformation taking place at that time. What is sought to be planted now is a congealed and solidified moment detached from its organic life, as Nissim Ezekiel would say of the process of writing poetry.

Postcolonial theory shows an abiding concern with the formation of the colonial and post-colonial 'subject'—a reincarnation of the old 'self' which suggested a measure of autonomy. How this subject conceives its identity and perceives the world around it is the subject of study here. The destruction of native languages and literatures through the imposition of western education was a clever move to convince the native of the latter's inferiority. The postcolonial writer would bring to light this fact and thus let the 'subject' understand his real identity.

Identity, as has been explained by the Postcolonialists like Said and Bhabha is relational. The self/other binary ought to be viewed in the deconstructive spirit—without prioritizing one term over the other. Moreover, in these times, the concept of identity has been proved to be an instable and shifting one. Therefore, it is meaningless to fix our identity in a unidirectional way as dished out by the colonizer of yore. As Bhabha has pointed out, the iterative acts of reinforcing such an identity only go to prove the inherent weakness of this discourse.

Our discussion of postcolonialism will not be complete without reference to the idea that postcolonial literature and theory have so far been strongly influenced by theorists primarily originating from the Middle East and Indian subcontinent. Many of their insights and concepts regarding postcolonial writing cannot, however, be transferred to other regions, like the settler societies. Accordingly, it is likely that African, Caribbean, Hispanic, and Irish voices, among others, give postcolonial literature and theory new vistas.

What Next?

Postcolonialism should ideally seek to take the academia out of the colonial straitjacketing of mind and provide it with the necessary insight to deal with the reality from an objective standpoint. That should mean mutual respect—a notion inherent in the term 'Postcolonialism' which hints at the world having moved beyond the colonial phase and the thinking tied to it. The recrimination over past injustices can be bloated to any extent. One could even ask for apology from the erstwhile colonizers. If Japan can demand and get apology from America for the wrongs done to it during WWII, the erstwhile colonized countries may also have a right to demand apology and compensation from the erstwhile colonizers.

Leela Gandhi concludes her brilliant book *Postcolonial Theory: A Critical Introduction* with the observation: "In its reflective modality, thus, postcolonialism also holds out the possibility of thinking our way through, and therefore, out of the historical imbalances and cultural inequalities produced by the colonial encounter. And in its best moments it has supplied the academic world with an ethical paradigm for a systematic critique of institutional suffering. So, after such knowledge, what forgiveness" (176).The post-postcolonial is said to be beyond the recrimination and revenge that informed the writing of the early postcolonial period, for the writer now, there is no implied European reader. Therefore, the writers are turning to themes which concern the present status of native societies. However, it would be wrong to assume that the Indian writer is not motivated by the desire to cater to the western reader. Despite the growing readership within India, readers in other countries who read English or translations in other languages form a sizeable market to which the Indian writers try to cater, as a critic avers, "On one hand, these writer write for and about the natives, but on the other hand, they have to include a wider audience in order to earn a decent living and reputation" (Deena 96). However, a writer is expected to be true to himself and not play to the gallery.

Looking at the colonial period as a transaction has been suggested by a section of the academia. The argument is that we have to move forward and not to get stuck at a point, so we ought to look at the colonial period as a negotiation between the colonizer and the colonized in which both sides gained something. While the colonizer exploited the native people and their resources to fuel the industries back home, the colonized were helped to usher in modernism through establishment of railways, industries, colleges, democratic institutions, etc. The ambivalent attitude of the colonizer reflected in the colonial texts is feted to buttress this viewpoint. Boehmer points out, "It was never as invasively confident or as pompously dismissive of indigenous cultures as its oppositional pairing with postcolonial writing might suggest" (4). Indeed, Western scholars like Jones, Charles Wilkins, Camille Bulcke, George Abraham Grierson, Ralph Lilley Turner, et al studied Indian languages and literature seriously, even as William Jones had the sub-agenda, "to domesticate the Orient and thereby turn it into a province of European learning" (Joshi 126).

There is no doubt that finally the decolonized nations have to put the past behind them and concentrate on development with the assistance of the technologically advanced West. Even otherwise, going back in time, no nation probably would have a history of being totally free of any external aggression or a period—short or long—of colonial repression, or having herself never been in the position of an invader. Culture, however, takes its own course of development and there is no way a line can be drawn at the re-examination of the past. The goal seems to be the postcolonial postnational dispensation at the global level. While the Marxists envision such a utopia on the basis of dissolution of state, the postcolonialists build the scenario on the basis of postmodernism which itself is highly dependent on commercial globalism with its digital revolution and corporate empire building. Be that as it may, the term post-postcolonialism as suggested by some scholars is an awkward choice for the simple reason that before long, need might be felt to define an even later phase. Shall we then coin the term 'post-post-postcolonialism'?

II

The Indian Scenario

The postcolonial writer of the initial phase in India was more concerned about debunking the Orientalist myth created by the colonizers. At the same time, he actually copied the metropolitan English of England thus proving Homi Bhabha's thesis of mimicry. The recurrent topic of academic debate is how a subaltern subject who writes in a European language can manage to challenge and fight against the very discourse which has moulded his subordinate identity. There is real concern about whether the subaltern can express himself in the colonizer's language. It has helped bring value to what was hitherto disparaged as vernacular. The use of culture-specific terminology from the native languages had always been there in English literature produced by the Western writers or the native ones, the only difference being its growing magnitude which shows the native writer is no longer hooked to the colonizer's English and can devise and use his own English rather confidently.

However, this is only half-truth. It is like showcasing of the ethnic food at high-end hotels. The truth is that in postcolonial societies like India, the structures of power have been controlled by the English-speaking elite. English is admittedly the language of power. It is a common sight to see people occupying seats of power—most of all the politicians—lament the domination of English language and vociferously espouse the cause of the regional languages (dubbed 'vernacular' by the colonialists), but send their children to English-medium schools within or better even outside the country.

Ordinary people too are attracted to use English words in plenty, courtesy the visual media. It is estimated that the Indians might soon be the largest number of English language users as a single nationality the world over. That should give us a measure of confidence in using English in our way. In fact, the British linguist David Crystal is on record as having stated that the future accent of English will be decided by the Indians. Now, while the people from the settler colonies like America, Canada and Australia do not mind speaking English in their own way, we in India still go by the British standard. Enormous amounts of money are spent to install language labs in schools to guide students to speak like the Englishmen even though we know it cannot be practically possible to copy them to the fullest extent. On the other hand, it creates problem for ordinary school children, sometimes taking the form of life-long diffidence. Why can't we think of speaking English confidently the Indian way, of developing the long suspended General Indian English project, and even rationalizing spelling as Americans have done?

In this, the colonial mindset of our countrymen is also to blame to a great extent. Before the English colonizers withdrew from colonies, they had painted the colony in their colours so that even after their withdrawal, educational institutions teaching English (and which ones are not teaching it?) continued to contribute to their coffers through payments for the original texts of English writers as also the critiques which were published in Britain. The orientalist discourse of the colonial times efficiently worked its way on the Indian psyche. The native texts translated into English at that time or even now take precedence over any translation done by native Indians. This is true of even our ancient philosophical and scriptural texts which the Indians by virtue of their having been born in the native culture should be best entitled to explain.

There is an additional concern expressed with regard to the area of research in English literature. There is widespread concern over non-inclusion of any Indian university in the top 200 ones in the world. While it is to the point to seek to sharpen the research and development capabilities of educational institutions in the country, it is known that the top list is readied by people in Europe and America and a kind of neo-colonial political manoeuvring is suspected at times as it in case of awards given to literary works at the international level.

The question that often crops up in the Indian context is: Have we really experienced Postcolonialism? Are we, in our attitude, conduct and creativity out of the colonial phase? An honest answer would be 'No.' Our standards of judgement with regard to common day-to-day life, cultural representations and guiding philosophies of life continue to be imported from the West. In fact, the agenda for intellectual orientation and growth as also and interpretation of the theory has been with the West. The non-West merely laps up whatever is dished out to it, and it is despite the Saids and the Bhabhas!

While in the academic institutions in India, the postcolonial literature forms an important and essential area of study, its study in the West includes the non-canonical and the marginal only. Our problem in the understanding of the Indian postcolonial is in the words of Dipesh Chakrabarty the 'asymmetric ignorance' where "third world scholars feel compelled to read a wide variety of Western texts, but Western scholars of Postcolonial Studies feel no such compunction to 'know' third world texts" (Boehmer and Chaudhuri 8). The fact is that whether it was Marx or Derrida or Foucault, the world ended for them with Europe. Leela Gandhi underlines this lack in the reckoning of Western scholars: "Thus, while Derrida brilliantly details the internal inadequacies, betrayals and elisions of what he calls the system of 'Western metaphysics,' he neglects adequately to theorize those external factors or civilisational Others which render this system unalienably 'Western.' So also, Foucault's scrupulous attention to the discursive structures and order of Western civilization remains culturally myopic with regard to the non-European world" (72-73).

Even as the academics debate the evolution of 'post-Postcolonial,' we in India at least can see the colonial mindset at work in all areas. From that standpoint, the pre-fix 'post' in post-colonialism does not seem to indicate any forward movement over colonialism. How this colonial mindset works can be in seen the way we make fun of the use of English language by ordinary Indians. Nissim Ezekiel's 'very English' poems are a case in point. Similarly, Anurag Mathur's novel *The Inscrutable Indian* uses this type of Indian-English throughout his novel to project a protagonist who cannot speak English correctly. No doubt, the language used herein reflects the reality but it also shows how fastidious we are with regard to a foreign language which will not be the case if we were using Hindi or any other Indian language. One wonders what our anglophile writers have to say about the phenomenon of creolization!

A key feature of postcolonial literature is its differentiated texture. The experience of each society with the colonization has been different. Therefore, what is relevant to Australia might not be true of India and so on. This feature sits comfortably with the contemporary perception of 'postcolonial' being an all-enveloping term that captures all that was previously viewed as the Other. Now, this term 'Other' is also applied to the literature that exists on the margins and is not considered canonical. Speaking about the literature written in English, it can be said that this language of the colonial times, in the hands of the colonized did not and certainly could not have remained the language that it once was. Also the time when postcolonial literature started being written is important for this study. In the 21st century, postcolonial writing is considered to be deregulated and anarchic as Boehmer notes: "The postcolonial therefore is associated with the metropolitan, diasporic, migrant, and minority spaces for which the nation as a horizon of expectation has retreated, to be replaced with the concepts of the anarchic [!] postcolony, the transgressive trans-local, and the infinitely co-optable multicultural" (247).

This tendency to go in for a certain anarchic writing practice cannot be viewed as a generalized phenomenon, as Emma Dawson Varughese avers in her study *Beyond the Postcolonial: World Englishes Literature*. Her critique focusses on the linguistic aspect of some fictional works produced in different countries, which she banks upon as markers of native culture gaining prominence in literary production there. True, language is a decisive marker of a culture but not the only one that subsumes all disparate strands of culture. There is the lifestyle pattern and the philosophy of life, decidedly of more import. The search for the postcolonial should impel us to include sociology, politics, history, etc. It would stand to reason to go along with Couze Venn when he states: "They [fields of study] overlap on the terrain of cultural theory, itself an eclectic bundle of concepts and theories from semiotics, literary studies, philosophy, ethnography, sociology, history, psychoanalysis assembled in opposition to conventional or authoritative protocols for describing the socio-cultural world" (6)

Even as I differ with Varughese in her identifying language as the sole marker of a culture, I shall go along with her broad premise of postcolonial writing: ". . . the multiple features that determine the voice of a World Englishes [postcolonial] writer are not defined by the notion of the voice being that of the subaltern—whether geographic, linguistic, cultural, ideological or all of the foregoing. World Englishes writers are less and less interested in their putative subalternity to a former colonial power and more and more interested in what constitutes (usually), positively, the identity of the culture from within which they write" (20).

The language aspect is a rather smaller symptom of the malady of anglophilia; there are other bigger problems. Literary evolution anywhere surely impacts similar development elsewhere in the world too. So, when postmodern writers in the West dislocate the logos and treat binaries as fluid, the concern for the cultural value system is gone and irreverence to popular societal icons becomes the norm. Contemporary popular writers like Ashok Banker and Amish Tripathi take the clue and re-write the sub-plots and re-fashion mythical characters like Rama and Shiva, who are treated as gods by common people. The protagonist of Arvind Adiga's novel *The White Tiger* refers to the deities in the temple as "two resident pairs of divine arses" (187).

The tendency travels across different media and we have movies, music and other forms of art using cultural and religious symbols in playful vein. So, we have the mercantile stuff like slippers and bathroom seats using images of these characters venerated by common people, as decorative (?) motif. Not every religion gets mocked at similarly, and indeed there are scholars who are proud of the Hindu tolerance and 'liberalism' in respect of these developments. Conversely, it can be seen as throwing baby with the bath water. In our zeal to do away with the centre/periphery binary, we may be re-creating periphery/centre binary.

Again, while it is good to discard superstitions, outdated beliefs, etc., does the postmodern ethos write off all that does not conform to logic and reason? All this harks back to the Enlightenment project which is being hotly debated at present. Is reason the sole criterion for our recognition of the 'human'? When we appreciate newer epistemologies detached from reason, what holds us back, if not that imperial nod from the West before we include this in our agenda? Dipesh Chakrabarty is rightly quoted as observing: "For generations now, philosophers and thinkers shaping the nature of social science have produced theories embracing the entirety of humanity: as we well know, these statements have been produced in relative, and sometimes absolute, ignorance of the majority of humankind, i.e., those living in non-Western cultures" (Gandhi 44). While it is nobody's case to totally reject all that comes from the West (indeed such a thing is impossible to envision more than ever in today's world), what is lamentable is to mortgage our thinking of the past and the present to 'their' approval.

Nativism

It would seem that the interpretation of the term postcolonial too has the ubiquitous Eurocentrism about it, as it has been in the case of Marxism and Feminism. This slant has given rise to the counter postcolonial notion of Nativism in India, which opposes the imposition of alien sensibilities, aesthetics and modes of articulation. At the level of thematics, Nativism in literature stands for "Indian outlook in socio-cultural and psycho-spiritual outlook of an author or even a society" (Paranjape 17). It is an integral approach that also takes into account stylistic aspects—the use of Indian words in English literature normally referred to as Indianism, and the narrative technique known as the Oriental or Eastern way of storytelling. Scholars like Makarand Paranjape, K. Sachidanandan, Bhalchandra Nemade. G.N. Devy, et al, have tried to outline Nativism in the field of Indian literature.

Devy views literary production as being language specific to which the standards of universal criticism should not be applied: "It [Nativism] views literature as an activity taking place 'within' a specific language, such as Marathi or Gujarati and bound by the rules of discourse native to the language of its origin. It understands writing as a social act, and expects of it an ethical sense of commitment to the society within which it is born. [. . .] It rejects the concept-specific method of 'universal' criticism" (119). Elaborating the tenets of Indian literary criticism, Devy is quoted to the effect that it "exhibits the models of the tripartite relation of the *bhaṣha* (vernacular/indigenous/local), the *marga* (Sanskritic/traditional/mainstream/national), and the *videshi* (colonial) tradition and that it is conditioned by a cultural laxity which still remains a fragmented discourse" (Krishnaiah 37).

While the language use is expected to show an Indian touch as Raja Rao commented in the introduction to *Kanthapura*,[3] we should also foreground, research and expand the genre of Indian poetics. It mainly follows the Sanskrit poetics, as we know. The Indian understanding of literature is that which addresses the common good (sahitya= sa+hit), and the 'good' is an uplifting moksha-oriented Dharmic one. In the criticism of poetry, the Indian notion of *reeti* deals with the linguistic style. Apart from it, the concept of *vakrokti* (literally 'crooked statement') as enunciated by Kuntak, means a less-than-direct route to meaning or deviance. It is an umbrella term which covers a number of stylistic, semantic and thematic distinctions. Out of the six classifications of *vakrokti*, three belong to the linguistic framework and refer to elements of deviation like phonological parallelism and amalgamation of registers, figures of speech like humanization and objectification, word selection and mutation, etc. The other mutations covered by the term address wit and irony and changes wrought in narrative to heighten a particular *rasa* (aesthetic pleasure).

Poetry and drama have been the indigenous forms but the novel is an import. It does not mean there was no story writing. We have the *Kathasaritsagar, Panchtantra, Vaital Pachisi*, etc., which have style that is different from the Western model of story writing. It has an oral orientation, relaxed pace and deviations at times. The overarching concepts of *rasa, dhawani, alankar* and *aucitya*, propounded by Bharatmuni, Anandvardhan and Kshemendra respectively play vital roles in narratology also. *Natyashastra* defined eight main variants of *rasa*, viz., the valorous (*veer*), the furious (*raudra*), the terrible (*bhayanak*), the pathetic (*Karun*), the erotic (*sringaar*), the comic (*haasya*), the disgusting (*veebhatsa*), and the fantastic (*adbhut*). The ninth *rasa*, viz., *shaant* or 'the peaceful' was added by Abhinavgupta. This *rasa* comes in the final stage of the plot when all action is supposed to resolve into peace—the epitome of all human endeavour—according to the Indian philosophy. There is no doubt that these concepts are like congealed concepts which have not been researched much or enriched, primarily due to our engagement with the Western stylistics and narratology. There is another objection that comes from the advocates of Dalit literature who feel that the mainstream aesthetics and literature neglect Dalit concepts and concerns. (Patteti 17-25). This objection is in correspondence with the one that subaltern groups raise to mainstream literatures the world over.

Makarand Paranjape divides the IE (Indian English) literature into 'marga,' desi and videshi categories and notes that the competition for dominance among these continues unabated, stating at the same time that IE literature, by virtue of its being in an elite language, constricted in reach, cannot be fully nativized, nor can it be one of our 'bhasha' literatures, even though it has a 'marga-like' position within the country. If it ever was in that position, it was during colonial times when this language was used purposely to subvert the colonial rule. The present position to which many critics would agree is that IE literature remains "isolated and distant from its audience because the linguistic skills of the latter are considered below par. The result, again, is a sedulous cultivation of imported styles and registers, best seen in advertising English, which is the most colonized of the various IE discourses, but also prevalent in our high-brow IE literature" (Parnajape 99). As such, the range of experience is also quite narrow and restricted.

More than the stylistic aspect, the thematic ones carry more significance in the Indian scheme of things. For appreciation, an artistic or literary creation should be placed in a "civilizational perspective" as Paranjape puts it: "Such a civilizational perspective makes it possible to separate the ephemeral from the lasting; it gives us the means to resist the power of the market or the hype and hoopla generated by the mass media; it enables us to evaluate works of art not just by narrower aesthetic or political standards, but by criteria which have a wider, national or universal significance" (88). What the critic means is the Indian way of looking at things which traditionally has been "dharmic view of life"[4], not to be identified with any particular religion.

This dharmic ethos may or may not find place in a literary work. Thus, modern fiction primarily focusing on alienation shows 'adharma' or the lack of 'dharmic' way at work, according to Paranjape, but he confounds the issue when he states, "Thus a Raja Rao or a Salman Rushdie despite their totally dissimilar values and philosophies, may be seen as similar in that they both wish to act upon society, to alter it in ways they consider good and beneficial. Both are, in that sense, practitioners and teachers of dharma, though one is traditional, the other modern; one vedantic, the other Leftist; one religious, the other secular; one majoritarian, the other minoritarian and so on" (96). In this, Paranjape seems to be taking 'dharma' as one's duty just as killing soldiers of the opposite army was Arjuna's dharma in the Mahabharata.

While growth and eclecticism are signs of its vibrancy and dynamism of a literary genre, it is expected to have an identity of its own—a unique core. This core consists of what we may call the Indian sensibility and ethos and brings into play the Indian value system and shared historical memories of a common culture. The core may or may not be strong enough to bring about total nativization of the alien elements but it must colour them in such a way that amidst the glitz and glimmer of the alien, shades of Indianness still show up. Against the Indian backdrop, this should not amount to the privileging of only the mainstream, canonical, traditional elements in the Indian society and culture, because the marginal and the peripheral too exist on the quintessential Indian page. As seen in the genre of criticism comprising of different critical idioms, Nativism means the plurality that has always been a feature of the Indian reality. The existence of myriad faith systems sanctified by the Sanskrit adage *Ekam sat viprabahudhavadanti* (Truth is one though scholars interpret it differently) with the atheistic philosophies is an indicator of this essential pluralism.

Indian English Literature

A fleeting review of the Indian English novel—this genre being the most prolific and capable of freely articulating ideologies and viewpoints—from the postcolonial/nativist angle will be in order here. The trajectory of the development of different genres ran thus: C.V. Boriah published the first prose work titled *Account of the Jains* in 1803; Henry Derozio the *Poems* in 1827; K.M. Banerjee the drama *The Persecuted* in 1831; and Kailash-Chander Dutt his fictional work *A Journal of the 48 Hours of the Year 1945*—a futuristic work—in 1835. (Naik 13-15).However, famous Bengali novelist Bankim Chander Chatterjee's *Rajmohan's Wife* (1864) was the first novel noticeable novel of the time. It portrayed a powerful woman character in a male-dominated society of rural Bengal. Chatterjee's other novels too had powerful women and the language showed Indianism. Thus, both theme and style proved his postcolonial leanings. Of the iconic Rabindranath Tagore's novels, *Gora* and *The Home and the World* which "appeared in approved English versions in his own life time" (Iyengar 107), the first deals with the issue of multiple identities which find resolution in the nationalist Indian identity finally. The second novel studies the impact of revolutionary fervor on individual life. The characters have been cast along the Indian understanding of human lives as being based on *triguna*, or the three attributes of human beings, viz. *sattwik, rajsik* and *tamsik:*

Till the end of the nineteenth century, stray novels and stories continued to appear in Bengal and Madras presidencies. A majority of these novels were social, historical and autobiographical ones modeled on British fiction. Mention must be made here of Behram Malabari's travel writing *The Indian Eye on English Life* (1885). True to its title, it presents a colonized's critique of the British as he saw them in London. "Though in a subject position, Malabari's discourse does not flinch from recording what he observed to be the shortcomings of the Master Race" (Bharucha 88)—clearly an early postcolonial approach. However, it is with the arrival on the scene of the trio—Mulk Raj Anand, R.K. Narayan and Raja Rao that Indian English Novel seriously takes shape. They are also the first important novelists of the nationalist phase in India. Anand, the most prolific of the threesome, seriously tried to nativise English novel by using Hindi and Punjabi words in transliterated as also in translated form. Such words include swear words and mis-spelt English words. He deals with the plight of the subaltern as in his first novel *Untouchable* (1935) produced during colonial times, he describes a day in the life of Bakha, a young sweeper. The day brings him three solutions to his predicament—proselytization,

Gandhian reform and mechanized sanitation; placing in this way the nativist view alongside others. His later novels *Coolie* and *Two Leaves and a Bud* also deal seriously with the social relations in Indian society.

R.K. Narayan presents a beautiful specimen of the postcolonial concern for the local with universal import. His little dramas of Indian life are enacted in Malgudi, an imaginary South Indian town. His main works are *Swami and Friends, The Guide, Waiting for the Mahatma,* and *The Man-eater of Malgudi*. Long before him, however, another novelist A. Madhaviah had criticized the Brahmanical dominance in his novel *Thillai Govindam.* Raja Rao's novel *Kanthapura* is perhaps the best portrayal in Indian oral *harikatha* style, of the Gandhian impact on rural people. *The Serpent and the Rope,* as also *The Cat and Shakespeare* are novels, in which Indian philosophy forms the substratum.

The post-Independence novelists deal with social issues. Of them, Bhabani Bhattacharya holds an important position with his novels. *So Many Hungers* set against the backdrop of Quit India movement and Bengal partition, deals with the theme of exploitation. Manohar Malgonkar's *The Princes* is his best novel which centres round the feudal life of the erstwhile rulers of states. His *The Devil's Wind* focusses on Nana Saheb's heroic role in India's First War of Independence waged in 1857, which is termed as a rebellion by the colonialists. He denigrates the view of British historians who had portrayed Nana Saheb as a villain. G.V. Desani's novel *All about H. Hatterr* with its mix of philosophy, vignettes of fake spiritual gurus, verbal jugglery and stylistic innovativeness is reckoned as a classic in Indian English writing.

Partition literature forms an important plank of the postcolonial literature. It centres around the partition of India effected by the colonial masters in 1947 in which around 1.5 million people migrated from India to the newly created Pakistan and vice versa. What marked this biggest one-time migration of people in human history was the large-scale bloodshed accompanied by violation of women on both sides of the border. This left behind a trail of painful memories which continue to find expression in literature even now. Some of the writers who have written novels on this theme include Chaman Nahal, Manohar Malgonkar, Khushwant Singh, Attia Hasan, Sunanda Sikdar, et al. It would be seen that the repetitive acts of producing partition literature do not act to efface the memory of this horrendous event; rather these perpetuate it.

Amitav Ghosh has much to his credit as a postcolonial novelist. While *The Shadow Lines* questions the imaginary boundaries dividing India and Bangladesh, his *The Hungry Tide* is a perfect piece of postcolonial ecological consciousness. He also touches upon Chinese history of the Opium War period by fictionalizing it in his novel *The River of Smoke.* Irvin Allan Sealy's *Trotter Nama* studies the cultural interface between several generations of an Anglo-Indian family and others in colonial India and uses the indigenous *Shahnama* style. Shashi Tharoor's *The Great Indian Novel* uses the Indian epic as the allegorical framework to tell the story of pre and post-independence India. Tharoor's novel *Riot* is also a piece of metafictional historiography as it presents multiple viewpoints based on memory thus questioning official history. There are many writers who have dealt with the Moghul period as also the colonial history in their novels; these include Basavraj Naikar, Sudhir Kakar, Indu Sundaresan, A.K. Srikumar, Tabish Khair, et al, though not all interrogate the official history.

Postcolonial concerns like the diasporic condition, cultural negotiation, subjectivity, subalternity, etc. have attracted a number of writers staying in India or abroad. Women novelists have particularly made their mark. While Booker winner Arundhati Roy's *The God of Small Things*, an excellent regional novel uses native words, Pulitzer award winner Kiran Desai touches upon the condition of the Indian immigrant belonging to the lower stratum of society. The diasporic condition has been dealt with by a number of writers as a large number of writers of Indian origin are based abroad to whom the personal experience of diasporic identity comes in handy. Such writers include V.S. Naipaul, Chitra Banerjee Divakaruni, Jhumpa Lahiri, Bharati Mukherjee, Anita Rau Badami, Boman Desai, Kiran Desai et al. The subaltern status of Indian women has been taken up by Kamala Markandaya and Shashi Deshpande in a remarkable and multidimensional manner. Other writers dealing with this issue include Anita Desai, Manju Kapur, Anita Nair and Namita Gokhale.

Two important landmarks in recent Indian fiction need to be noted: one, Salman Rushdie initiated the postmodern phase in Indian English literature with a bang, winning the Booker prize in 1981 for his *Midnight's Children*. In this, as in *Shame*, he not only used the recent history of the Indian sub-continent as his thematic material but also applied the Indian narrative form of story-telling with ample doses of Indianism in the use of language. On his own admission, he went in for the "chutnification" of language and history—a potent postcolonial concern. The lead in using magic realism—a form developed in the Third World—was followed by others like Shashi Tharoor, Boman Desai, Rukun Advani et al.

The second landmark is in the form of thee rise of popular novel with the advent of Chetan Bhagat. Popular novel as a non-canonical and marginalized genre, in its various forms like campus novel, career novel etc. has come to occupy a place of prominence in postcolonial times. Chetan Bhagat with six novels to his credit till date, is an icon in Indian English fiction. There have been writers of this type before him also, as for example, Shobha De, but Bhagat has inspired a large number of writers as also professionals to write novels and the Indian English fiction is richer for all this. The extent of enthusiasm in this regard can be gauged from the fact that since 2000 AD, more than 700 novels have been written in English. This figure does not take into account the story books and novels translated from other languages into English. The themes touched by these novels include campus and office comedies, professional life, live-in and extramarital relationships, science and murder mysteries, thrillers, mythology, current events and fashions, etc. Important writers of popular fiction include Ravi Subramanian, Sagarika Ghosh, Anuja Chauhan, Amish Tripathi, Ashok Banker, Anita Nair, Jaishree Misra et al.

The emergence of popular novel in India admits hardly of identification with any ideology—nationalism or socialism—rather it is emblematic of personal expression. Considering that its content is almost entirely shaped by personal journeys, attachments, memories, losses, Leela Gandhi observes, "It seems more than a little curious that these iterative and skillful portraits of artists as young—and not so young—men should be authorized to represent the public voice of the postcolonial world" (164-65).

It is clear from the foregoing discussion that the postcolonial touch to serious Indian English literature is seen from the very beginning in the form of focus on Indian culture, as also its interface with Western culture. Literature has always been linked to the psychological, social, political and cultural issues of the time. It is only the greater stress on the marginalized sections of society which has received impetus due to postcolonial movement. The cause of the marginalized communities and castes too has been taken up by writers like Rohinton Mistry, Aravind Adiga et al. However, a comparison of Indian English literature with the literature produced in regional languages throws up surprises. The involvement of the regional language writer in the native milieu and the proximity of expression to the native lifestyle is far greater than that of the Indian English writer. Writers like Rabindranath Tagore, Munshi Premchand, Sharatchandra Chattopadhyaya, U.R. Ananthamurthy, Krishna Sobti, R. Krishnamurthy, et al have few parallels in Indian English literature. Postcolonialism has also resulted in the centre-staging of non-canonical literature produced by writers with no great literary reputation but bearing the stamp of authenticity, coming as they do from marginalized background. The voice of the subaltern and the Dalit, however, gets articulated in regional languages. Such writers like Baba Valangkar, Kisan Bansod, Omprakash Valmiki, Faustina Bama, Sharankumar Limbale, C.K. Janu et al have their unique value.

Summing up, I would like to refer to Makarand Paranjape's classification of IE literature along three axes. He divides it into broad categories of subaltern, sub-imperial and imperial, based upon the power enjoyed by a text or a culture and aligns other categories with them. He finds the Indian English literature as national marga-like position even through it is not truly native. The following is his thought-provoking scheme of categorization:

Subaltern	**Sub-imperial**	**Imperial**
Desi	Marga	Videshi
Regional	National	International
Native	National	Non-native
Peripheral	Semi-peripheral	Core
Colonial	Sub-metropolitan	Metropolitan
Folk	Literate	Super-literate
Local	National	Global
Non-elite	Elite	Super-elite
Bharat	India (n)	West (erner)
Resident Indian	Resident Non-Indian/Non-Resident Indian	Non-Indian

And so on. (90).

On the whole, it can be said that the postcolonial Indian English fiction has emerged as a rich genre that deals with multiple themes concerning the Indian psyche and situation in the contemporary globalized setting increasingly using an Indian idiom and narrative styles. It is a great link between India and the rest of the English speaking world. By winning multiple awards, it has brought prestige to Indian English literature. However, its representational potential is limited in the sense that it has not engaged itself with the quintessential Indian reality in a serious way. Thus, many metropolitan writers in English, whether residing in India or not, continue to produce works that reflect the outlook of a relative outsider. In comparison, the regional novel in other Indian languages proves its Indian credentials in a better way. Therefore, while Indian English writers need to do more to represent, within the limitations of linguistic representation, the Indian reality, critics need to widen their critical lens far beyond their current focus.

NOTES

1. National consciousness is indicated in ancient Indian literature, as for example, an ancient Sanskrit couplet mentions the boundaries of Bharat: "*Uttaramyatsamudrasyahimadreshchaivadakshinam/ varsh tad Bharatamnaamambhartiyatrasantati*" (That part of the earth which is situated north of the ocean and south of the Himalayas is called Bharat and its children are called Bharati.) Similarly, Chanakya gives the measurement of ancient India: "*Himvatsamudrantarmudicheenamyojansahasraparimanam*" (From the ocean down south to the Himalayas in the north, the country measures one thousand *yojan*.).
2. The present position is that whereas Islam is practised by a majority of people in Turkey, Kosovo and Albania, it has sizeable devotees even in France and England. There have been problems enforcing secular measures like even banning scarfs and veils in schools and public places in France. With the lengthening shadow of the conflict in the Middle-east over Europe and its youth, a worrying number of whom is getting attracted to terrorist outfits like ISIS, how far will the call of secularism carry the people along is anyone's guess.

3. Raja Rao, in the foreword to his acclaimed novel *Kanthapura*, makes a comment meant to guide the Indian writers which has often been quoted. Mentioning about his difficulty in telling the story "from the contemporary annals of my village," he says, "The telling has not been easy. One has to convey in a language that is not one's own the spirit that is one's sown. One has to convey the various shades and omissions of a certain thought-movement that looks maltreated in an alien language. I use the word 'alien,' yet English is not really an alien language to us. It is the language of our intellectual make-up—like Sanskrit or Persian was before—but not of our emotional make-up. We are instinctively bilingual, many of us writing in our own language and in English. We cannot write like the English .We should not. [. . .] After language the next problem is that of style. The tempo of Indian life must be infused into our English expression, even as the tempo of American or Irish life has gone into the making of theirs."
4. Makarand Paranjape elaborates the concept of dharma to coincide with what is morally sound, spatially and temporally. He states, "Dharma is common to Hinduism, Buddhism, Jainism, Sikhism, the indigenous religions, and to Zoroastrianism, Islam and Christianity, faiths which have their origins outside our land but which have many local adherents now. That is why, the faith of this country is known as *sanatana* dharma, the eternal dharma, and is not to be identified with anyone form of what has now come to be known as Hinduism. Hinduism, as we know it, may or may not survive, [Indeed there was no such term in use prior to the advent of Islam in this country, Dharma having been used in generic sense since ages.] but the *sanatana* dharma is imperishable. The same is true of other faiths too. Religions come and go; ways of practicing them also change. But underlying them is the eternal dharma which always remains, though it find newer and varying expressions" (85).

Works Cited

Adiga, Aravind. *The White Tiger*. New Delhi: HarperCollins, 2008, Ninth Impression 2009.

Anderson, Benedict. *Imagined Communities*. London: Verso, 1983.

Boehmer, Elleke. *Colonial and Postcolonial Literature*, Second ed. New Delhi: Oxford, 2006.

Boehmer, Elleke & Rosinka Chaudhuri. *The Indian Postcolonial: A Critical Reader*. London: Routledge, 2011.

Bertens, Hans. *Literary Theory: The Basics*. Oxford: Routledge, 2001.

Bhabha, Homi K. *The Location of Culture*. London: Routledge, 1994.

Bharucha, Nilufer E. *World Literature: Contemporary Postcolonial and Post-Imperial Literatures*. New Delhi: Prestige, 2007.

Chakrabarty, Dipesh. *Provincializing Europe: Postcolonial Thought and Historical Difference*. New Jersey: Princeton, 2000.

Chatterjee, Partha. *Nationalist Thought and the Colonial World: A Derivative Discourse*. London: Zed Books, 1993.

Deane, Seamus, ed. *Nationalism and Colonial Literature*. Minneapolis: University of Minnesota Press, 1990.

Deena, Seodial. "Colonial and Canonical Control over Third World Writers. *Postcolonial Discourse: A Study of Contemporary Literature*. Ed. R.K. Dhawan. New Delhi: Prestige, 1997.

Devy, G.N. *After Amnesia*. Bombay: Orient Longman, 1992.

Fanon, Franz. *The Wretched of the Earth*. London: Penguin, 1967, Reprint 1990.

Gandhi, Leela. *Postcolonial Theory: A Critical Introduction*. New Delhi: Oxford, 1998.

Groden, Michael et al ed. *The John Hopkins Gide to Literary Theory & Criticism*. Second Edition. Baltimore: The John Hopkins University Press, 2005.

Iyengar, K.R. Srinivasa. *Indian Writing in English*. New Delhi: Sterling, 1985, reprint 1995.

James, Paul. *Nation Formation: Towards a Theory of Abstract Community*. London: Sage, 1996.

Joshi, Swati, ed. *Rethinking English: Essays in Literature, Language, History*. New Delhi: Oxford, 1994.

Krishnaiah, B. *The Native Tradition and Recent Indian Novel*. New Delhi: Prestige, 2010.

Lau, Lisa & Om Prakash Dwivedi. *Re-Orientalism and Indian Writing in English*. Hampshire, UK: Palgrave Macmillan, 2014.

Menon, Nivedita. "Thinking through the postnation."*The Indian Postcolonial: A Critical Reader*. Eds. Elleke Boehmer and Rosnika Chaudhuri. London: Routledge, 2011. pp. 316-33.

Mongia, Padmini, ed. *Contemporary Postcolonial Theory: A Reader*. New Delhi: Oxford, 1997, Ninth Impression, 2012

Naik, M.K. *A History of Indian English Literature*. New Delhi: Sahitya Akademi, 1982, Reprint 2010.

Nandy, Ashis. *The Intimate Enemy: Loss and Recovery of Self under Colonialism*. New Delhi: Oxford, 1983.

Parnajape, Makarand. *Towards a Poetics of the Indian English Novel*. Shimla: IIAS, 2000.

Patteti, Raja Sekhar. "Can the Dalit Speak?: Fluctuating Subjectivity and Fragmented Postcolonial Identity," *Postcolonial Literatures: Discourses on the Praxis and the Pedagogies*. New Delhi: Prestige, 2008, pp. 17-25.

Rao, Raja. *Kanthapura,* Second Edition. New Delhi: Oxford, 1989.

Said, Edward. *Culture and Imperialism*. London: Chatto & Windus, 1993.

Sheshadri, Vijay. "Connecting Worlds: A Study of Arun Mukherjee's Postcolonialism: My Living."*India in Canadian Imagination*. Ed. R.K. Dhawan et al. New Delhi: Prestige, 2003, pp. 184-92.

Varughese, Emma Dawson: *Beyond the Postcolonial: World Englishes Literature*, London: Palgrave Macmillan, 2012

Venn, C. *The Postcolonial Challenge: Towards Alternate Worlds*. London: Sage, 2006.

‘A Bag of Tricks’: Silence and Power in the Novels of Amitav Ghosh

DIANE YERKA

In Amitav Ghosh’s novel *The Calcutta Chromosome* (1995), the character Phulboni, a famous writer, gives a speech at an award ceremony. Using words that echo through this novel, Phulboni says, “Mistaken are those who imagine that silence is without life; that it is inanimate, without either spirit or voice. It is not” (*Calcutta* 29). Phulboni spends many years of his life in search of the voice behind the silence, and indeed, the silence he speaks of is the central element of this novel. Characters who are silent in most novels tend to be those with subaltern status, such as Friday in *Robinson Crusoe* or Estha in *The God of Small Things*. Postcolonial literature, or literature coming out of countries which were once colonized, often attempt to give voice to groups of people who have been voiceless in the past or people who were subaltern in some way. Much of the literature that is considered postcolonial, then, focuses on characters who are given voices (and in many cases, power) where they previously had none, such as J.M. Coetzee’s (1940-) character Friday in *Foe* (1986).

Amitav Ghosh (b. 1956), an internationally-bestselling writer who was raised in India, educated in Egypt and England, and currently resides in New York City, provides an alternate perspective of silence and speech. In this paper, I will trace the trope of silence through two of Ghosh’s works, *The Hungry Tide* (2005) and *The Calcutta Chromosome*. I argue that instead of conforming to the traditional view of silenced subaltern characters having little power in their history or narrative, Ghosh creates subaltern characters that are in some way silent, either by choice or by circumstances, but who retain power to control either their own lives or the experiences of other characters.

Silence, of course, is a common point of discussion among critics of postcolonial works. In 1988, Gayatri Chakravorty Spivak's seminal essay "Can the Subaltern Speak?" raised awareness of who is allowed to speak and who isn't within the narratives of postcolonial work and within modern systems of governance.[1] Since then, postcolonial literary criticism has explored her ideas further, reaffirming or arguing against Spivak's notion that dominant groups cannot (or should not) speak for subaltern ones. R. John Williams, in his analysis of Nuruddin Farah's "Sweet and Sour Milk," argues that for the subaltern, speaking is a method of revolution. He writes,

> In Subaltern Studies, 'silence' forms the basis for a three-part trajectory: 1) There is an imposition of silence by a colonial or neocolonial state . . . . 2) An insurrectionary act of drawing attention to that silence, calling it out, mapping its genealogy, and identifying the hypocrisy of its boundaries—a process fueled by resentment. 3) A revisionary act of speaking from that silence, giving it a voice, an identity, and eliminating its absence. (163)

In this way, Williams argues that speech can remove the subaltern status for a person, because it removes the silence that comes with subalternity. He writes that the third part of this trajectory, the part where writers begin to speak from the silence, is where postcolonial literature originates and should, therefore, be the focus of postcolonial criticism.

But not all critics agree that gaining the ability to speak will make a person no longer subaltern. In *Framing Silence*, Myriam Chancy argues that "oppression should not be conflated with identity" (33). The reality of being oppressed, of not being allowed a voice, does not necessarily dictate who a person is, and, additionally, the ability to speak does not necessarily make or not make someone subaltern. She writes that since "the 'subaltern' is always speaking, and since oppression still exists, it follows . . . that the 'subaltern' continues to exist in her/his state of oppression even as she/he speaks" (33). In other words, speaking does not necessarily bring a person out of subalternity, which explains her use of scare quotes around the term. In fact, silence can be a power in and of itself. In *Language and Silence* (in a chapter titled "The Retreat from the Word" and devoted to considering the idea that speech is not the only method by which we communicate), George Steiner writes, "We live inside the act of discourse. But we should not assume that a verbal matrix is the only one. . . . . There are actions of the spirit rooted in silence. It is difficult to speak of these, for how should speech justly convey the shape and vitality of silence?" (12). Lewis MacLeod takes this one step further in his analysis of J.M. Coetzee's *Foe*, a reinterpretation of Daniel Defoe's *Robinson Crusoe*, to argue that silence itself is a way of preserving identity for a subaltern. MacLeod points out that one of the characters in *Foe* who is literally silenced (his tongue has been cut out) is given power over his own narrative because of his silence. In refusing to speak, Friday "refuses to put the story . . . of his life into anyone else's hands. . . . Friday's silence prevents him from becoming the raw materials of someone else's narrative" (6). Friday is subaltern to the character of Susan, but he retains his identity through his silence. Silence gives him power to keep from being narrated by Susan.

Ghosh's characters are also allowed power, despite real or apparent silence. Claire Chambers argues that Ghosh "suggests that the act of putting anything into writing inevitably distorts the 'truth' of the thing it seeks to describe" ("Network" 53). In other words, as soon as words have been put together to describe something, it is changed, much the same that an outsider will change the dynamics of a group when he comes to study it. In his 1992 hybrid travelogue-autobiography-history narrative *In an*

Antique Land, Ghosh works as an anthropologist doing fieldwork in Egypt. He attempts to relate to readers what people in the small Egyptian village are like, but he also acknowledges that his presence there changes what those people are like. His conversations with the Imam, for example, take place only because Ghosh is an outsider. The Imam would never have the same arguments with people on the inside. Spivak argues that this is why it is difficult to speak for subalterns. She writes, "There is no unrepresentable subaltern subject that can know and speak itself" (27), but to speak for them is to change them. Linda Alcoff and others would ask: How can anyone truly get in the mind of another person and speak for that person? Chambers argues in response that "Ghosh's preoccupation with silence . . . may be an ethical response to the economic and social gags of colonialism. Ghosh's creation of a space for silence . . . may come as a reminder that we should not 'speak for' the subaltern, but rather recognize, with Spivak, the unrepresentable aspects of the Other's experiences" ("Networks" 57). The speaker, or in the case of postcolonial literature, the writer, will always have the voice, will always be the one to make decisions about what parts of the subaltern are represented. Thus, Ghosh has to write about these subaltern characters, because that is the medium he chooses for the tales he is telling, and in doing so he must to some extent remove their authority to represent themselves. But he does so in a way that still allows for silence on the part of his characters, allowing them to retain at least some portion of their fictional identity that is not created by the author or read by the reader.

Before I explain how Ghosh uses silence and power in two of his novels, I will explain exactly what I mean by these terms, because the perspective I am taking is not necessarily the most common one. By silence, I do not mean someone who never speaks (although Ghosh does create a few characters who speak very little). Instead, I mean characters that are silenced in a myriad of ways, either by virtue of never getting to tell any of the narration in their own words, or choosing not to speak to other characters, or even simply choosing carefully what information to give to other characters or readers. For example, in Ghosh's first novel, *The Circle of Reason* (1986), the primary protagonist Alu is a quiet boy who grows into a quiet man, speaking only when required to and preferring weaving to human company. In *The Shadow Lines* (1988), the narrator has no name, leading readers through the events of the novel (including the death of another arguably-silenced character, Tridib) without ever having a firm identity himself. Ghosh's memoir *In an Antique Land* centers around a slave who is mentioned only briefly in an ancient letter written by an Indian and is barely involved in Ghosh's memoir. The characters Dolly and Uma are best friends in *The Glass Palace* (2000), yet there is considerable silence between them in the form of many things they don't talk about, such as Uma's loneliness. All of these characters are like the hidden threads of Alu's tapestries, supporting the bright colors of more noticeable characters without being seen much themselves.

When I refer to having power, I am not necessarily referring to the type of power we would generally think of, like governmental power or strong charisma that leads to social change. Instead, I wish to show that these characters are able to control, to at least some extent, their immediate surroundings and the characters they interact with. As an example of the antithesis of the type of power I refer to here, consider Estha from Arundhati Roy's (1961-) *The God of Small Things* (1997), who is victimized throughout his life, by his mother, other relatives, the sexual-molesting theater-employee, the police, and, possibly, his own sister and cousin. Estha is forced away from home and becomes silent by choice shortly thereafter when he stops talking. But Estha never gains power, in spite of or because of his silence. He continues to be subaltern to the other characters in the novel. Ghosh presents a much different picture, and particularly in the two novels which I will spend the rest of this essay exploring. These two novels offer the best examples of silence in Ghosh's novels. I will begin with *The Calcutta Chromosome*, which is explicitly about silence, and then follow up with a more subtle reading of *The Hungry Tide*.

The Calcutta Chromosome, like most of Ghosh's works, has many different time periods occurring at the same time. In the present we have Antar, an Egyptian living in a near-future New York City, who struggles with recurring malarial fevers. He works as a glorified keyboard cruncher, sifting through old items with so little conscious thought required that when his personified computer isn't looking, he can read novels projected on the walls. At the very beginning of the novel, Antar comes across the ID card of an old colleague. That colleague, Murugan (or Morgan, as he sometimes goes by) had spent much of his life trying to track down the history of Ronald Ross's 1898 discovery of the source of the malaria virus in Calcutta. To the disdain of the scientific world, Murugan thought he had discovered that Ross was not the original discoverer at all, but only a pawn to the people who had done real work on the virus: Murugan has found a group of Indians that weave in and out of the history of Ross's discovery. This silent group serves as a palimpsest to the western scientists who pursue the cause of malaria, acting, once again, as the hidden threads behind a rich tapestry. They are silent in that they are never noticed by the scientists around whom they work, nor are they ever entirely discovered even by those who deliberately seek them, including Murugan and Phulboni, the fictional author I quoted at the beginning of this essay. Murugan explains his theory to Antar in the following way:

> You know all about matter and antimatter, right? And rooms and anterooms and Christ and Antichrist and so on? Now, let's say there was something like science and counter-science. Thinking of it in abstract, wouldn't you say that first principle of a functioning counter-science would have to be secrecy? The way I see it, it

> wouldn't just have to be secretive about *what* it did (it couldn't hope to beat the scientists at that game anyway); it would also have to be secretive *in* what it did. It would have to use secrecy as a technique or procedure. It would in principle have to refuse all direct communication, straight off the bat, because to communicate, to put ideas into language, would be to establish a claim to *know*—which is the first thing that a counter-science would dispute. (104-5)

In other words, the modus operandi for the counter-science group is silence. They trade in silence, they discover in silence, and they move silently through the novel, never fully coming into the narrative strongly enough for readers to know if they even actually exist or are just part of Antar's malarial fevers. Antar traces this counter-science group from his living room, using the resources of AVA, his computer, and the research that Murugan has already done for him. He is trying to track down something so silent that it leaves no trace of itself, just as other characters in the novel have done before him, and just as readers do right along with him. Although Antar does (possibly) come across answers, we never really hear the voice of the counter-science group. Anshuman Mondal, in his book-length study of Ghosh's works, argues, "Silence as a metaphor for subalternity is . . . one of the key motifs of *The Calcutta Chromosome*" (146). They are subaltern in that they are outside the normal, Western view of science and culture, and they are silenced by the very nature of their group, as well as by the discourse of the novel. Yet, despite their status and their silence, this group is intensely powerful within the lives of all the characters.

Murugan travels to India to try to track down more information about this counter-science group. In India, we meet several characters that are either influenced by, or part of, the counter-science group (and a few who will eventually be both, as several of the characters end up joining the counter-science group). Beginning in the late 1800s, the counter-science group is pulling the strings behind the western scientists who are working on the malaria virus. The counter-science group seems to originate with Mangala, an Indian woman who works for the first of the British scientists, Cunningham. When describing her to another Englishman, Cunningham says, "Don't pay the slightest attention to her. . . . She's just the sweeper-woman" (142). But she is not just a sweeper woman; she is, as far as the novel allows us to know, the originator of the counter-science group. She makes things happen in Cunningham's lab that he never would have accomplished without her. Another assistant, whom we discover is also part of the counter-science group, is not even given the dignity of an introduction. Ghosh writes, "Since the man was a menial employee Farley was not surprised that Cunningham had not taken the trouble to tell him his name" (143). Cunningham does not realize that behind his back, Mangala and the other Indian assistants are controlling almost everything that happens in the lab. Farley, the Englishman to whom Cunningham is talking, sees more than the laughably-oblivious Cunningham can. Throughout his stay at Cunningham's lab, Farley catches glimpses of the power that the so-called assistants have over the lab. For example, Ghosh writes, "It was she [Mangala] who selected the slides that were to be presented to him for examination. Watching carefully, Farley saw her picking them out with a speed that indicated she was not only thoroughly familiar with the slides but knew exactly what they contained" (144). Strange, for a woman who is just the sweeper-woman, to know what the slides contained well enough to purposefully give Farley slides containing no hint of the malaria virus. When he pushes further against this counter-science group, demanding to see the truth of what they're doing, Mangala eventually shows him the true malarial slides and reveals herself to be in control of the lab. But he has now broken their silence, and he is punished for it. At the end of the chapter, we learn that when he leaves the lab, he boards a train and is never seen again (154).

Like Cunningham, Ronald Ross, the British scientist who ostensibly discovered exactly what mosquito carries malaria, also never realizes that he's being led by the counter-science group. This subaltern group remains behind the scenes all the way through Ross's experiment, even though they are intricately connected to it. They send him an assistant, Laakhan (or Lutchman, as Ross calls him in an indifferent resistance to learning his assistant's name[2]), who becomes vital to Ross's experiments but is never considered by Ross to be anything other than an Indian coolie. They point him in the direction of the right mosquito, and they send him an Indian who has the exact blood type to be studied, even keeping away any other Indians who might want to earn a few rupees by sharing their malarial-infested blood with the scientist (73). All through this, Ross never realizes that he is being manipulated. He happily determines that he must be brilliant, while the counter-science group pulls strings like a puppetmaster in the background. Ross is credited with the discovery that it is the female Anopheles mosquito that causes malaria without ever knowing that his assistant (and his assistant's counter-science group) did most of the work.

Murugan is the only one who is able to put the pieces together, through scraps of documents and inferences he collects throughout his lifetime. But even poor Murugan is not able to penetrate the secrecy and silence of the counter-science group. At the end of the novel, he does not get to find the answers he so desperately craves. Instead, as he explains it to Urmila, "My part in this was to tie some threads together so that they could hand the whole package over in a neat little bundle some time in the future, to whoever it is they're waiting for" (307). Murugan only learns as much as he does about the silent counter-science group, we discover, because they wanted him to. They want Urmila, and it is through Murugan that they are able to get to her. In a conversation between Murugan and Antar, Murugan says:

> "What these guys were after was much bigger; they were after the biggest prize of all, the biggest . . . ball game any human being has ever thought of: the ultimate transcendence of nature."
>
> "And what might that be?" Antar asked politely.
>
> "Immortality," said Murugan. (107)

In order to achieve this immortality, the members of the counter-science group transcend their own bodies and move their souls (or spirits, or personalities, depending on one's interpretation) to other bodies. Thus, the main characters Urmila and Sonali become part of the counter-science group, after Urmila has heard the whole story from Murugan. Mrs. Aratounian, a woman who was ostensibly just a landlady, is actually Mangala after several incarnations. While it is unclear exactly what happens, it appears that at the end of the novel, she seems to transcend her body, becoming first Urmila and then Tara (or possibly Sonali and then Maria). In the same way, the character Laakhan takes many bodies, including Roman, Sonali's lover; Lucky, Tara's friend; and eventually (as it is implied) Antar (although it can be argued that all of the counter-science group ends up embodied within Antar; the ending is ambiguous enough to allow for a multitude of readings). This is perhaps the ultimate manifestation of silent power: taking over someone's body with (or without, depending on how you read it) their approval. These moments of transcendence indicate a great deal of power, since they require the moving of a soul from one body to another (possibly, although the novel is not explicit about how this transcendence occurs). But the moments of transcendence are also silent: we never witness what actually occurs in a transcendence. The closest we get is when Sonali sees part of a ritual involving Mrs. Aratounian, but before she knows what is going on, she faints (*Calcutta* 167).

The best example of the counter-science group as both silent and powerful comes from their interactions with the fictional author Phulboni, who is as obsessed as Murugan is with finding the counter-science movement. Phulboni, however, does not think about them in terms of science, but rather in terms of a personified (or possibly even deified) silence. Throughout the novel, we catch snippets of Phulboni's speeches (for a man seeking after a deified Silence, he spends a lot of time making speeches) in which he talks about silence. In the first speech, which Murugan hears by accident through a loudspeaker, Phulboni says, "that which is hidden has no need of words to give it life; . . . sustenance [is] precisely where it appears to be most starkly withheld—in this case, in silence" (*Calcutta* 25). These words seem particularly pertinent to Murugan, but for some reason, he does not stop to consider them. Two sentences after this quote, Murugan is meeting two women, Sonali Das and Urmila, and Phulboni is forgotten. Poor Phulboni gets ignored through much of the novel. Although we discover that Sonali is actually his daughter, she pays no attention to his speeches. After one speech, she reacts, "Just listen to him! He's really worked himself up today" (*Calcutta* 29). In his most impassioned speech, Phulboni cries, "For more years than I can count I have walked the innermost streets of this most secret of cities, looking always to find her who has so long eluded me: Silence herself. I see signs of her presence everywhere I go, in images, words, glances, but only signs, nothing more" (*Calcutta* 123-24). Phulboni is desperate to find this goddess that he is worshipping, the goddess of silence. Unfortunately for him, he is given no chance to find it. In the middle of this speech, Mrs. Aratounian (not coincidentally, one of the members of the very group that Phulboni is trying to find) turns off the TV, cutting Phulboni off in a way that is both humorous and poignant. We learn at the end of the novel that Phulboni has actually encountered the counter-science group in a strange, surreal visit to a train station that may or may not exist, attended by a stationmaster who may or may not exist. This experience affects Phulboni so profoundly that he spends the rest of his life trying to understand it, trying to find meaning behind the silence that is the only after-effect. He wants so badly to join their group, but he is never able to. Their silence influences and afflicts Phulboni for most of his life.

It is interesting that Ghosh assigned Phulboni a role as a writer. Other than the fact that Phulboni is well-liked enough to be giving speeches, there seems to be no particular reason that he would need to be a writer. His books do not make much of an appearance in the novel. I would argue that Phulboni can be considered, at least to some extent, a stand-in for Ghosh himself. Ghosh is attempting to track down the silences behind subaltern people throughout India's history, from the Burmese war in *The Glass Palace*, to the poppy disputes in *Sea of Poppies*. His novels, like many of those by postcolonial India writers, bring history to life through round, realistic characters that have been ignored in the historiography of both the colonized and postcolonized India. Anshuman Mondal writes that Ghosh's "focus on the histories of 'the people,' or subalterns, which had previously escaped the notice of nationalist and colonial historians, was . . . an affirmation of the role of subalterns in the historic formation of the modern Indian nation" (27), much the same way that Phulboni and Murugan are attempting to affirm the role of a subaltern group within scientific history. What does it mean, then, that Phulboni is never able to find the substance behind the silence? While this fact drives Phulboni to obsession and disappointment, Ghosh seems less frustrated by the silence. In an interview with Claire Chambers, he says, "there are certain things that can't be verbalized. That's what I was really trying to get at, to say there are certain things that can't be said. . . . [I]t's a constant idea in mysticism: that which cannot be perceived, that which cannot be articulated, which can be apprehended but not known" (Chambers, "Absolute" 32). He is playing off not only Gnosticism, but possibly Buddhism or Taoism, in which, as George Steiner explains, "The soul is envisioned as ascending from the gross impediments of the material, through domains of insight that can be rendered by lofty and precise language, toward ever deepening silence. The highest, purest reach of the contemplative act is that which has learned to leave language behind it" (12).Ghosh does not seem perturbed by what he can't know, or can't explain in language. Indeed, as he explains to Chambers, he starts *The Calcutta Chromosome* telling himself "if you're seriously trying to write a book that's about resistance to knowledge, then you have to accept that there's stuff *you* don't know" or at least can't write about (Chambers, "Absolute," 32).

While *The Calcutta Chromosome* explores the silences behind power struggles in science and cultures, Ghosh's sixth novel, *The Hungry Tide* (2005), is a more subtle example of Ghosh's ability to weave silences into human relationships. This novel follows the journey of Piyali Roy, a young woman who is Indian by ethnicity but raised in America. She is a cetologist (a scientist who studies marine animals) who has come to the Sunderbans, on the east coast of India, to study the Irawaddy Dolphin. The narration of the novel alternates between Piyali (or Piya, as she is familiarly called) and Kanai Dutt, a translator from Delhi who is exploring his family origins in the tiny Sunderbans village of Lusibari. Piya and Kanai meet at the very beginning of the novel, but are separated for much of the narrative. The focalization of the novel primarily moves back and forth between these two, with some additional chapters showing instead the journal of Kanai's uncle Nirmal. While these two are the main protagonists, several other characters move on the periphery of the narration. The most important of these, I would argue, is Fokir, a crab fisherman who lives in Lusibari with his wife Moyna and his son Tutul. Piya first meets Fokir when she is out on the river with two hired men, trying to find the Irawaddy dolphin. From the first meeting that Piya and Fokir have, two things become clear: first, that Fokir is a silenced subaltern, and second, that Fokir is going to have at least some of the power over their relationship.

How is Fokir silenced? He is silenced by the narrative itself, which is focalized through Piya, but he is also silenced through the language barrier between him and Piya. When we first meet Fokir, we discover that he speaks only Bengali, which is a problem for Piya who, despite her Indian heritage, speaks no Bengali. From the moment she comes across him in his boat while she is being ferried by two hired government officials, her conversations with Fokir are limited to pictures, music, and gestures. Their very first interaction occurs when Piya asks the forest guards piloting her boat to stop Fokir so she can ask him about the dolphin. Ghosh writes:

> She lowered herself to one knee and when their heads were level she held out the card [showing a picture of the dolphin]. She tried to give him a smile of reassurance, but he would not meet her eye. He glanced from the card to her face and raised a hand to point upriver. The gesture was so quick and matter-of-fact that for a moment she thought he had misunderstood. Then she looked into his eyes and he nodded, as if to say, yes, that's where I saw them. (40)

Much of the beginning relationship between Piya and Fokir takes place exactly like this: she asks some question that she isn't sure he understands, he answers it using gestures which she interprets for herself and for readers. When Piya attempts to pay Fokir for the use of his boat, he is alarmed. Ghosh writes, "A loud exclamation followed as Fokir retrieved the money. . . . [H]e peeled a single note from the bundle and held it aloft. She understood that he was telling her that he would accept that one note as a compensation for the money that had been taken from him" (55-56). Although that may be exactly what Fokir was attempting to tell Piya, readers do not get to know what he was actually saying. We get only Piya's view of the event, and only Piya's interpretation. They are, as Piya later says, "people who could not exchange a word with each other and had no idea of what was going on in one another's head" (118).

Fokir is also clearly a subaltern character at the beginning of this novel. The two hired men that are ferrying Piya are forest guards who think of Fokir as a poacher, someone over whom they hold legal authority. Ghosh writes, "The guard barked a question that elicited a muttered response from the fisherman" (39), and the guard tells Piya his suspicion that Fokir is a poacher. From this short sentence, we get a picture of Fokir as rebellious, but subservient to the two government employees, who seem to hold all the power over Fokir here. They can require him to stop his boat, they can bark questions, and, as Piya realizes shortly after, they can require him to "pay either a bribe or a fine" (39). In all of this, Fokir has no opportunity to talk back to them; he must allow himself to be treated as a subaltern by these government officials.

Despite the enforced silence and subaltern status shown here, Fokir does in fact have some power over the situation. While he can't simply row his boat away or tell the guards to leave him alone, he is able to influence the narrative at this point. Piya has stopped Fokir's boat to ask him where the dolphins are, something she has asked many other people in the past. Fokir is the first person who is able to respond that yes, he does know where these dolphins are. In her jubilation, Piya attempts to pay Fokir for the good news, and in the attempt, she is thrown overboard. While Piya's two hired men stand and watch, Fokir jumps into the water to save her life. After pulling her out of the water, he gives her CPR until she is breathing again (48). In this way, Fokir has taken literal power over Piya's life: he is the source by which she is able to continue living. Furthermore, he has done so in front of the uncaring hired men, indicating to readers a moral power that the hired men do not possess. It is no wonder that Piya gets off the hired boat to ride with Fokir instead. In addition, through Fokir's rescue of Piya, he has written himself into her story and her life, becoming part of the means by which the story is being produced. It is only through his rescue of Piya at this point and his knowledge of the dolphins later on that the rest of the story is able to be told at all.

On his boat, Fokir maintains this balance between silence and power. I quoted earlier the passage in which he lets Piya pay him only a small amount, again indicating the sort of moral power that he holds (especially compared with the guard from the hired boat, who tried to con Piya out of more money than he had originally agreed to). This power continues when Fokir strings some fabric across a corner of the boat to give Piya some privacy. Piya is "at first a little embarrassed to think that it was he rather than she herself who had been the first to pay heed to the matter of her modesty" (60). Fokir has taken control even of Piya's privacy, giving her some when she was not expecting it (or worried about it, having spent considerable amount of time living with men on boats in the course of her research). Even more impressively, Fokir manages to make Piya feel, not like a passenger, but a member of a family, something she has not experienced in a long time (or ever, depending on how one reads the passages about her childhood). Ghosh writes, "It was not just that he had thought to create a space for her; it was as if he had chosen to include her in some simple, practiced family ritual, found a way to let her know that despite the inescapable muteness of their exchanges, she was a person to him and not, as it were, a representative of a species, a faceless, tongueless, foreigner" (60). Surely this represents a type of power over the experiences of another character, for a man who is a subaltern even within his own people to give a sense of family and home to a rich American researcher whose language he does not even speak.

Fokir and Piya spend several days on his boat exploring the Sunderbans, spending time fishing for crabs and marking the migration route of the Irawaddy dolphins. During this time, they become close in a way that defies their lack of verbal communication. Shameem Black, in *Fiction without Borders*, writes that "[r]ather than identifying with another's process of perception, communion takes place outside of their minds in the convergence of their gaze upon a shared object" (190). They are both so focused on finding the dolphins that Fokir's subaltern status is irrelevant. Back in Lusibari, Fokir's home island, however our second protagonist Kanai is getting a very different picture of Fokir from Fokir's wife, Moyna. According to Moyna, while Piya and Fokir are dawdling around the rivers, trying to find traces of the dolphins and acquire enough crabs, Moyna is back on Lusibari working and training to become a nurse. She is worried that Fokir has been gone so long, but she is also terribly frustrated with him. She tells Kanai that Fokir will "be off on his own somewhere without another human being in sight. . . . That's just how he is, Kanai babu. He can't help himself. He's like a child" (129). Fokir doesn't stay with the adults the way he is supposed to, the way Moyna would and does, and he would rather be off by himself. Alone, and therefore silent. By casting him in the role of the child, Moyna is making Fokir subaltern even in his marriage relationship.

Later, we see Moyna and Fokir together for the one and only time in the novel. At the hospital, Kanai and Piya are talking with Moyna, and Piya asks where Fokir is.

> "There."
>
> Turning her head, Piya saw that Fokir was squatting in the dwelling's doorway, half hidden by a grimy blue curtain. He did not look up and offered no greeting nor any sign of recognition: his eyes were lowered to the ground and he seemed to be drawing patterns with a twig. . . . There was a fugitive sullenness about his posture that suggested he would rather be anywhere but where he was. (172-73)

Fokir's very existence as a human being is hidden in this situation, where he is behind a "grimy blue curtain." Although previously he had been warm and compassionate to Piya, now he ignores her and everyone else. His relationship with Moyna is so strained, so silencing, that it affects what had been good rapport with Piya. Perhaps Moyna, like Piya, has had to interpret Fokir, rather than letting him speak for himself, and her interpretation has been less complimentary to Fokir. After years of this, it is no wonder that Fokir is silent around Moyna. Unfortunately for him, this means that one of the few people in the novel he actually could talk to that speaks his language is unavailable to him. He is silenced even in the most intimate relationship he has, his marriage.

Once again, however, the apparent silence that Fokir has around Moyna is somewhat misleading. Despite the appearance of frustration and disappointment that Moyna has for Fokir, she is not only dependent on him for at least some of her livelihood, she also is inexpressibly attached to him. When Kanai asks Moyna why she married him after she has explained all her problems with Fokir, Moyna replies, "It doesn't matter how many languages you know. . . . You're not a woman and you don't know him. You won't understand" (130). Towards the end of the novel, Moyna's feelings about Fokir are more clearly illuminated in a conversation between Kanai and Piya. Kanai says:

> "There's so much I want to tell you, Piya, and maybe it would be easier to put it into words if I didn't want to so much. It's like Moyna says."
>
> Piya was jolted by the sound of that name. "What does she say?"
>
> "That words are like the winds that blow ripples on the water's surface. The river itself flows beneath, unseen and unheard."
>
> "What did she mean?"
>
> "She was talking about how she feels about Fokir," Kanai said.
>
> "And?"
>
> "He means everything to her, you know, although you wouldn't think it." (277)

The passion Moyna feels for Fokir (and the passion we discover he holds for her too) is evident despite the angry words she levels at him and the silence he gives her. They have a bond that is stronger than language or silence. Shameem Black writes that "the erotic connection between Moyna and Fokir is presented as a communion beyond the reach of language" (192). Moyna is loyal to Fokir throughout the novel, even while she is berating him for his lack of ambition or the fact that he takes their son fishing instead of sending him to school.

As the novel progresses, Fokir becomes more and more important to Piya's research. After a few days in Lusibari, Piya, Fokir, Kanai, and another character head back out onto the river to continue to hunt for Piya's dolphins. Fokir is only one who doesn't speak any language in common with Piya, a fact that Kanai keeps reminding her of (primarily out of jealousy, as Kanai likes Piya and doesn't want her to be dependent on Fokir). Kanai says things like, "You see, Piya, if I hadn't been here to tell you, you'd have had no idea what he'd seen," after Fokir points out a crocodile (222). While it may be true that Fokir couldn't tell Piya in words exactly what he was pointing at in the water, Piya still wants to travel with Fokir, even in his silence, rather than Kanai, who can tell her verbally what is going on. She tries to explain Fokir's importance to Kanai:

> "You saw how he spotted that dolphin back there, didn't you?" said Piya. "It's like he's always watching the water—even without being aware of it. I've worked with many experienced fishermen before but I've never met anyone with such an incredible instinct. It's as if he can see right into the river's heart."
>
> Kanai took a moment to chew on this. "So do you think you're going to go on working with him?"
>
> "I certainly hope he'll work with me again." . . .
>
> "Is there anyone else you could work with?"
>
> "It wouldn't be the same, Kanai," Piya said. "Fokir's abilities as an observer are really extraordinary." (221)

Throughout this passage, Kanai attempts to move Fokir back into the subaltern status that he believes Fokir should inhabit as a low-class fisherman among higher-class researchers and translators. But Piya will have none of it. She grants Fokir the accolades he deserves, showing off Fokir's power to the doubting Kanai. It isn't until later in the novel, when Kanai and Fokir are alone on an island with a Bengal tiger, that Kanai acknowledges that Fokir might know something that he, Kanai, does not. This revelation comes at a time when Fokir is no longer even with him, having left Kanai alone on the island with a Bengal tiger. By the end of Kanai's fearful experience with the tiger, he has realized that Fokir's choice not to speak is not hiding stupidity, as Kanai has been led by Moyna to believe. At this point, Fokir has power over Kanai's life, and he chooses to exercise it in a way that will forever change the way Kanai thinks about him.

At the end of the novel, Piya and Fokir get caught in a tidal wave that strands them on an island with nothing but mangrove trees and a single tiger around them. To save their lives, Fokir straps the two of them to a tree, sticking Piya between himself and the tree to protect her as much as possible. The first half of the tidal wave leaves them breathless and exhausted, but essentially unharmed. The back half of the tidal wave, however, has changed directions, and the mangrove tree they are strapped to is no longer between them and the debris. As a result, Fokir's body is pummeled by an uprooted stump. It hits "him so hard that she too had been crushed against the trunk of the tree they were sitting on. The sari had kept them attached to the trunk even as he was dying" (323). As he dies, we learn later, Fokir whispers the names of his wife and son. The actual moment of his death is not described at first by the narrative. Readers see Piya and Fokir just as the storm is hitting them, and then not until after Piya has been rescued. While his death is silent in the fact that, unlike most of the events of Fokir's interactions with Piya, we are not shown his death in real time (getting the events only later after she is rescued), it is crucially important to the plot, as it is only through his death that Piya is protected. He sacrifices himself, without ever being able to explain to her why he is doing it. Once again, as at the beginning when he saves her from the river, her life is in his hands, and he gives it to her while relinquishing his own, slipping into an eternal silence.

But even after his death, Fokir still has power in the course of Piya's research. Fokir's knowledge of the region's animals and weather is instrumental in helping her accomplish her goal of finding the traveling patterns of the Irawaddy dolphins. Before the storm hit, he had taken her in his boat to every place where the dolphins frequent, and she keeps all the pertinent information from this trip in her GPS. After Fokir's death Piya names her project after him, "since his data are going to be crucial to the project" (328). Fokir may be silenced as a character, but within the structure of the novel, he has a great deal of influence over Piya's work. His sacrifice furthermore allows an even more subaltern group to be allowed a voice: the Irawaddy dolphin. Because of Fokir's knowledge, Piya is able to find the information she needs to gain support for the dolphin. In addition to her work, however, Fokir has taught her something about communication on a level deeper than the verbal (which is arguably all that Kanai offers her through much of the novel). Piya and Fokir understand each other. Ghosh writes, "Wasn't it better in a way, more honest, that they could not speak? For if you compared it to the ways in which dolphins' echoes mirrored the world, speech was only a *bag of tricks* that fooled you into believing that you could see through the eyes of another being" (132, emphasis added). Piya and Fokir function so well together because they do not see a need to understand one another on a verbal level. They can, as Black puts it, "cut through social differences and arrive at a space beyond conventional categorization" (190). Fokir is a subaltern who is silent in several ways throughout the novel, but he clearly has a kind of power that returns again and again in almost every relationship that he has.

Two necessary complications exist for my argument that the silenced characters in Ghosh's novels do, in fact, have power. First of all, the fact that these characters exist at all as people in a novel suggests that they are, in fact, not silenced. If they were truly silent, they would not exist in this literature at all. Indeed, the character of Bomma from *In an Antique Land*, who is central to the motivations Ghosh had to write the book, is barely contained within its pages. He makes only a few appearances in the history that Ghosh provides. Of course, the slave leaves no record to draw from, but Ben Yiju also has little record, and yet Ghosh draws a great deal of inference about him. Certainly Fokir and the counter-science group have more voice than poor Bomma the slave. But Ghosh's purpose in writing literature is to give voice to people who had no voice, and the writing of silence is a necessary contradiction. He attempts, then, to give them life without usurping their voices. As Mondal writes, "Ghosh scrupulously refrains from translating the subaltern past into a 'document' that could be assimilated into the idioms of historical discourse" (148). In other words, Ghosh gives his characters the capacity to resist becoming part of the dominant culture, but he still puts them in his novels.

The second objection is that Ghosh is really making these characters more subaltern by denying them voices. Perhaps Fokir is as subaltern in Ghosh's book as other Indians are in colonial literature. Perhaps the counter-science group never existed at all. It may be true that the characters I've discussed are not given the same amount of voice, say, Kanai or Piya or Dolly or Rajkumar or any of the other protagonists in Ghosh's works; on the other hand, the fact that they are there at all, and that they refuse to be narrated, speaks to some kind of power over their own fictional lives. As Lewis MacLeod writes, their silence "becomes a kind of heroic resistance, a triumph of individual agency against insistent demands that [they] participate in some kind of master narrative and the discourse it posits" (12). They do not have to become part of a narrative in order to make their influence felt. They do not have to conform to Western ideals.

For Ghosh, the silence even in his own books has power. He doesn't need to know everything about his characters, or even about his narratives. He admits to Claire Chambers that even he doesn't know what happens at the end of *The Calcutta Chromosome*. And it doesn't matter. To Ghosh, the act of exploring the silences of the subaltern people, giving some of them voice but allowing others to remain silent, is a way of retaining power. He awakens his readers to the idea that there might be voices in the silence of colonial history, just as his colleagues in the Subaltern Studies project are doing. But unlike some of the other writers, Ghosh does not force his characters to speak or else remain subaltern. Instead, he shows that even those who are silent have power in their way, and that is something we as interpreters of their silence need to understand. Michael Wood, in his excellent book *Children of Silence: On Contemporary Fiction*, argues, "We can't speak for others, and we can't be them; we can't even hear them as long as we're talking all the time. But there are silences where we may meet; it is possible to imagine others if we listen hard enough to their silence" (181). In *The Hungry Tide* and *The Calcutta Chromosome*, we are given the opportunity to imagine the subaltern characters of Fokir and the counterscience group, and in the act of taking time to imagine these fictional characters, we are giving them power over our actual lives, even if only for a brief period.

NOTES

1. Many critics take issue with Spivak's argument, stating that the attitude that states that subalterns cannot speak or be represented is defeatist and doesn't allow for any attempts to represent subalterni-

ty. But Spivak herself does not go so far as to state that no one should attempt to represent those who are subaltern. She writes, "the intellectual's solution is not to abstain from representation" (27); in other words, people should not give up entirely on speaking for those who are subaltern, but should be aware of the limitations and risks of doing so. Furthermore, as Linda Alcoff explains in "The Problem of Speaking for Others," Spivak is attempting to foster the idea that those for whom we are speaking might have alternative views on things, which, as Alcoff writes, "allows for the possibility that the oppressed will produce a 'countersentence' that can then suggest a new historical narrative" (23).

2. Ross's inability (or lack of desire) to learn his assistant's name is a great example of Edward Said's foundational idea of Orientalism, which Said describes as "the corporate institution for dealing with the Orient—dealing with it by making statements about it, authorizing views of it, describing it, by teaching it, settling it: in short, Orientalism as a Western style for dominating, restructuring, and having authority over the Orient" (Said 88). In refusing to allow Laakhan his own name, Ross believes himself in control of his assistant. Little does Ross know, of course, that Laakhan, at least in Ghosh's version, is not only the one pulling the strings, but that Laakhan himself allows his name to be changed according to the function that he is fulfilling at a particular time, making Ross's butchering of his name part of a plan rather than a subjugating experience.

Works Cited

Alcoff, Linda. "The Problem of Speaking for Others."*Cultural Critique* 20 (Winter 1991): 5-32. *JSTOR*. 11 April 2013.

Black, Shameem. *Fiction across Borders: Imagining the Lives of Others in Late-Twentieth-Century Novels.* New York: Columbia UP, 2010.

Chambers, Claire. "'The Absolute Essentialness of Conversations': A Discussion with Amitav Ghosh."*Journal of Postcolonial Writing* 41.1 (2005): 26-39. *EBSCOhost*. 12 Nov. 2012.

_____ . "Networks of Stories: Amitav Ghosh's *The Calcutta Chromosome.*" *Ariel: A Review of International English Literature* 40.2-3 (2009): 41-62. *Free E-Journals*. 7 Nov. 2012.

Chancy, Myriam J.A. *Framing Silence: Revolutionary Novels by Haitian Women.* New Brunswick, N.J.: Rutgers UP, 1997.

Ghosh, Amitav. *The Circle of Reason.* Boston: Houghton Mifflin, 1986.

_____. *The Calcutta Chromosome*. Boston: Harper Perennial, 1995.

_____ . *The Glass Palace*. Boston: Houghton Mifflin, 2000.

_____ . *The Hungry Tide*. Boston: Houghton Mifflin, 2005.

_____ . *In an Antique Land*. New York: Vintage, 1994.

_____ . *The Shadow Lines*. Boston: Houghton Mifflin, 1988.

Guha, Ranajit, and Gayatri Chakravorty Spivak. *Selected Subaltern Studies*. Oxford: Oxford UP, 1988.

MacLeod, Lewis. "'Do We of Necessity Become Puppets in a Story?' of Narrating the World on Speech, Silence, and Discourse in J.M. Coetzee's *Foe*." *Modern Fiction Studies* 52.1 (2006): 1-18. *Project Muse*. 7 Nov. 2012.

Mondal, Anshuman A. *Amitav Ghosh*. Manchester, New York: Manchester UP, 2007.

Roy, Arundhati. *The God of Small Things.* New York: Random House, 1997.

Said, Edward. "Orientalism." *The Post-Colonial Studies Reader*. Ed. Bill Ashcroft, Gareth Griffiths, and Helen Tiffin. London: Routledge, 2002. 87-91.

Spivak, Gayatri Chakravorty. "Can the Subaltern Speak?" *The Post-Colonial Studies Reader*. Ed. Bill Ashcroft, Gareth Griffiths, and Helen Tiffin. London: Routledge, 2002. 24-28.

Steiner, George. *Language and Silence.* New York: Athenaeum, 1967.

Williams, R. John. "'Doing History': Nuruddin Farah's 'Sweet and Sour Milk,' Subaltern Studies, and the Postcolonial Trajectory of Silence." *Research in African Literatures* 37.4 (2006): 161-176. *JSTOR*. 7 Nov. 2012.

Wood, Michael. *Children of Silence: On Contemporary Fiction.* New York: Columbia UP, 1999.

Literary and Cultural Hybridity in Tayyeb Salih's *Season of Migration to the North*

DAHOOD EL-OQLA

This essay explores Tayyeb Salih's representation of the hybridity and plurality of the Sudanese African-Arab culture in *Season of Migration to the North* (1969). The novel's hybridity results from merging Arabic narrative techniques like *Hakawati* style and genres like *Maqamat* and *Mu'aradah* with the Western literary genre of the novel (Harlow 74). Salih's use of these three Arabic forms highlights indigenous narrative techniques and values, such as orality, circularity, and collective experience. In addition, the novel's formal hybridity is paralleled by a thematic and ideological hybridity, which is revealed by examining the divided loyalties of the two main characters, the unnamed narrator and his friend Mustafa Sa'eed (Makdisi 814). The novel emphasizes this by describing these personas' multiple Western, African, and Arab characteristics. Both Sa'eed's and the narrator's Western personas attract them to an English education and lifestyle, which intensifies their struggle to maintain a traditional and conservative Sudanese cultural identity because of European secular and technologically advanced culture. The division within these two characters is also paralleled by a layer of division within the Sudanese community during the postcolonial era in the 1960s and '70s. The novel illustrates how different socio-political forces (colonial vs. postcolonial, patriarchal vs. feminist, progressive vs. traditional) struggle against each other. Through these multiple forces Salih represents a more vibrant image of the complexity of postcolonial Sudan, one that subverts the traditional reductive representation of African realities as national allegories or exotic figments of Western imagination. In analyzing the hybridity, plurality, and cultural complexity of the Sudanese community, this essay draws on Mikhail Bakhtin's concept of parody, which facilitates the emergence of multiple voices and explains the intertextual and ideological dependencies and interconnections between Western and indigenous cultures in postcolonial times.

To illuminate this rich and culturally vibrant representation of the Sudanese community in Salih's fiction, Wail Hassan and other critics interpret the text in light of Bakhtin's theories of discourse, parody, and heteroglossia. Hassan, for example, argues that Salih's fiction reflects Bakhtin's concept of novelistic discourse because it brings together different "competing sociolinguistic strata [and therefore ideologies] that are constantly engaged in 'dialogic' interaction" (11). Hassan connects the "dialogic" nature of Salih's fiction to Bakhtin's concept of parody. According to Hassan, parody implies a kind of "double-voicedness" that allows Salih's novel to respond to "previous European and Arabic texts that thematize the cross-cultural encounter between Europe on the one hand and Africa and the Arab world on the other" (83). Thus, the concept of parody illuminates the interaction between Arabic literary forms like the *Hakawati* style, *Mu' aradah*, and *Maqamat* and the Western literary genre of the novel. While Hassan limits Bakhtin's concept of parody to the intertextual influences between Arabic and Western literary traditions, I plan to extend Hassan's theory in examining these intertextual connections and to show the role of parody in creating hybrid characters and communities—especially the two main characters. The "double-voicedness," even *multiple-voicedness* I argue, allows both characters to adopt different Western, African, and Arab personas. Parody in this sense becomes a form of mimicry that gives the two characters a hybrid status and allows them to express and grapple with their cross-cultural experiences. The narrator and Sa'eed exhibit tremendous attraction to Western and Sudanese cultural values and lifestyles, thereby occupying conflicted and divided spaces of hegemonic colonizer and dominated colonized simultaneously. This ideological parody is also paralleled by formal one that facilitates the presence of Arabic literary forms like *Mu'aradah* and *Maqamat* within the genre of the novel.

The novel opens with the unnamed narrator's recent return home after spending the past seven years studying English poetry in Britain. His feelings of assurance and comfort on returning to his homeland are soon disturbed by an encounter with a stranger named Mustafa Sa'eed and by the prevalence of Western technology in his indigenous community. Mustafa Sa'eed triggers the curiosity of the narrator, who starts a quest to learn about Sa'eed's life, history, and origins. The narrator begins a friendship with Sa'eed and eventually learns about his academic and cultural experiences in Europe. Sa'eed tells the narrator about his sexual exploits with European women for whom he invented fabrications that reinforce the stereotypical, exotic, and fantastical associations that many Europeans attach to the African/Arab "other." Sa'eed reveals how he managed to lure many European women through his "lethal lies," pushing at least one woman, Isabel Seymour, to commit suicide. Sa'eed also tells the narrator about his trial that resulted from murdering his wife Jean Morrison. After serving seven years in prison, Sa'eed goes back to Sudan and chooses to settle down among the indigenous Sudanese in an obscure village at the bend of the Nile. He marries Hosna, the daughter of one of the villagers. In Sudan, Sa'eed helps the poor villagers combat the corruption and exploitation of rich farmers.

While learning about the life of Mustafa Sa'eed, the narrator develops a fascination, bordering on an obsession, with Sa'eed, and he notices connections and parallels between Sa'eed's life and identity and his own. After Sa'eed's sudden disappearance, the narrator becomes the guardian of Sa'eed's children and develops love for Hosna. In learning about the narrator's empathy with Sa'eed, we also learn about different forms of oppression and exploitation within the indigenous community. The narrator criticizes the elite class and high government officials for their corrupt and unproductive tactics, which have created division and conflict among the differing socio-political factions within the indigenous community. The narrator's dissatisfaction with his indigenous culture is also evident in his critical attitude toward patriarchal practices, which eventually lead Hosna to murder old Wadd Rayyes and commit suicide after she is forced to marry him.

The bicultural experiences of the two main characters and the complex realities of postcolonial Sudan mark hybridity and plurality as the ultimate modifiers of the Sudanese Arab culture. This hybridity is best represented in Salih's novel by the formal and ideological plurality that facilitates the merging of Western and indigenous literary forms and cultural values. Salih's novel draws upon the ancient Arabic literary technique of *Mu'aradah*, a form that, in highlighting the social issues and literary forms pertinent to indigenous Arab (here Sudan) culture helps redefine the Western literary tradition, including the novel genre. The narrative's constant literary allusions push many critics, including Barbara Harlow and Benita Parry, to read the text as a *Mu'aradah*, "a form literally meaning opposition or contradiction in which at least two voices participate, the first composing a poem that the second will undo by writing along the same lines, but reversing the meaning" (74). The novel takes up its role of Arabic *Mu' aradah* in contrast to the colonial discourse is by deconstructing colonial gender difference. Ania Loomba argues that colonial discourse tends to highlight gender differences between the self and the other, showing the colonizer as a master/rapist and the colonized as a feminized victim:

> We have seen how a wide spectrum of representation encodes the rape and plunder of colonial countries as master/rapist. But the threat of native rebellion produces a very different kind of colonial stereotype which represents the colonized as a (usually dark-skinned) rapist who comes to ravish the white woman who in turn comes to symbolize European culture. (79)

Season follows Loomba's argument when the Sudanese resistance to colonial discourse becomes a form of sexual violence against the European female body. Sa'eed contends that he plans on liberating Africa with his "penis" (100), and most of his sexual experiences in London involve the exploitation of European women. Salih's narrative, however, deconstructs many of the Western misconceptions regarding the "other" through the characterization of Mustafa Sa'eed, who exploits Western stereotypes of the "other" as exotic and libidinous energy. To emphasize the fantastical, illusionary nature of Sa'eed's otherness, the narrator states:

> Occasionally the disturbing thought occurs to me that Mustafa Sa'eed never happened, that he was in fact a lie, a phantom, a dream or a nightmare that had come to the people of that village one suffocating dark night, and when they open their eyes to the sunlight he was nowhere to be seen. (39)

As a consequence of the fabrications which Mustafa Sa'eed uses to build his whole existence in Europe, he ends up destroying himself and the lives of many innocent people around him.

The narrative's implementation of the *Mu'aradah* techniques enables Salih to subvert the thematic assumptions regarding European colonialism in Africa and the realistic narrative techniques of Western novels like Joseph Conrad's *Heart of Darkness.* The opening lines of Salih's narrative, "It was, gentlemen, after a long absence—seven years to be exact, during which time

I was studying in Europe—that I returned to my people" (3), echo Joseph Conrad's opening when Marlow addresses his companions and crew on board the Nellie: "'And this also,' said Marlow suddenly, 'has been one of the dark places of the earth'" (5). The beginnings of both novels mark the multilayered structure of these narratives, for Salih's and Conrad's unnamed narrators tell their audiences about the stories they have learned from Sa'eed and Marlow respectively.

By invoking a similar opening to that of Conrad, Salih's narrative echoes another Arabic literary tradition, the *Hakawati* style, which mandates the interaction of a speaker and a listening audience, a strategy that foregrounds the collective experience of the indigenous culture and subverts the theme of alienation of the modern person dominant in Conrad's narrative. Sari Makdisi points to the Arabic *Hakawati* characteristics of Salih's narrative. He argues that these features dominate the beginning of the novel but disappears later in the narrative. Makdisi adds that this change marks a shift to a European modernist novel, shatters colonial binary oppositions, and allows the narrative to evolve into a hybrid postcolonial status (814). It is important to remember that the *Hakawati* style is not marked simply by an opening with a central speaker addressing a group of people. Rather, it highlights a larger oral tradition that depends on circular and repetitive techniques, rhymed prose, refrain, and alliteration. These characteristics persist within Salih's narrative, in fact, until the final paragraphs of the novel, despite what Makdisi argues. Although he attempts to highlight the hybridity of Sudanese culture by examining the change and transformation he perceives within Salih's narrative techniques, Makdisi inadvertently reinforces the binary opposition he intended to deconstruct. In other words, Makdisi's insistence upon distinguishing between earlier *Hakawati* and later European modernist techniques confirms the dualism his argument intends to undermine.

Contrary to the argument that Makdisi presents, the narrative actually accentuates the circular and oral feel of the *Hakawati* style by repeating key phrases, expressions, and motifs at both early and later stages of the novel. The motif of fabrication, for instance, occurs in every chapter of the narrative. Words such as "lie," "illusion," and "phantom" are used many times to describe Sa'eed and the narrator. The motif of tension between water pumps and the Nile attract the narrator's attention when he returns from England at the beginning of the novel and last until the final scene of the novel: "I heard the reverberation of the river and the puttering of the water-pump" (138). It is this very circularity that undermines the linear narrative approach of Western epistemology. For instance, despite the apparent recursive structure of Conrad's narrative, with its framed structure, there is no doubt of its linear progression, for the narrative presents the incidents of Marlow's journey into the Congo chronologically. While deconstructing Western narrative techniques, Salih also subverts European ideological assumptions regarding the colonizing mission. Although *Heart of Darkness* indicts Belgian colonialism, the narrative still centers on a European male's psychological development, rather than the material conditions of Africa or the cultural disintegration of its people at the hands of colonialism. *Season of Migration to the North*, on the other hand, constantly reminds the reader of the violent and destructive aspects of this mission every time there is an Eastern-Western encounter. Salih's novel, more importantly, centers on the damaging effects colonial and cultural encounters have on two Arab, rather than European, men. The narrative contextualizes this theme by emphasizing the destructive impact Western technology has on the indigenous landscape like the Nile; the pumps enhance the "thrusting of the water," which leads to the "retreat" of the Nile banks (6). This choice of violent diction reflects the negative impact that results from Western technology on the Sudanese indigenous eco-system.

Season also makes continuous references to William Shakespeare's *Othello*, in an attempt to deconstruct racist and stereotypical Western assumptions regarding the identity of the other as a sexual and cultural threat. During his trial for the murder of his wife Jean Morrison in London, Sa'eed states that the violent and sexually uninhibited Sa'eed "does not exist. He's an illusion, a lie" (28).Sa'eed compares himself to Othello, who is also characterized as a "lie" (80). Salih's criticism of these stereotypical images of the African "other" is reflected in his ironic tone. Sa'eed's exaggerated characterization as sexually unbridled and psychologically unstable, whose personal, sexual, and cultural involvement with European females usually ends with the murder or suicide of these females, becomes an ironic parody of Shakespeare's Othello or, more generally, European fantasies regarding the African-Arab Moor, who is repeatedly seeking the European "Desdemona" or the European female body.

Season's tendency to parody Arabic forms predating the novel is also evident in its adaptation of the literary tradition of *Maqamat*. Critic Amina Shah states that *Maqamat* literally means to "stand up" in an "assembly" and denotes "discourses delivered or conversations held in any such assembly" intended for didactic and instructive rather than entertaining purposes (vii). This echoes the *Hakawati* style, which literally means the teller of *hikayat* (stories), for both *Maqamat* and *Hakawati* imply the centrality of a single speaker or narrator addressing a group of people. The *Maqamat*, however, highlights the didactic element due to its multilayered narrative, or narrative within a narrative, which turns it into a form of cautionary tale. This strategy is characteristic of Salih's novel and is evident in English novels, including *Heart of Darkness* and *Frankenstein*. Like many European cautionary tales, *Season* warns against the dangers associated with cultural encounters, especially reinforcing fabrications regarding the Eastern and/or Western "other," as well as the violent and traumatic effects of oppressive systems like colonialism and patriarchy. Although Salih's novels adopts the didactic nature within European novels, it does so by undermining, rather than underscoring, the dominant colonial, patriarchal, and racist assumptions in its representation of marginalized classes. The novel's narrative techniques also diverts from European norms in order to highlight indigenous African oral and circular narration.

Salih's novel also imitates the narrative technique of *Maqamat* because of the double relationship it develops between the two main characters. It is common within the *Maqamat* tradition for writers to create two characters, and the curiosity of one pushes the other to physically and psychologically follow the other in a demand to learn about his origin, life, and adventures (Shah vii). In Abu Mohammed Al-Hariri's eleventh-century *Maqamat*, for instance, the author establishes a double relationship between Abu Zayed Al-Saruj and Harith Bin Hamman, who follows Al-Saruj into different cities wishing to learn about his life (Shah vii). Likewise, this doubling relationship exists in Salih's novel between Sa'eed and the narrator. The similarities between the two characters are striking: both characters have been to the West, where they received their formal educations and experienced cultural familiarity with European nations. Sa'eed has such a strong impact on the narrator that he haunts the narrator even after Sa'eed's death. "Thus Mustafa Sa'eed has, against my will, become part of my world, although in my brain, a phantom that does not want to take itself off" (42). The narrator even sees his own story and existence as an extension of that of Sa'eed and decides "to begin where Sa'eed had left off" (111).

The narrator's and Sa'eed's narrative voices intermingle and their stories overlap at multiple points, and Sa'eed's narrative even impinges upon that of the narrator. This merging of characters and stories is underscored when the narrator enters Sa'eed's lib

> I struck a match. The light exploded my eyes and out of the darkness there emerged a frowning face with pursed lips that I knew but could not place. I moved towards it with hate in my heart. It was my adversary Mustafa Sa'eed. The face grew a neck, the neck two shoulders and a chest, then a trunk and two legs, and I found myself standing face to face with myself. This is not Mustafa Sa'eed—it's a picture of me frowning at my face from a mirror. (112)

The obsessions of one character with the other present a detailed picture about the life and history of this character, as is the case with the narrator and Sa'eed. In this sense, the *Maqamat* becomes a bildungsroman, a novel that traces the growth and development of the main character. Discussing the Arabic influences of the *Maqamat* on the European picaresque novel, James T. Monroe argues: "the *maqamah* genre is pre-novelistic, for in the novel the reader is allowed to follow the adventures of the protagonist from a specific moment in his life (e.g., from birth), to a moment when the hurdles life offers in that specific novel are eventually overcome (e.g., marriage and living happily ever after), all in chronological and spatial order." (8)

Although Salih's narrative reinforces the bildungsroman tradition through its intense focus on the growth and development of Sa'eed's character, it diverts from the linear and chronological narrative by deploying circular and repetitive narratives, like recurring motifs, themes, and expressions. This strategy allows Salih to employ some characteristics of the *Maqamat* tradition while subverting some of the Western adaptations to this tradition as evidenced in the bildungsroman. In discussing the significance of geo-historical circumstances within the contemporary Arabic novel, Hosam Aboul-Ela argues that Salih's novel provides an excellent example of the Arabic circular narrative technique. "The sense of causality and orderly progress that one senses in Dickens's novels is replaced by the episodism and emphasis on the scene as the primary building block," and this subverts linear and straightforward narrative of "the Anglo-European *Bildungsroman*" (12). Although the *maqamat* creates unity within the whole (usually composed of fifty *maqamah*, singular for *maqamat*) by reinforcing the development and evolution of the main character, each single *maqamah* can stand on its own as independent work of art. These *Maqamah* (s), then, could be seen as a series of short stories or mini episodes within a larger work. Salih divides his novel in a series of fully developed chapters that can stand on their own as independent works. Each of these chapters focuses on a single aspect or phase of the narrator's life, some dealing with his personal life like his love or marriage and others dealing with his career in Khartoum and disillusionment with the corruption governments and unproductive officials.

Another way in which the narrative echoes the *Maqamat* is its drive towards social criticism, change, and reform. Al-Hariri's *Maqamat*, for instance, features a wide range of characters representing different social institutions, such as judges, sultans, clerics, and intellectuals throughout its different episodes and reveals their corruption. Similarly, *Season* empowers traditionally marginalized perspectives like those of women and peasants allowing them to criticize elitist and patriarchal social institutions, a topic that will be fully examined later in this essay.

When Salih draws heavily on Arabic literary forms like *Mu'arada* and *Maqamat* in crafting his novel, he manages to create a hybrid literary piece that combines indigenous and Western narrative traditions. This formal plurality is also paralleled by an ideological hybridity that reveal the socio-political diversity of the Sudanese community, which is reflected specifically in the identities of the two main characters. Both Sa'eed and the narrator "parody" and espouse different personas, Western and indigenous alike. In his analysis of African-Arab culture, Shaden Tageldin insists upon the strong interconnection between Arab, African, and European cultural components in defining the

African-Arab identity. He finds fault with critics like Ngugi wa Thiong'o who exclude Arabic language and ethnicity as alien to an "authentic" African identity. In contrast, he applauds intellectuals like Kwame Nkrumah, who

> sought a post-independence Africanness that would "allow the combined presence of traditional Africa, Islamic Africa and Euro-Christian Africa" [and] Frantz Fanon—who . . . urged post-independence Africa to reject the temptation of the color line: the division of Africa into a "white" North and a "black" South and the demonization of Arabic and Islam as alien to African identity. (86)

Tageldin's argument regarding the hybrid nature of African identity, including the African-Arab identity, aptly describes the character of Mustapha Sa'eed in *Season*, whose hybrid identity is reflected in his mixed genealogy and ancestry. Sa'eed descends from a northern Arab (Egyptian-Sudanese) father and Southern black mother: "His father was from the Ababda, the tribe living between Egypt and the Sudan. . . . It is said that his mother was a slave from the South, from the tribes of Zandi or Barai—God knows" (45). Moreover, Sa'eed's early attraction to different cultures and geographies reinforces his multiple identities. In a letter he addresses to the narrator, Sa'eed admits both his happiness and contentment in the simple life of the village people while admitting his attraction to "faraway places": "Rationally, I know what is right: my attempt at living in this village with these happy people. But mysterious things in my soul and in my blood impel me towards faraway parts that loomed up before me and cannot be ignored" (56). Sa'eed is characterized as a chameleon who takes up multiple personalities that correspond and fit both African and Western cultural values. While receiving his education in England, he takes on a different persona with each sexual experience, for he was "Hassan and Charles, and Amin and Mustafa and Richard" every time he had sex with a different English woman (31). The names Sa'eed takes with each sexual adventure come from different origins, Arab, European, and African.

Sa'eed's Western persona is revealed when he adopts the dominant and hegemonic identity of the European colonizer, particularly his obsessive fascination with having an English education and speaking the language. Despite that Salih's Sudanese people shy away from sending their children to English schools because they saw them as "a great evil that had come to them with the armies of occupation," Sa'eed finds English schools and receiving an English education appealing from his early childhood (19). Sa'eed excels in the English language, the language of the colonizer, which facilitates his espousing Western cultural perspectives. Describing his fascination with the English language and its mysteries, Sa'eed states that his "brain continued on, biting and cutting like the teeth of a plough. Words and sentences formed themselves before me as though they were mathematical equations; algebra and geometry as though they were verses of poetry" (21). The privileged and empowering status of English in Sa'eed's time is later affirmed when a Sudanese civil servant describes it as "the key to the future" (44).

But such a tacit acceptance of English as "the key to the future" undermines the validity of the indigenous language, a form of cultural annihilation that in turn reinforces the values and interests of colonizing nations. English is the language of the empire and its dominance underscores the cultural dependency colonized countries struggle with as a result of the traumatic experience of colonization. Language is part of the ideological apparatus through which colonial nations reinforce their hegemony over colonized countries. Ironically, although Sa'eed aspires to an empowering status when developing an attachment to English language and education, he ends up accentuating colonial hegemony. Sa'eed's English education paradoxically co-exists alongside his non-Western heritage, for he states that while in Britain, he "by day lived with the theories of Keynes and Tawney and at night [he] resumed the war with bow and sword and arrows" (30). Just as the colonizer uses weapons to oppress the colonized nations, Sa'eed uses traditional weapons that fit the indigenous culture and its warfare to describe his figurative cultural and sexual, but very ambivalent, wars against the English woman Isabel Seymour. This association between Sa'eed and indigenous traditional weaponry reminds us again of his African-Arab heritage.

By validating the language and education of the colonizer, Sa'eed signals the cultural dependency associated with colonial conquest, for language is an ideological system that shapes and serves the interests of the dominant group. That is why, as Ania Loomba reminds us in summarizing Gauri Viswanathan's seminal work *Masks of Conquest: Literary Studies and British Rule in India*, English literature was promoted and taught in the colonies: "to play a key role in attempting to impose western values to the natives, constructing European culture as superior and as a measure of human values, and thereby in maintaining colonial rule" (85). Ironically, Sa'eed's attraction to English education and adoption of the English language, which can be perceived as subversive for Western culture, proves European domination and hegemony over African-Arab nations.

Sa'eed not only embraces a Western persona through education, but also through inverting traditional colonial discourse. In England, Sa'eed characterizes himself as an invader and takes up the persona of a colonizer. He confirms that during his trial, he experienced a sense of superiority towards the judge and the jury that stems from his feelings of significance and worth, for he sees himself as the "colonizer," the "invader," and the "intruder" (79). He even perceives the trial itself as a battlefield that reminds him of ancient histories and colonial relationships:

> In that court I hear the rattle of swords in Carthage and the clatter of the hooves of Albany's horses desecrating the ground of Jerusalem. The ships at first sailed down the Nile carrying guns not

> bread, and the railroads were originally set up to transport troops; the schools were started so as to teach us how to say 'yes' in their language. . . . Yes, my dear sirs, I came as an invader into your very homes. A drop of poison you injected into the veins of history. "I am no Othello. Othello was a lie." (79)

Sa'eed sees his trial as an opportunity to expose and respond to the historical atrocities associated with colonial trauma. According to Sa'eed, colonialism destroyed the religious and cultural heritage of the indigenous culture. Mona Amyuni believes that a major concern of Salih's novel is to reveal the traumatic effects associated with the colonial encounter, specifically those reflected in the character of Sa'eed, whose sexual exploits of British women parody the colonizers' exploitation of indigenous land: "when the colonizer reaches the heart of the colonized world, he implants his banner at the top of the official buildings, sits in them, appropriates the land, and the people of the land" (211).

Sa'eed further promotes his colonizer's personality by perceiving his experience in Europe as a sexual revenge. In his analysis of the double-relationship between the narrator and Sa'eed, Musa Al-Halool argues that Salih's novel "attests to a conceptualization of colonialism as rape and anti-colonial struggle as a sexual revenge" (31). Sa'eed's sexual revenge, I would add, depends largely on destabilizing gender roles in terms of his relation to London and English women. From his earliest encounter with the European female body, Sa'eed associates the West with sexual pleasure. Sa'eed exhibits tremendous sexual attraction to Western women like Mrs. Robinson, a British expatriate in Egypt who sponsors Sa'eed's education in Cairo:

> At that moment, as I stood at the station platform amidst a welter of sounds and sensations, with the woman's arms round my neck, her mouth on my cheeks, the smell of her body—a strange, European smell—tickling my nose, her breast touching my chest, I felt—I, a boy of twelve—a vague sexual yearning I had never previously experienced. (22-23)

Since Sa'eed sees his journey to England as counter-colonization, his intention to feminize Europe is necessary to facilitate the process of domination—for he intends to liberate Africa with his "penis" (100). Sa'eed's reversal of the power dynamic is signaled by emphasizing his male gaze. Describing his first encounter with Jean Morrison, for instance, he states, "She opened the door and lingered; she appeared to my gaze under the faint lamp-light like a mirage shimmering in the desert" (26). Sa'eed's emphasis on the role of his gaze in his encounter with European females registers his intentions to return the colonial gaze and affirms his masculine dominating status. As Edward Said argues, the hegemonic relationship between East and West within colonial discourse is established upon feminizing the East. For many years, the East has been perceived by the Western audience as feminine domain suitable for fulfilling the exotic fantasies of the European male traveler (188). In reversing the idea of sexual exploitation, Sa'eed commits the same thing he accuses the colonizer of doing—both of which are at the expense of women, regardless of race or culture. Salih does not promote misogynistic ideologies but provides us with us with a range of characters, one of whom is pushed to commit atrocious acts because of his anger and frustration. As we will see later in this essay, Salih valorizes voices, perspective, and experiences of female characters in the novel.

In spite of adopting a Westernized persona, Sa'eed shows a strong loyalty and attachment to the Sudanese indigenous culture, and this double connection intensifies the hybrid nature of his identity. Sa'eed exhibits tremendous appreciation of the traditional and simple lifestyle of his rural Sudanese community. After long years of living and travelling in different European countries, he chooses to spend the rest of his life and establish a family in a small village in rural Sudan. He even wants the same for his children and asks the narrator to raise them in the village:

> If they grow up imbued with the air of this village, its smells and colors and history, the faces of its inhabitants and the memories of its floods and harvesting and sowing, then my life will acquire its true perspective as something meaningful alongside many other meanings of deeper significance. (55)

That is, Sa'eed wants his children to be brought up in the village so that they can develop a deeper and more meaningful understanding of its culture and history. Sa'eed's desire to teach his children the value of indigenous history and memories reflects his appreciation of the Sudanese collective experience. Sa'eed does not want his children to experience the cultural alienation and displacement he had in his earlier life.

Moreover, being part of a larger community and tradition gives both Sa'eed and his children a deeper perspective and purpose in life. After settling down in the Sudan, Sa'eed becomes highly invested in the lives and best interests of the indigenous community. His work with the Agricultural Project Committee empowers the peasants and relieves them from the exploitative practices of rich farmers. Sa'eed's economic ideas help the peasants establish their own mill and buy their own lorries to transfer their own products. These economic measures reduce the peasants' dependency on the rich farmers and their advanced equipment, upon which agricultural processes depend. The ideas that Sa'eed brings to the community effectively deconstruct the hierarchical structure within the village and create more social justice and democratic values by giving the working farmers more economic and agricultural autonomy. His honest desire to reform the indigenous community and empower the marginalized peasants reveals a genuine sense of belonging and a true desire to give back to his own Sudanese people.

In addition to his genuine interest in the well-being of the Sudanese indigenous community, Sa'eed reflects his traditional identity by satirizing and subverting Western stereotypes of "exotic" and "primitive" African culture. Sa'eed, as we have seen, compares himself to Othello many times in the novel, insinuating that the fabrications surrounding Othello and himself are part of Europe's long tradition of exoticizing the East and the "other." Laura Rice believes that Sa'eed's fabrications are intended to reveal the lies associated with the other, for Sa'eed "embodies all the lies the English have told about him. He gives them what they wanted to see, and in doing so, he becomes a mirror exposing their lies" (133). Sa'eed's appropriation of Africa's exoticism aims at deconstructing rather than intensifying the stereotypical association of the exotic other. Even when Sa'eed uses these fabrications to lure English women sexually, he exaggerates these fantasies in order to ridicule their illusory and unrealistic nature. Relating his first encounter with Isabel Seymour, Sa'eed states:

> I related to her fabricated stories about deserts of golden sands and jungles where nonexistent animals called out to one another. I told her that the streets of my country teemed with elephants and lions and that during siesta time crocodiles crawled through it. Half credulous, half believing, she listened to me, laughing and closing her eyes, her cheeks reddened. . . . There came a moment when I felt I had been transformed in her eyes into a naked, primitive creature, a spear in one hand and arrow in the other, hunting elephants and lions in the jungle. . . . "Yes. Our house is right on the bank of the Nile, so that when I am lying on my bed at night. I put my hand out of the window and idly play with the Nile waters till sleep overtakes me." (32-34)

Both Sa'eed and the "half credulous, half believing" Isabel understand that his stories are no more than entertaining exaggerations that preface their sexual intimacy. Moreover, Sa'eed's excessive exaggerations establish his ironic attitude toward European fantasies. This ironic attitude is one of the means through which Sa'eed subverts European stereotypical perceptions. The satirical effects of Sa'eed's representation of Africa as primitive and exotic are linked to his notions of theatricality, for Sa'eed constantly states that his bedroom has turned into "a theater of war" (29) at times and like "an operating theater in a hospital" at others (27). In his analysis of the representation of the Orient within Western literature, Said points out the significance of theatricality: Turning the Orient into a stage transforms and distorts the original reality of the Orient in order to meet the fantasies and imagination of the Western audience (67). Similarly, by playing with this notion of theatricality, Sa'eed offers a caricature of African culture. Theatricality intensifies Sa'eed hybrid character and allows him to adopt multiple personas, for he becomes a different character each time he gets on the stage.

The parallels and interconnections the reader can draw between the experiences of Sa'eed and the narrator reinforce the argument that, just like Mustafa Sa'eed, the narrator espouses both Western and indigenous identities. The narrator's traditional, indigenous identity is evident in his attachment to and celebration of the traditional aspects of the Sudanese community. When the narrator returns from his studies in Europe to his Sudanese culture after a seven-year absence, he foregrounds his feelings of "assurance" and comfort (4). He enjoys the "warmth of his tribe" over the "cold" and unpleasant English weather (3). The narrator states that he "feels a sense of stability" when he sees the Nile River and the farmers working in the fields surrounding it (6). The narrator also takes pride in the histories his grandfather is able to recount about former Turkish colonization and the genealogy of every individual in the village. The narrator's admiration for his grandfather indexes respect for the indigenous tradition:

> By the standards of the European industrial world we are poor peasants, but when I embrace my grandfather I experience a sense of richness as though I am a note in the heartbeats of the very universe. He is no towering oak tree with luxuriant branches growing in a land on which Nature has bestowed water and fertility, rather is he like the sayal bushes in the deserts of Sudan, thick of bark

> and sharp of thorn, defeating death because they ask so little of life. (62)

As we can see, the narrator relies on establishing binary oppositions between Eastern and Western cultures in order to highlight his strong connection and admiration for the traditional and ancient features of his indigenous culture. Comparing his grandfather to the "sayal bushes," the narrator establishes a strong relationship between his people and their landscape, which reinforces their sense of cultural identity. Ties between the land and the people is later used by the narrator to secure his own place within the Sudanese community: "but I am from here, just as the date palm standing in the courtyard of our house has grown in our house and not in anyone else's" (41). In order to underscore his sense of belonging, the narrator reiterates his knowledge of the "village, its people, streets and houses" (40).

The narrator's identification with his traditional community is also reflected in his discomfort at the presence of Western technology and culture within the indigenous community. For example, he experiences great discomfort that shakes his feelings of assurance and confidence at the presence of water pumps along the Nile River instead of the traditional waterwheels:

> From my position under the tree I saw the village slowly undergo a change: the water-wheels disappeared to be replaced on the banks of the Nile by pumps, each one doing the work of a hundred water-wheels. I saw the bank retreating year after year in front of the thrustings of the water, while in another part it was the water that retreated. (6)

The presence of European technological advances, the water pumps, disturbs the natural flow of the Nile River and the natural layout of the indigenous landscape and registers the violent impact, the "thrustings," that result from the introduction of Western technology. The water pumps also establish a sexual dynamic that feminizes the indigenous landscape and underscores

Western hegemony. But the most disturbing presence of Western culture within the Sudanese community is Sa'eed himself, as well as his fluent knowledge of the English language and European culture. Sa'eed is also a constant reminder to the narrator about the futility of literary studies. This complicates the narrator's struggle for identity because it raises uncomfortable questions about his productive role in the community. Sa'eed tells the narrator: "We have no need for poetry here. It would have been better if you'd studied agriculture, engineering or medicine" (9). In questioning the value of English literature, Sa'eed makes the narrator feel like an outsider and emphasizes his own productive role within the indigenous community.

Complicating the narrator's discomfort at the presence of Western technology within the indigenous culture, he sometimes perceives it as an acceptable part of the Sudanese postcolonial situation. When the narrator goes to meet with Sa'eed for the first time, he speaks in English. Even Sa'eed, the epitome of Western presence in indigenous Sudan, criticizes the narrator for speaking in English and asks, "[H]as your long stay in England made you forget Arabic or do you reckon we've become anglicized" (14). Later, the narrator's passive acceptance of the country's cultural and economic dependency after decolonization seems to actually provide justification for the colonial project:

> The fact that they came to our land, I knew not why, does that mean that we should poison our present or future? Sooner or later they will leave our country, just as many people throughout history left many countries. The railways, ships, hospitals, factories, and schools will be ours and we'll speak their language without either a sense of guilt or a sense of gratitude. (41-42)

The narrator's stance normalizes the dangerous, traumatic effects of colonialism, and this creates a kind of complicity, even if unconscious, between the colonizer and the narrator. The narrator therefore ignores and dismisses the traumatic and tragic effects resulting from colonial violence and exploitation, as well as cultural and economic domination. This attitude can be seen as his tacit approval, accepting and justifying the colonial project as something productive and positive rather than traumatic.

The narrator's association with Western identity and perspective is evident in his attraction and attachment to Sa'eed's wife Hosna Bint Mahmoud, whose marriage to Sa'eed has turned her into a stereotypically Western type of female. Extremely liberal, assertive, and Westernized, Hosna's presence in Sudan becomes a reminder of Sa'eed's, and possibly the narrator's, sexual and cultural attachment to Western culture and women. The change that characterized Hosna's personality after her marriage to Sa'eed is noticeable by many members of the village community. The narrator's childhood friend Mahjoub, for instance, believes that Hosna went under "indescribable change" turning into a "city girl" (84). Hosna is even seen by the narrator's mother as a "hussy" because she asks the narrator to marry her in order to rescue her from a forced marriage to Wad Rayyes (102). It is obvious from these examples that Hosna's relationship with Sa'eed has affected her personality and transformed her into an independent and assertive woman, characteristics that are not typical of mainstream Sudanese and Arab women.

Nevertheless, these assertive, liberal characteristics are the source of the narrator's physical and emotional attraction to Hosna. During one of their conversations, Hosna laments the loss of her husband, but her perfume and sobbing are perceived as inviting to the narrator, and they trigger his sexual attraction. Describing her sobbing in the darkness, the narrator states: "I listened to her sobbing as though it came to me from afar, mingled in my mind with scattered noises which I had no doubt heard at odd times but which all intertwined in my brain like a carillon of church bells" (80).Hosna's voice reminds the narrator of an experience that is part of Western culture, perhaps a Christian holiday, rather than the indigenous culture. The narrator's attraction to Hosna illustrates his association with and desire to take on Sa'eed's sexual role. The narrator admits, "[I]n one form or another [I] was in love with Hosna Bint Mahmoud" (86). It is only through this attraction that we learn about the sexual and romantic sides of the narrator's character, as we never get a glimpse into his intimate life in either Europe or Sudan. Hosna seems to be the ideal, or an approximation, of what he desires as well as a reminder of his bond to Sa'eed.

The narrator's admiration of and sexual attraction to Hosna exemplify his disconnection from the Sudanese indigenous community. When he learns about the tragic death of Hosna as a result of her forced marriage, the narrator is shocked at his people's indifference and inability to empathize with her. The narrator feels like a stranger to his own community: "[T]here is no room for me here. Why don't I pack up and go? Nothing astonishes these people" (107). His friend Mahjoub reinforces the narrator's outsider status, telling him that "schooling and education has made [him] soft" (107).

As critic Maurizio Calbi argues, the narrator's "outsider" status is a sign of division within the Sudanese community, particularly the gap between the upper classes like the elites and educated and lower classes like peasants and the working class (352). Calbi's assertions describe the state of many characters in Salih's narrative, including the narrator who negotiates his place within differing and conflicting social groups. The narrator's in-between social status, for he comes from a humble, working class family with an education that connects him to elitist, upper classes, complicates his sense of belonging to either group. This divided status again explains the narrator's and Sa'eed's simultaneous attraction to Western and indigenous cultural values. Their drive toward espousing, or "parodying," multiple indigenous and Western identities, explains their attraction to English education and European culture. Their multiple identities also give them a critical perspective that reveals the shortcomings of both exploitative Western colonization and corrupt indigenous culture. Moreover, the multiple and plural identities of the main two characters reflect the diverse and hybrid nature of the postcolonial Sudanese community.

The diverse, sometimes conflicting, cultural affiliations exemplified in the two main characters mirror the complexities of postcolonial Sudan, particularly the presence of multiple and differing Western and indigenous cultural values and socio-political forces. In addition to showing the impact of colonial influence on the Sudanese community, the narrative reflects the divisions within the indigenous community between traditional and progressive views, secular and spiritual perspectives, and patriarchal and feminist ideologies. Colonial interference leads to the introduction of new and different Western cultural perspectives and values within the indigenous community of Sudan. These perspectives and values create conflict and tension among liberal, secular, and conservative factions and highlight the weaknesses and shortcomings of local officials. On one of his trips to his village from Khartoum, the narrator, for instance, encounters a civil servant on the train and strikes up a conversation that shows how colonial practices/policies create division and instability within the indigenous community. The civil servant explains:

> They [English officials] would employ us, the junior government officials who were natives of the country, to bring in the taxes. The people would grumble and complain to the English commissioner, and naturally it was the English commissioner who was indulgent and showed mercy. And in this way they sowed hatred in the hearts of the people for us, their kinsmen, and love for the colonizers, the intruders. (45)

This hatred for specific elitist and government groups, as well as its divisive and destabilizing consequences, is reinforced by neocolonial tactics. As mentioned earlier, Calbi believes that the hybridity and division within the main two characters, signs of the divisions and conflicts within the Sudanese indigenous community, result from their cultural contact with European nations (352). Despite the fact that colonizers eventually cleared out during decolonization, they left behind a culturally colonized people—the elites and high government officials—who still think and speak like their colonizer. The interests of those who govern the country after the departure of the colonizer conflict with the interests of the majority of the Sudanese community. According to the civil servant, colonization upsets the social hierarchy of the community by "show[ing] favor to nonentities—and it was such people that occupied the highest positions in the days of the English" (45). What is interesting about these "nonentities," traditionally marginalized groups within the mainstream Sudanese culture like, is that they understand the language, interests, and logic of the colonizer. Colonial interference, then, not only enhances favoritism for specific social groups, but also upsets the longstanding indigenous social hierarchy in a way that serves the colonial nations. This creates a kind of complicity between the colonizer and indigenous elitist factions that destabilizes the socio-political harmony within the indigenous community. Upsetting and undermining the traditional social hierarchy within the indigenous community, in turn, creates social and political instability that takes decades after the colonizers' departure to repair. These destructive colonial practices depend on principles of divide and conquer that slow the process of cultural, political, and economic independence of indigenous communities.

Frantz Fanon, the seminal scholar of postcolonial psychology, points to the damaging effects of physical and psychological colonization, specifically the divisions and conflicts among different social and political forces within the indigenous community during periods of colonization and decolonization.

> The country people are suspicious of the townsman. The latter dresses like a European; he speaks like the European's language, works with him, sometimes even lives in the same district; so he is considered by the peasants as a turncoat who has betrayed everything that goes to make up the national heritage. The townspeople are "traitors and knaves" who seem to get on with the occupying powers, and do their best to get in within the framework of the colonial system. (112)

Fanon later argues that this antagonism and mistrust results because some groups benefit, like the elites and townspeople, from the colonial systems while others, like peasants and dwellers in rural areas, are excluded from these benefits. Fanon's argument applies very well to Salih's representation of Sudanese postcolonial realities. For example, the conversation between the narrator and civil servant reveals the antagonism between elites and high government officials and the rest of the Sudanese indigenous community. The interests of both segments of the community, the powerful and marginalized, do not meet.

Critics like Muhsin Al-Musawi have argued that one of the major concerns of postcolonial Arabic novels during the second half of the twentieth century is "to target the roots of corruption in Arab regimes, and to tackle the misery and tragedy" of the indigenous communities (25). Musawi's claim is illustrated well in Salih's narrative, which focuses on the bureaucracy and corruption of government officials who exploit the wealth of the nation with little consideration for the development and progress of peasants and the masses. For example, Mahjoub, the narrator's close friend and President of The Agricultural Committee, expresses his frustration with the shortcomings of the government and its ineffective attempts to build and develop schools and hospitals for an indigenous community that struggles to meet even basic needs in education and healthcare. The narrator also wonders about the government's corruption, lack of interest in the indigenous community, and exploitation of national wealth.

From his perspective as a government insider, the narrator states that Mahjoub

> will not believe the facts about the new rulers of Africa, smooth of face, lupine of mouth, their hands gleaming with rings of precious stones, exuding perfumes from thick cheeks, in white, blue, black and green suits of fine mohair and expensive silk rippling on their shoulders like the fur of Siamese cats, and with shoes that reflect the light from chandeliers and squeak as they tread on marble. (98-99)

The "smooth" and "gleaming" features of the government officials signal their corruption and detachment from the harsh realities of the Sudanese community. Moreover, the "lupine" features of the elite highlight their exploitative and predatory habits that consume the natural wealth of the nation. The narrative highlights the parasitic bourgeoisie classes within the indigenous community by criticizing their Westernized lifestyle, especially lavish spending in European cities and plush, air-conditioned houses and offices:

> "If we do not tear out this disease by the roots we shall have with us a bourgeoisie that is in no way connected with the reality of our life, which is more dangerous to the future of Africa than imperialism itself": how can I say to Mahjoub that this very man [the Minister of Education] escapes during the summer months from Africa to his villa on Lake Lucerne and that his wife does her shopping at Harrods in London, from where the articles are flown to her in a private plane, and that the members of his delegations themselves openly say that he is corrupt and takes bribes, that he had acquired whole estates, had set up businesses and amassed properties, has created a vast fortune from the sweat dripping from the brows of wretched, half-naked people in the jungle. (99)

The narrator describes the government's corruption as a damaging "disease" that separates officials from the actual realities of the indigenous community, thereby alluding to division and socio-political instability that could result from the elites' detachment. The narrator likens this disease to imperialism, pointing to the complicity between corrupt governments with colonial and oppressive nations, a complicity based on exploiting the wealth and "sweat" of indigenous masses.

In addition to criticizing those who exploit the nation's wealth, the narrative is critical of those who do little to impact the lives of the indigenous people in a positive way. One of these ineffective elites is the narrator himself, who admits his lack of productivity when compared to people like Mahjoub, whose work as the Chairman of the Agricultural Project proves to have a lasting, positive impact on the lives of the ordinary people. The narrator explains: "[Y]ou influence actual life in the country. We civil servants, though, are of no consequence" (82). The narrator's uncle Abdul Mannan also expresses a similar critical attitude toward corrupt and ineffective officials when he states that Sudan witnessed better days during English colonization than during independence because of the corruption and inefficacy of local governments. When the narrator asks his uncle about an unfinished hospital, he states,

> They have been at it for a whole year and can't finish it. It's a hopeless government. . . . All they're any good at is coming to us every two or three years with their hordes of people, their lorries and their posters: Long live so and so. We were spared all this hullaballoo in the days of the English. (53)

Although Abdul Mannan belongs to the traditionally marginalized lower group of the masses, the narrative gives him voice to criticize the shortcomings and corruption of local governments and compare it to colonial rule. Not only do the powerful and well-educated voice their opinions about the damage resulting from colonialism and the elites' complicity with colonial nations, but uneducated peasants like Mahjoub and Abdul Mannan can also express their dissatisfaction with their corrupt, greedy, and inefficient government.

Salih also emphasizes ideological diversity in the narrative by empowering the critical voices of women, giving female characters enough space to express their emotional and physical desires, and at the same time exposing and subverting the oppressive and violent practices of patriarchal institutions within the indigenous Sudanese community. One of the most prominent female characters is Bint Majzoub, who espouses a masculine rather than a feminine persona that allows her to seek and express sexual pleasure openly. Bint Majzoub defies the conservative traditions of the Sudanese patriarchal culture, for she associates with the prominent men of the village, smokes, and drinks alcohol. Her voice is characterized as a "manly voice made hoarse by too much smoking" (63), and her rhetoric is masculine, for she advocates divorce, a privilege reserved for men only in Sudanese culture. Her "daring and uninhibited" (64) conversations allow her to express her past sexual experiences and the pleasures associated with her eight marriages without any reservations: "'May I divorce,' said Bint Majzoub, freeing the ash from her cigarette on to the ground with a theatrical movement of her fingers, 'if his thing wasn't like a wedge he'd drive right into me so I could hardly contain myself'" (63). But the most prominent aspect of empowering female characters is giving Bint Majzoub a daring voice to speak the "unspoken," a strategy that usually subverts and interrogates systems of oppression like patriarchy. For example, when the narrator asks the villagers about the details of Wadd Rayyes's suicide, Bint Majzoub is the only person with the courage to pronounce the violence and horror associated with the murder. In doing so, Bint Majzoub lets the reader in on the violent and traumatic acts that can result from male oppression:

> The red straw mat was swimming in blood. I raised the lamp and saw every inch of Bint Mahmoud's body was covered in bites and scratches—her stomach, thighs and neck. The nipple of one breast had been bitten through and blood poured down from her lower lip.

> There is no strength and no power save in God. Wadd Rayyes had been stabbed more than ten times—in his stomach, chest, face, and between the thighs. (105)

Hosna's decisive act to murder Wadd Rayyes and commit suicide reinforces the text's drive to empower women characters against patriarchal oppression. Throughout the novel, Wadd Rayyes is perceived as the symbol of patriarchal sexual pleasure. His stories about his past sexual experiences please most male characters in the text and tease their unconscious desires. When Hosna kills him and herself, she rejects her forced marriage and reclaims her body from the oppressive and violent patriarchal practices of her community. Moreover, Hosna's daring acts subvert male patriarchy by depriving men of the main object of their sexual pleasure, the female body. Stabbing Wadd Rayyes between his thighs becomes a symbolic assault on patriarchy that Hosna manages to free her body from, directing threatening and emasculating hits to this oppressive system.

To emphasize the traumatic effects of patriarchal domination of women, the narrative connects the sexual abuse of women to other violent acts like the colonization of Sudan. The sexual exploits of Wadd Rayyes, whose phallus is compared to a "British cannon," are highly criticized by the narrative over and over again (70). The narrator is shocked at old Rayyes's belligerent unwillingness to accept young Hosna's refusal of his marriage proposal. Rayyes's insistence on owning Hosna for his sexual pleasure reminds the narrator of Sa'eed's sexual abuses against European females, for both become symbols of colonial and patriarchal oppressive practices against the female body, Western and Eastern alike. Both Sa'eed and Rayyes are indifferent to the feelings, sentiments, and well-being of their female Partners, Jean Morrison and Hosna respectively. Although Salih exposes colonial and patriarchal atrocities, exemplified in both Sa'eed's and Rayyes's obsession with fulfilling their sexual drives and control over women, the author bestows upon female characters a tremendous degree of agency. In both murders, women are the initiators of the killing. Although Jean Morrison is the one who is murdered, Sa'eed is only responding to her plots. Jean Morrison is the one who drives Sa'eed to commit murder by triggering his jealousy, undermining his masculinity, and reinforcing Western stereotypes about the "ugly" and violent African-Arab.

Finally, Salih's vibrant representation of the Sudanese African-Arab hybrid and complex identities in *Season of Migration to the North* is reminiscent of Achebe's representation the Igbo culture and people in *Things Fall Apart*. Although both writers represent different geo-historical African realities, Igbo transition into colonial rule and Sudan independence in Achebe and Salih respectively, their complex representation reveals the cultural plurality of their nations. Both writers draw upon Western and indigenous narrative techniques and genres in order to reflect the differing socio-political forces within the indigenous communities. Like Achebe's emphasis on Igbo oral culture's repetitive and circular narrative technique, and its appreciation for storytelling, folklore, and mythology, Salih draws upon literary techniques characteristic of the *Maqamat* and *Hakawati* style and the *Mu'aradah*, techniques that reflect African-Arab oral cultures. Salih also benefits from the novelistic narrative techniques dominant in European picaresque and bildungsroman traditions in his development of his main characters and criticism of the shortcomings of his indigenous culture. But even when he borrows from the western literary traditions, Salih subverts some of its techniques, particularly the linear storyline.

The merging of these African, Arabic, and Western narrative techniques allows writers like Salih to create hybrid literary masterpieces that reflect their regions' mixed cultural identities. These culturally vibrant representations reflect the complex realities of these nations in periods of change and transition, including newly independent Sudan in Salih's novel. His narrative exposes the oppressive systems of European colonialism and indigenous patriarchy, and valorizes traditionally marginalized perspectives, like the men and women who struggle against these systems. In short, Salih shows us the damaging effects of colonization, specifically the proliferation of socio-political factions within indigenous culture. Like Achebe, he refuses to romanticize the latter, describing, for example, corrupt government officials and gender imbalances. But it is by presenting us with these rich, hybrid representations of the cultural, historical, and social realities of his community that Salih subverts the reductive and stereotypical representations of Arab-African cultures common in Western writers. Like Achebe, Salih shows us that these cultures are every bit as complex and sophisticated as their western counterparts.

Works Cited

Aboul-Ela, Hosam. "Writer, Text and Context: The Geographical Location of the Post-48 Arabic Novel."*Edebiyat* 14.1 (2003): 5-19.

Achebe, Chinua. *Things Fall Apart*. New York: Norton, 2009.

Al-Halool, Musa. "The Nature of the Uncanny in *Season of Migration to the North.*"

Arab Studies Quarterly 30.1 (2008): 31-38.

Al-Musawi, Muhsin Jassim. "Postcolonial Matters in Arabic Narrative."*The Postcolonial Arabic*

Novel: Debating Ambivalence. Boston: Brill Academic, 2003. 21-69.

Amyuni, Mona. "The Arab Artist's Role in Society. Three Case Studies: Naquib

Mahfouz, Tayeb Salih and Elias Khoury."*Arabic and Middle Eastern Literature* 2.2 (1999): 203-22.

Bakhtin, Mikhail M. "From *The Dialogic Imagination*: Four Essays." *A Critical Anthology: Theory of the Novel*. Ed. Michael McKeon. New York: John Hopkins UP, 2000. 321-55.

Bhabha, Homi. "Interrogating Identity: Frantz Fanon and the Postcolonial Prerogative."*The Location of Culture*. London: Routledge, 1994. 28-57.

Calbi, Maurizio. "*Othello*'s Ghostly Remainders: Trauma and Postcolonial 'Dis-ease' in Tayeb Salih's *Season of Migration to the North*." *Shakespeare's World/World Shakespeare*. Eds. Richard Fotheringham, Christa Janshon, and R.S. White. Cranbury, New Jersey: Associated UP, 2008. 342-57.

Conrad, Joseph. *Heart of Darkness*. New York: Penguin Group, 1999.

Fanon, Frantz. *Black Skin, White Masks*. Trans. C. L. Markman. London: Pluto Press, 1986.

Harlow, Barbara. "Sentimental Orientalism: *Season of Migration to the North* and *Othello*," in *Tayeb Salih's "Season of Migration to the North": A Casebook*, ed. Mona Takieddine-Amyuni. Beirut, 1985. 75-79.

Hassan, Wa'il. "Introduction." *Tayeb Salih: Ideology and the Craft of Fiction*. NY: Syracuse UP, 2003.1-15.

Loomba, Ania. "Introduction: Situating Postcolonial Studies." *Colonialism/Postcolonialism*. London: Routledge, 1998. 1-103.

Makdisi, Saree. "The Empire Renarrated: *Season of Migration to the North* and the Reinvention of the Present."*Critical Inquiry* 18.4 (1992): 804-20.

Ngugi, wa Thiong'o. *Decolonizing the Mind: The Politics of Language in African Novels*. Portsmouth, MD: Heinemann, 1986.

Parry, Benita. "Reflections on the Excess of Empire in Tayeb Salih'*s Season of Migration to the North*."*A Journal of Modern Critical Theory* 28.2 (2005): 72-90.

Rice, Laura. "Heimlich Un-Heimlich: of Home as Heterotopia in Salih, Tlili, and

Mokeddem."*Of Irony and Empire: Islam, the West and the Transcultural Invention of Africa*. Albany, NY: State U of New York P, 2007. 125-49.

Salih, Tayyeb. *Season of Migration to the North*. NY: NYRB Classics, 2009.

Shah, Amina, trans. Introduction. *The Assemblies of Al-Hariri: Fifty Encounters with the Shaykh Abu Zayd of Seruj*. London: Octagon Press, 1980.

Tageldin, Shaden M. "The African Novel in Arabic." *The Cambridge Companion to the African Novel*. Irele F. Abiola, ed. Cambridge: Cambridge UP, 2009. 85-102.

Lady Winterbourne in the Harem: Rewriting the Fantasy in Ahdaf Soueif's *The Map of Love*

KELLY MEYER

> For her, her whole life will change. Her people will be angry with her. And the British here will shun her. And even if they soften, it will be difficult for her, as your wife, to visit them or receive visits from them. She will be torn off from her own people. Even her language she will not be able to use . . .
> If she feels for you as you feel for her, she will throw away the world and come to you. But if you take her . . . you will be everything to her. If you make her unhappy, who will she go to? No mother, no sister, no friend. Nobody. It means if she angers you, you forgive her. If she crosses you, you make it up with her. And whatever the English do, you will never burden her with the guilt of her country. She will be not only your wife and the mother of your children—insha' Allah—but she will be your guest and a stranger under your protection and if you are unjust to her God will never forgive you.
>
> Ahdaf Souief, *The Map of Love*[1]

> And insofar as these people exist between the old and the new, between the old empire and the new state, their condition articulates the tensions, irresolutions, and contradictions in the overlapping territories shown on the cultural map of imperialism.
>
> Edward Said[2]

The sobering words of Zeinab Hanim to her love-struck son, Sharif, when he is contemplating marriage to British traveler

Anna Winterbourne are a potent reminder of the incredibly vast gap between the British, as the colonizer of Egypt during this time, and the colonized Egyptian people. There is no precedent for this relationship, which is the romantic center of Ahdaf Soueif's novel *The Map of Love*. In his article "The Politics of Desire in the Writings of Ahdaf Soueif," Joseph Massad articulates the tensions at play in their love story, namely, "the ostracism to which Anna was subjected by the English *colons* in Cairo on account of her marrying an Egyptian and the questions raised about Sharif's nationalism by Egyptian nationalists on account of his marrying a colonizer" (81). Just as Anna would be leaving behind everything she knows, Sharif enters uncharted territory in his relationship with a woman from another world, from the ranks of the powerful British imperialists who oppress his people. Indeed, Zeinab Hanim warns Sharif that he must not attribute England's guilt as something innate to the Englishness of his future wife.[3] The work Anna and Sharif must do to make their relationship a success will be a great challenge, and Anna will bear the brunt of the alienation and isolation as she is fully and utterly *away from home*, in every sense of the phrase. Contemplating her upcoming marriage, Anna writes, "Piece by piece it is coming to me: the distance I am placing between myself and those I have known and cared for all my life" (310). Despite all such future obstacles, Zeinab Hanim, as evident in the counsel she gives her son, sees the potential for two people from supposedly opposing sides to create a harmonious whole.

Within Said's description of the "cultural map of imperialism" in the epigraph above, I find many layers of meaning to the new postcolonial world he evokes, from geographical, political, and cultural applications to questions of individual identity, interpersonal relationships, and all the complications inscribed therein. His quote speaks to the unprecedented number of "refugees, migrants, displaced persons, and exiles" in our modern postcolonial world (*Culture*322). It certainly applies to the characters within *The Map of Love*, who live their lives in a state of in-betweenness as Egyptians inextricably linked to the Western world but yearning for freedom within their own sovereign nation. In fact, as Said was Soueif's "personal friend and her intellectual mentor," it is fitting to draw links between Said's writing and the characters and themes of her novel (King 143). Scholars writing about *The Map of Love* note the connection between Said himself—as writer, activist, intellectual hero, and even the founder of postcolonial studies—and Soueif's rendering of Sharif as well as Omar, who is Sharif's grand-nephew and counterpart in modern New York. But so too are Said's postcolonial philosophies applicable to the character of Anna, whose life during the course of the novel comes to be defined by "tensions, irresolutions, and contradictions." She is an aristocratic British woman who seeks out the company of the colonized, namely, a family of Egyptian nationalists who are active enemies against the British occupation in Egypt. As the foremost exile in the novel, Anna indeed encounters difficulty, as her mother-in-law predicts, but she also has the opportunity to revise her positioning, to rewrite her identity and locate it on the new map of a postcolonial world. As Said articulates regarding this postcolonial condition, "Exile, far from being the fate of nearly forgotten unfortunates who are dispossessed and expatriated, becomes something closer to a norm, an experience of crossing boundaries and charting new territories in defiance of the classic canonic enclosures, however much its loss and sadness should be acknowledged and registered" (*Culture* 317).

For all that she has lost, we see the exiled Anna, who narrates her story through her journals and letters, challenge the "classic canonic enclosures" of British epistolary and travel writing traditions. And Anna's story is deftly handled by Soueif, whom Said himself described as "one of the most extraordinary chroniclers of sexual politics now writing" (qtd. in Massad 77). Indeed, in the novel, the personal and the political intertwine, and Anna's politics of desire hold ground with the male-dominated politics of a nation. For all that she loses, Anna—an unsatisfied wife and then widow—has much to gain, and she does so, first and foremost, by transgressing the indifferent world she lives in. She rejects British imperialist ideology, upper-class patriarchal expectations, and even the confines of her own native language as she embraces love, desire, and sexuality through her boundary-crossing travels and relationships.

In this essay, I will situate the historical relationship between imperial Europe and Egypt as a backdrop for Anna's positioning as a British woman who is intrigued by Orientalized representations of the East. When she chooses to travel in Egypt and explore Arab culture, to see for herself how the paintings and stories ring true, Anna situates herself in the Victorian tradition of women's travel writing, but she also subverts it. Through her journals and letters, I will establish the factors that both limit and embolden Anna and how she must free herself from an indifferent environment in order to pursue her desires. It is only by willingly exiling herself in multiple senses that Anna is able to follow her desires, ultimately finding freedom, peace, and physical and emotional intimacy with a man whose mind and heart matches her own.

Writing the East, Fighting the West

In his book *The Arabs: A History*, historian Eugene Rogan reminds us, "For centuries, Europeans had traveled to the Middle East and written books on the manners and customs of the exotic people they found there" (86). In a three-year project that accomplished such feats as the discovery of the Rosetta Stone, the world's first Egyptologists, working for Napoleon himself under the banner of scientific discovery, perpetuated this introduction of an ancient nation to the Western world. As journalist Nina Burleigh describes in her book *Mirage: Napoleon's Scientists and the Unveiling of Egypt*,

> Those *savants* who survived produced an exhaustive encyclopedia of Egypt, twenty-three outsize volumes, delicately printed with engravings of the buildings, rocks, people, plants, and thousands of the beasts, birds, bugs, and fish that dwelled in Egypt circa 1800. *La Description de l'Égypte* (The Description of Egypt) comprised the ultimate work of the scientists. Their encyclopedia is a record of the impressions of European civilian participants in the first large-scale interaction between Europeans and Muslims in the modern era. (xiii-xiv)

For all the "firsts" that Burleigh attributes to these men and the books they authored, Said situates the project in a colonial context, as the first and best example of how an effort to know the Other could be formalized and deployed for the benefit of a European colonizing agenda. As Said relates in *Orientalism*, Egypt was an important staging ground for the later endeavors of colonialism that flourished in the Victorian age. Burleigh herself grants that the French government of the time saw Egypt as belonging to nobody (xi). In the novel, Sharif explains that this fascination with the exotic East originated with the West, in the West, and for its own interests—with the Eastern people themselves an afterthought to the intent: "This attraction is born in the European while he is still *in his home country*. When he comes here, he finds that the land is inhabited by people he does not understand and possibly does not much like" (481, emphasis in the original). Wanting to "render it completely open, to make it accessible to European scrutiny," Napoleon gave no thought to the Egyptian people who were already the keepers of their own stories; rather, he sought to transform Egypt into "a department of French learning" (*Said Reader* 104). In an effort to commodify a strange, exotic culture for the easy digestion of Europe, Napoleon's Egyptian "project" produced the commanding body of knowledge that Burleigh references, which was rooted, not in "empirical reality," but in a Western construction of "ideas and myths culled from texts" (*Said Reader* 101). However, as Said clarifies regarding such products of Orientalism, they are not "a mere collection of lies":

> Orientalism, therefore, is not an airy European fantasy about the Orient, but a created body of theory and practice in which, for many generations, there has been a considerable material investment. Continued investment made Orientalism, as a system of knowledge about the Orient, an accepted grid for filtering through the Orient into Western consciousness, just as that same investment multiplied—indeed, made truly productive—the statements proliferating out from Orientalism into general culture. (*Said Reader* 72-73)

Indeed, these efforts of Orientalism held power and served great purpose in constructing the Orient for the benefit of the West.

Such knowledge about the Orient, which Anna would have been exposed to, is then skillfully constructed and repurposed as part of a colonizing power-knowledge regime. The human element dissolves into the metaphorical as a Western power seeks the means—any means necessary—to make a play for the territory of the Other. While, as Said discusses, "it was characteristic of all Orientalist projects before Napoleon's that little could be done in advance of the project to prepare for its success," these French endeavors to contextualize Egypt—to *textualize*it, really, through the *Description de l'Égypte* volumes—served as valuable weapons to facilitate Napoleon's thrust for power. The French leader "wanted nothing less than to take the whole of Egypt, and his advance preparations were of unparalleled magnitude and thoroughness" (*Said Reader* 100). As Said explains, Napoleon's project in Egypt set a precedent for future European colonizing enterprises, which would use a Western-constructed knowledge base as a tool in acting against a real people:

> His plans for Egypt therefore became the first in a long series of European encounters with the Orient in which the Orientalist's special expertise was put directly to functional colonial use; for at the crucial instant when an Orientalist had to decide whether his

> loyalties and sympathies lay with the Orient or with the conquering West, he always chose the latter, from Napoleon's time on. As for the emperor himself, he saw the Orient only as it had been encoded first by classical texts and then by Orientalist experts, whose vision, based on classical texts, seemed a useful substitute for any actual encounter with the real Orient. (*Said Reader* 100-1)

In the novel, Sharif articulates a similar sentiment based on his experience living under the British occupation of Egypt: "Europe simply does not see the people of the countries it wishes to annex—and when it does, it sees them in accordance with its own old and accepted definitions: backward people, lacking rational abilities and subject to religious fanaticism. People whose countries—the holy and picturesque lands of the East—are too good for them" (483). Anna echoes this sentiment, observing of the blatant racism in her Thomas Cook guide to the Middle East, "So far I have found that the book, like my friends at the Agency, has a fairer view of the land than of its inhabitants" (209). Drawing their conclusions separately, Sharif and Anna both identify a particular quality of colonial relations: Western indifference to dark-skinned fellow humans which denies their subjectivity as well as their rootedness in their lands, histories, and cultures. Drawing a link between the historical Said and Soueif's character of Sharif, Katherine Callen King explains the connection in her article "Translating Heroism: Locating Edward Said on Ahdaf Soueif'*s The Map of Love*": "[L]ike Said, Sharif talks about the invisibility of real modern Egyptians to the European eye and about Europeans' insistence that intellectual Egyptians get their ideas from elsewhere and are not representative of the mass of their people" (145). Indeed, Sharif's justified indignation is palpable as he decries the British rule: "What are we? A nation of infants? . . . After five thousand years? Do we have to keep going back to the beginning?" (364-65). For all their supposed knowledge and "special expertise," the Orientalist savants—as Said describes them and Sharif experiences them—are voyeurs, feigned scholars, spies. Perhaps is it precisely because the Orientalist has not sought out a "real" encounter with the culture he studies and does not "see the people," as Sharif laments, that the question of loyalty Said poses is no question at all.

Napoleon's specific choice of Egypt—as this earliest of battlegrounds on which the colonizer's knowledge-as-power advantage played out—was far from an arbitrary one. As Anna describes Egypt, it is an "amazing land, this conjunction of the two mighty continents of the Ancient World" (210). Regarding the "cultural, geographical, and historical significance" of the nation, Said states, "Egypt was the focal point of the relationships between Africa and Asia, between Europe and the East, between memory and actuality" (*Said Reader* 104). Joseph Fourier's original preface to the *Description de l'Égypte* offers an explanation as to why Egypt, and *only* Egypt, would do as the staging ground for modern European colonization of the exotic Orient:

> Placed between Africa and Asia, and communicating easily with Europe, Egypt occupies the center of the ancient continent. This country presents only great memories; it is the homeland of the arts and conserves innumerable monuments . . . It is therefore proper for this country to attract the attention of illustrious princes who rule the destiny of nations.
>
> No considerable power was ever amassed by any nation, whether in the West or in Asia, that did not also turn that nation toward Egypt. (qtd. *Said Reader* 105)

This most ancient of nations, then, becomes an important pawn in the modern power games of Western nations—and its own sovereignty is negligible when "illustrious princes" step up to play. Said continues, describing Egypt by another metaphor, that is, the stage on which new histories unfold:

> Because Egypt was saturated with meaning for the arts, sciences, and government, its role was to be the stage on which actions of a world-historical importance would take place. By taking Egypt, then, a modern power would naturally demonstrate its strength and

> justify history; Egypt's own destiny was to be annexed, to Europe, preferably. (*Said Reader* 105)

To "justify history," then—indeed, to legitimize a worldwide colonizing enterprise—it becomes understandable that Britain has turned its imperial gaze toward Egypt in the turn-of-the-century world in which Soueif situates Anna Winterbourne.

Moreover, because the stakes are so high as to lose their "own destiny," it is just as understandable why Egyptians, including Anna's eventual husband, Sharif, would fight back—and why Egyptian-born Soueif would portray such struggles of world-historical significance at play in the individual lives of her novel's characters. As seen through Sharif's thoughts, his people were not unaware of the British cultural gaze. He playfully reminds Anna of such stereotypes when they reminisce about their first encounter:

> "Weren't you afraid of me? The wicked Pasha who would lock you up in his harem[4] and do terrible things to you?"
>
> "What terrible things?"
>
> "You should know. They're in your English stories." (153-54)

Indeed, the unique nature of their romance itself recalls—and challenges—the British literary canon of the time, which offered voyeuristic narratives that further bolstered a Western imperialist agenda. Just as Napoleon carefully crafted his Egypt project for the benefit of his own empire, so too did "colonial romances express the fears and fantasies of Western publics about their empires" (Davis). Noting such texts as Sir H. Rider Haggard's *King Solomon's Mines* and Edgar Rice Burroughs' *Tarzan of the Apes*, scholar Emily S. Davis explains that "the romance's tradition of male questers seems to lend itself all too well to narratives of imperialism as grand adventure." In her article "Romance as Political Aesthetic in Ahdaf Soueif's *The Map of Love*," Davis sets the context for *The Map of Love*'s subversive power as a novel within this very same genre, which "proved well suited to the xenophobic nationalism of the colonial project." While certainly not all English literary romances of the time reinforced or even engaged with such ideology, Davis's discussion characterizes the backdrop against which Soueif's novel exists. In *The Map of Love*, we see an insightful female traveler, rather than a "male quester," encountering the East—not to conquer it as a representative of the Empire but as an individual who refuses to be penned in by the indifference of her mannered British world. Indeed, because Anna and Sharif's romance cuts across national lines rather than reinforces them, it transgresses the agenda of the national romance. Davis explains: "While in the national romance, idealized love is threatened by the same forces that undermine national unity, Soueif's evocation of the colonial romance tradition necessarily complicates the nationalist equation. Sharif's relationship with Anna cannot function simply as a tale about national unions, because Anna's position as imperial white woman makes her an icon of the very forces that undermine national unity." Written a century later, this romantic center of Soueif's novel reaches back to the genre to reshape the colonial romance to a postcolonial and transnational agenda, with Anna functioning importantly as the instigator of this new sort of romantic adventure.

As King explains, the author situates her romance—and particularly the "darkly handsome romance figure" of Sharif—within a "politically deromanticized Egypt," using the seductive draw of a love story to showcase an important "political struggle between imperialist Britain and occupied Egypt" (143). Resisting the Orientalist's gaze is part and parcel of a larger effort to fight European colonization. In her article "Narrating England and Egypt: The Hybrid Fiction of Ahdaf Soueif," Susan Muaddi Darraj explains how, using Sharif and Anna's relationship, "Soueif speaks back to the colonialist vision of the Arab in order to correct it" (103). Darraj contextualizes Sharif and his compatriots, as Soueif portrays them, as part of a historical anti-colonial movement that fought against total British colonization. While England "had, indeed, colonized Egypt for decades, the Egyptian people, especially the intellectual class, prevented that colonization from being complete" (102). Darraj continues,

> There was a thriving anti-colonial movement, as well as a recognition by the Egyptians of the orientalist veil English attempted to thrust upon them. The colonization was not a complete victory, as the Egyptians refused to be colonized quietly. Instead, there existed an almost two-way relationship, and when England finally left Egypt, it was not totally unchanged by its experience. (102)

Even marking on their colonizers, Sharif's historical counterparts prevented a complete political and cultural takeover of Egypt. Both through her romance and her individual autonomy, Anna herself becomes a participant in the resistance, and we can see how her early writings shape her distinctive anti-colonial stance.

Becoming 'That Son'

Particularly in the light of Egypt's place in these modern power games, the resulting postcolonial world, as Said describes in this essay's epigraph, is difficult to define and, for the characters of the novel, even more difficult to navigate, whether in the context of the early 1900s or the 1990s portion of *The Map of Love*'s intertwining plots. As a sheltered woman who fearlessly seeks out her own answers to the doubts and unknowns that have begun to torment her, Anna commits remarkable acts of rebellion just by questioning the imperialist ideology of her own British culture. First we meet Anna as she writes in her journal in 1897, when she articulates her struggles in living up to the domestic expectations of her feminine role regarding her husband, Edward: "I did strive—do strive—to be a faithful and loving wife and companion" (11). As we quickly see, Anna's desire for an expanded sense of female autonomy is linked to her desire to see a broader world than the sheltered, aristocratic one she has lived within thus far. While she doesn't join in the men's talk on British colonizing enterprises and racial sovereignty, the views of her father-in-law, Sir Charles, stir up her curious mind:

> The question of whether savage nations had a right to exist came up, George arguing—from Darwin and the survival of the fittest—that they had none, and the rest of the company being of much the same mind. Sir Charles was much incensed and ended the conversation by saying (somewhat strongly) that the British Empire had done so much harm to so many people that it deserved to perish and then it would be too late to say or do anything. Edward was, for the most part, silent, I fancy because he really agreed with the younger set but was careful of offending his father. Sir Charles's only ally was John Evelyn, who declared his intention of sending his son up the Nile to "learn Arabic, keep a diary and acquire habits of observation and self-reliance and not to imbibe Jingo principles." I wish—if that is not too wicked a wish—I wish I were that son. (13)

Anna's recollection of this conversation is important in establishing her character. While she doesn't explicitly place herself on either side of the debate, she doesn't automatically subscribe to the predominant apathetic sentiment toward "savage nations." What's more, her fragile desire to travel and learn more of other cultures emerges here, even though she knows it is a far-off fantasy because of her role as a married British woman.[5] She doesn't want to be sheltered from the larger world by her positioning.

It was not unprecedented, however, for a British woman to travel and write of foreign lands. The publications of such women as Mary Louisa Whately, Amelia Edwards, and Lady Mary Wortley Montagu, all of whom traveled in and wrote from the Middle East, shaped the historical genre for Anna's writing as seen in *The Map of Love*. Anna specifically references "the letters of Lady Duff Gordon" and meets Lady Anne Blunt while in Egypt, both of whom published their personal writing from travels in Egypt and the surrounding Arab region. As her grandniece Amal reads through Anna's journals and letters decades later, she describes Anna as "a little self-conscious, perhaps, a little aware of the genre—*Letters from Egypt, A Nile Voyage, More Letters from Egypt*. . . . Perhaps she is thinking of a future publication. In any case, I forgive her the mannered approach as she feels her way into my home" (58). Such Victorian travel writing by women detailed encounters with the East, often reinforcing stereotypical images such as the harems depicted in Edward William Lane's English translation of *Arabian Nights*. Anna was familiar with these influences as well—even, no doubt, influenced by them herself—as she references Lane and is fascinated by the works of British Orientalist painter John Frederick Lewis. Darraj examines Anna's exposure to such depictions to illustrate "how deeply England was drowning in its culture of orientalism—a culture that allowed the English to imagine the Arabs as exotic 'other' " (102). Regardless of the Orientalist images some of her historical counterparts reinforced, Anna chooses her true inspirations carefully,[6] drawing from Lady Gordon and Lady Blunt as open-minded, fearless women who traveled more deeply into unknown areas of the Arab desert than was considered proper. And Anna will eventually do so herself, dressed as a man, making her spark of interest in being "that son," autonomous and free, a fantasy that Anna is able to fulfill in spirit.

Exploring ideas that will later inform her perspective as a female traveler-writer in Egypt, Anna carefully listens to such talk as she relates in her journal entry, unable to ignore a nagging sense of disapproval for the colonizing enterprises most of her fellow British companions blindly support. After Edward returns from military service in Africa during the Boer War, Anna links her concern about her husband's strange behavior to her burgeoning critique of the "invented" British Empire, as her father-in-law characterizes it (32). Edward shows symptoms of post-traumatic stress, and his father, Sir Charles, has the ammunition removed from the guns kept in the house for fear that his son will do himself harm. As Anna and Sir Charles discuss how Edward's service in the Boer War has wreaked havoc on his sanity, Sir Charles criticizes his son for his willing role: "If he had not the stomach for it, what drove him to go? He requested that commission—he would not be denied." Anna more sympathetically contemplates Edward's motives: "'He believed he was doing the right thing.' And also, she thought, he wanted action, adventure, purpose, a mission." This afterthought in particular is a desire which Anna shares for her own life. Representing his view on the British imperializing mission that sent his son to the Sudan, Sir Charles says, "I told him, though. I told him this was not an honest war. This was a war dreamed up by politicians, a war to please that widow [Queen Victoria] so taken with her cockney Empire" (30).

Following her father-in-law's lead and seeking to understand what her husband has experienced, Anna continues to question the British imperialist agenda with its particularly aggressive approach to nationalism. It is clear that she is beginning to gain an awareness of the disturbing truth beneath the surface of what she, as a British citizen, has been told about this "war." She wonders, "What had they done beyond taking the Soudan and restoring order? . . . I long to ask my husband what this means, for my instinct is that there is a key here to what ails him, but I am afraid." Repeating a euphemism for colonization she has no doubt heard time and again—"restoring order"—Anna is unsettled by what underlies Edward's post-traumatic symptoms: "But Edward will not speak and I am afraid. I have not dared voice the thought, but I am afraid we are in the grip of something evil—my husband is in the grip of something evil, something that will not allow him to shake off this illness and come to himself" (31). She watches her husband grow sicker by the day, unable to keep down anything he eats, of which Anna observes, "I fancy he is attempting to purge himself of—all manner of things" (33).

Rather than deny them and retreat into the sanctuary of a polite British life, Anna follows her intuitive thoughts about the "evil" nature of the British war in Africa. As she watches her husband fade away and finally die in the months after his return, Anna comes to a conclusion about the nature of Edward's experiences and how they have irrevocably changed him:

> Oh, I do so completely fear for my husband now, for if it is true and if he took part in those terrible deeds, he who puts honour above all else and truly thought that in embarking on this expedition he embarked on a brave and honourable task, I cannot see now how he can put it behind him—most particularly when he is so ill in body and at the mercy of the fever which burns him up for hours and leaves him, when it does, limp and so weakened that he can barely take the water that we put to his lips. (35)

Anna knows that Edward's illness is the physical parallel to a deeper psychological trauma. And Edward's condition hearkens a larger British complicity, as Catherine Wynne explains in "Navigating the Mezzaterra: Home, Harem and the Hybrid Family in Ahdaf Soueif's *The Map of Love*": "The Victorian section of *The Map of Love* not only establishes an anti-imperialist theme in terms of its politics but also domesticates it, as the sins of the empire return to haunt the British home" (57). A man of honor, as Anna knows Edward to be, who is used—indeed, used up—in a dishonorable war simply cannot recover, as the "sins of the empire" follow him home. Edward's personal encounter with the "terrors" and the "evil" of the British colonizing rampage in Africa has sapped his soul, rendering him, in the end, a shell, emptied of will and emotion, indifferent to his own existence.

Her husband's death pushes Anna from a nebulous curiosity about distant lands to convictions about empire and dominion, honor and dishonor. Ultimately, she leaves behind the polite salons of British aristocratic life, along with the restraint and naivety that characterizes women in her position, never allowing herself to turn to the willful ignorance that would be required to step back into her former life. Rather than push down nagging thoughts, squash her curiosities, and disguise her distresses, Anna faces what haunted her husband to his death head-on. Realizing that he would never find relief from his painful experiences—and that she would never be fully free in her station—Anna reluctantly acknowledges the freedom his death endows her. She describes a "terrible thought: that in this grief I have no thought for myself. I have not once found myself thinking: what shall I do without him—" (41). In that admission, we see that, deep down, Anna knows just what she will do without him, what she is *able* to do because he is gone. She will be able to travel and write and see a part of the world she never thought she would. However, it is a difficult decision for her to reach. She continues her polite but stunted grief for Edward, denigrating herself for not making him happier in life, but she also blames the dishonorable war, knowing she could find peace if she "could believe that he died for a noble cause" (44). Finally, when she sits listening to a moving opera, she lets herself be overcome, surrendering herself to emotion for perhaps the first time in her quiet, modest life:

> It was as though I had been holding myself very still, holding a door shut, holding something down; something which the music swelled and strengthened until it broke through. And for many days later, although I could not put my feelings into words, much less write them down in my journal, it was as though I felt that music coursing through my body and as it went, like a river in full flood, it churned up its bed and its banks, and I was most ill with a fever and—poor Caroline tells me—delirious and impossible for many days till one morning I woke up and—I had not quite returned to the world, but I had seen the door by which I might return. (44)

Typically able to craft her thoughts and feelings in words, Anna experiences something unprecedented, something that defies being precisely articulated in the careful writing of a lady's journal.

This breaking free, breaking loose, and giving in to what she has so carefully kept at bay is an awakening for Anna on numerous levels. Indeed, as she hereafter becomes gravely ill and then recovers, it is a rebirth, as symbolized by "one last cluster of blossom like a small pink chandelier" that has lived longer into the fall season than any other foliage. She observes, "I was overcome with gratitude as though it had stayed there to say to me, Look! It is not too late" (45). Anna won't wither away as a young widow in an empty London house haunted by the sins of imperialism. It is not too late, and she doesn't need to continue living indifferent to her desires or indifferent to the realities of the world. She is reborn as a bold traveler.

Anna will even fulfill another part of the original fantasy when she learns Arabic. As she dives into the language, her quest for freedom and self-discovery runs parallel to her education in the Arabic language and culture alike. In that way, Anna goes beyond many of her fellow female Victorian writers. Indeed, she leaves behind the "mannered approach" Amal sees in her early writing, no longer preoccupied with conforming to the British literary style of a particular genre. As Anna dives into the rich Arabic language, she becomes more and more enlightened as to the reality of life in Egypt, with its respective struggles and beauties. Just as Soueif offers untranslated Arabic within her English text—and uses her characters to illuminate these words' complex, nuanced meanings and connotations—Anna discovers that one language alone, particularly the language of the colonizer, is not enough for her new life. Articulating her linguistic journey as part of a larger experience, Anna describes the different types of love that exist within the Arabic language and, indeed, within the entire novel:

'Hubb' is love, 'ishq' is love that entwines two people together, 'shaghaf' is love that nests in the chambers of the heart, 'hayam' is love that wanders the earth, 'teeh' is love in which you lose yourself, 'walah' is love that carries sorrow within it, 'sababah' is love that exudes from your pores, 'hawa' is love that shares its name with 'air' and with 'falling,' 'gharam' is love that is willing to pay the price. "I have learned so much this past year, I could not list all the things I have learned." (386-87)

Beyond learning a language, observing a culture, and rejecting aggressive "Jingo" nationalism, as John Evelyn wishes for his son, Anna experiences more because of her positioning as a woman. She deeply loves a proud Egyptian man, she finds mutually fulfilling friendships with women in the inner sanctum of the harem, and she fulfills sexual desires as well as personal ambitions. She learns things she cannot articulate, in that way rejecting an Orientalist sort of commodification of her new life in the Arab world. Anna protects her experience as a personal gift, feeling "a strange unwillingness to provide a detailed picture of 'life in the Harem' " to her British friend Caroline. Instead, Anna recognizes some things as untranslatable using words alone: "If she were to visit, however, I would be glad to have her as my guest for it is only then, I think, that she would gain a true picture of my life here" (354).

With Edward's death, Anna steps up to become the son of her father-in-law, who has served as her political and intellectual mentor. She becomes "that son," not of John Evelyn, but of Sir Charles. As she experiences Egypt, becoming involved in the inner lives of an Egyptian family who is fighting British rule, Anna observes, "I had the strangest feeling of life expanding and opening out. I found myself thinking about Sir Charles, wondering what he would make of this Egyptian Pasha into whose house I had landed in so odd a fashion. And then came the thought that under the same circumstances, Sir Charles himself would probably have acted in the same way" (144). In this way, Anna writes her own fantasy, fulfilling herself but also replacing her husband as the child his father always wanted: one who both sees the world and sees herself in it.

Frustrated Female Agency and Desire

Within the same journal entry in which she articulates her desire to travel far and freely, Anna identifies other passions, specifically sexual "stirrings," which give us a sense of just how her feminine world limits her. Regarding her feelings of dissatisfaction after her husband visits her bedroom, she says,

> I have long thought it was a mark of the waywardness of my character that on such occasions I was beset by stirrings and impulses of so contrary a nature that I was like a creature devoid of reason: I wept into my pillows, I paced the length of my chamber, I opened the casements to the cold night air and leaned out and wished—God forgive me—that I had not been so resilient in physical health that I might not catch a fatal chill and make an end of my unhappiness. (13-14)

Anna identifies her passions as unnatural, "contrary," and "devoid of reason." In that way, her thoughts and feelings are set against the backdrop of a British culture that is indifferent to female sexuality, a culture that expects the individual woman to be indifferent to any such passions or desires within herself. As Stoler explains in *Race and the Education of Desire*, "Male sexual anxiety focused on more than suitable Christian marriage partners for European women and on the transmission of property, but on the unmanaged desires of women themselves" (41). At the heart of this need to control and define women—and the resulting indifference to their lack of fulfillment and agency—is the ever-present fear of being undone by the Other, in this case the feminine Other. As Stoler continues, the "unmanaged sexuality" of European women "was considered a threat to these different social bodies," namely, the "Christian nation" (41-42).

Knowing she would have more autonomy as a man, Anna invests her desires in that fantasy, rather than ones in which she envisions herself fulfilled—sexually and otherwise—as the woman that she is. As the novel's author eventually situates Anna and her sexual desires in the context of a colonized Egypt, some insights on the sexuality of Arab women at this time is certainly applicable in understanding Soueif as an Egyptian-born "chronicler of sexual politics." Amal Amireh extrapolates the fear over female sexuality as a reinscription of men's own fears of violation, of being unmanned or rendered impotent in a time when the nation itself was vulnerable. As Amireh explains—echoing Stoler's assertions regarding European patriarchy—within Arab culture there circulated a "dominant traditional ideology according to which female sexuality is legitimately realized only in marriage, wifehood, and motherhood" (763). As such, without finding sexual satisfaction as a wife, Anna has no recourse for her frustrated desires. It is ironic, then, that she should find it by traveling to this region with perhaps more stringent parameters on female sexuality and through her transgressive relationship with an Arab man.

As the earliest pages of Anna's journal reveal, because such indifference to her human sexuality is the truly unnatural state, she simply can't deny that certain passions, desires, and curiosities exist within her, however shameful she deems them to be. Indeed, before she goes down to breakfast after such nights of pent-up anguish, she makes every effort to hide any sign of her distress from her British family, and she even questions the good her journal writing does, as it gives her a place to express her wayward, "wicked feelings." Anna attributes these to "some weakness of my feminine nature" and has "devised small stratagems" to distract herself, trying to bridle her feelings and her desire for freedom by living a carefully ordered life (14). Until Anna is freed from all such trappings of her current life, she is not able to pursue the avenues of fulfillment that her journal writing foreshadows. What Anna feels here is a fluttering, a hint at future sexual and personal freedom. And the process of reaching that end, Massad asserts, is more important than the end itself. He describes an "unfolding" that is particularly applicable to the character of Anna: "The journey of [Soueif's] characters is not one where liberation is the necessary telos, but rather the complex process through which the unfolding of desire (s)—sexual, social, economic, and political—is shaped by the characters themselves and all that surrounds them" (75).

As a passionate, desiring British woman in the colonial context of *The Map of Love*, Anna inhabits a truly unique position, one transected by her gender, her race, and her class. Anna's kinship with Arab women in a patriarchal culture is evident; however, she is undeniably born and bred of—though, as we see, not fully interpellated by—British culture. As Anne McClintock relates in her book *Imperial Leather: Race, Gender and Sexuality in the Colonial Context* of colonial women, "Barred from the corridors of formal power, they experienced the privileges and social contradictions of imperialism very differently from colonial men." These colonial women were rarely people who "reaped the vast profits" of the system: "The vast, fissured architecture of imperialism was gendered throughout by the fact that it was white men who made and enforced laws and policies in their own interests." However, McClintock asserts, the white privilege of these women cannot be denied: "Nonetheless, the rationed privileges of race all too often put white women in positions of decided—if borrowed—power, not only over colonized women but also over colonized men" (6). Although Anna doesn't seek to wield this sort of power in her travels to Egypt, her unique positioning remains: "As such, white women were not the hapless onlookers of empire but were ambiguously complicit both as colonizers and colonized, privileged and restricted, acted upon and acting" (McClintock 6).

Similarly, Anna's upper-class status both limits and emboldens her; she must be a proper well-born lady, but she has influence and the means to travel on her own terms. And these terms, really the *only* term she stipulates, is that she see the "real" Egypt,[7] to walk behind the façade of the Orientalist harem paintings and encounter Egyptian people—not as a colonizer but as a woman exploring a liminal space on multiple planes, both restricted and free, as a traveler seeking a home for her soul, and as a fellow human full of passions and desires. Given her complicated positioning, it is, perhaps, symbolic that she recognizes "the oddity of Egypt's position" as it is pulled three ways by its complicated political identity: a theoretically independent nation which is still part of the Ottoman Empire but ultimately governed by the British Agency (57). Indeed, the political and the personal intertwine as the Egyptian effort of nation-building portrayed in the novel juxtaposes Anna's quest for freedom from the various constraints upon her.

'Life in the Harem': Fantasy Fulfilled

We see that Anna has, according to Darraj, "rejected her country's orientalist and racist notions of the Arabs," and she tries "to understand Egypt on its own terms" (102). Anna has also found a measure of female autonomy simply by leaving the expectations of a proper widowed life behind her, applying her intellect and her passions to the same enterprise through her travels to and within the Middle East. Placing herself outside of the realm of patriarchal and Orientalist discourses gives Anna subjectivity within a new discourse. As El Naga explains of such female agency, "It is a discourse that emanates from a liminal space, joining a feminist consciousness with a cultural awareness. . . . For these women, identity does not invite binaries or antagonism. . . . Put differently, this discourse explores new margins that are capable of subverting old binaries" (71). It is from this liminal space, from "new margins," then, that Anna finds the freedom of feminine self-definition along with the freedom to interrogate the Empire.

For a time, her only companions are other British travelers, "who feel it their duty to assist and chaperone an unprotected female in a strange land" (60). But Anna did not travel this far to be among her countrymen and women. She has seen the bazaars and the pyramids, but, she laments, "I sit here in my room at Shepherd's Hotel possessed by the strangest feeling that still I am not in Egypt" (102). The idea of joining a guided expedition to see the Sinai region sounds distasteful, as Anna knows she would be hampered by the perspectives of fellow British tourists: "I would have remained within the world I knew. I would have seen things through my companions' eyes, and my mind would have been too occupied in resisting their impressions to establish its own . . . [T]here was a strong part of me that did not wish to be in the company of my own kind here" (213). Indeed, when given the opportunity to engage with Arab culture on her own terms, Anna's wholehearted enthusiasm and innocent, childlike wonder contradicts the typical British attitude Arabs expect. As her future sister-in-law relates of Anna,

> She had none of the arrogance or the coldness we were used to imagining in her countrymen, so that we almost forgot that she was English except that she would wonder at things and admire things that we were so accustomed to that we no longer saw them or thought about them, and the result of this was to make us look afresh at the things surrounding us and, seeing them through her eyes, find them fascinating once again. (372-73)

For Anna, it is not enough of an experience to engage with careful, sanitized bits of Egyptian culture as the other British do. She observes that they criticize anyone who seeks out more than nominal contact with the Egyptian people, culture, and land. Such a person "they regard as a crank who chooses to live in the desert, and they use of him the phrase 'gone over' by which I assume they mean he sees matters from a different point of view" (70). Discussing this man who has "gone native,"[8] Anna feels kinship with him. She writes, "But I feel it would be a little odd to come all the way to Egypt and learn nothing except more about your own compatriots" (71). In pulling away from the enclave of British society in Cairo, Anna gives herself an adventure but also the peace she has been seeking. She finds solace—and a "soul free to contemplate" (213). As we can see, Anna is not a tourist, really. She doesn't simply "tour" in the culture of others, but she looks to find her soul—to be irrevocably moved and marked upon and changed—through the unique experiences she seeks out and, especially, the people she meets.

Echoing Sharif's sentiment about the invisibility of Egyptian people, Anna thinks, "And yet I wonder whether it is possible for a conquering ruler to truly see into the character of the people whom he rules." Thinking of her own maidservant, Anna questions, "How well, in fact, I have found myself wondering, do I know Emily?" (99). Trying to find a parallel in her own life, Anna is not ignorant of or indifferent to the colonized Egyptian people who live under British rule, and she refuses to have her knowledge limited by her gender and race. With that, Anna devises a plan to travel uninhibited into realms and regions that would be potentially dangerous for a woman by dressing and behaving as a man. Her actions come at a price, though, as she is mistaken for an important British man and she and her traveling companion, Sabir, are kidnapped. Because the crime becomes worse when her gender is discovered, Anna's first instinct is to protect Sabir from the fallout of "this episode," as she calls it:

> My thoughts run mainly on my friends at the Agency and how I should prevent any word of this episode ever reaching their ears. As to consciousness of danger, I can truthfully say I have had none, nor do I have any now. Any fear I might feel is conjured up more by the imagined visage of Lord Cromer than by the actual circumstances in which I find myself. I know that he will blame Mr. Barrington most severely for encouraging my foolishness, and will probably insist on his dismissing poor Sabir and that will make him most unhappy. Sabir will also be deprived of both his protector and his income. I am determined not to let this happen. For myself, the thought that holds most terror for me now is to be-

> come known in London as "that Lady Anna Winterbourne who was abducted by the Arabs." (105)

Anna even seeks to protect her well-mannered captors, whom she feels do not deserve the wrath of Lord Cromer and the British Agency. She writes of these Egyptian men, who have kidnapped her in hopes of gaining some kind of leverage against the British toward the goal of Egyptian self-governance:

> It was a great pity that I was not able to converse with them, and find out the nature of their grievance, and how they thought this wild action would bring them closer to redress. Is this event the reason I felt Fate draw me to Egypt? How odd it would be if—through me—the Egyptians got their longed-for Constitution. But I am not important enough, nor will this affair reach that proportion, for I do believe that once they have found out that I am a woman and a mere visitor, they will send me on my way with courtly apologies. (106-7)

She neither wants to be rescued nor prevented from having future adventures, so Anna makes the most of her abduction. She sees it as an opportunity, finally, to meet real, proud Egyptian people, ones who aren't in the pocket of the British, including her eventual husband, Sharif, and his sister, Layla, who will become Anna's lifelong friend. And, in her own way, she soon becomes "important enough," even as a woman, to participate in the political realm as a partner with Sharif in working for full Egyptian independence. Indeed, before she has even married Sharif, Anna takes up the causes of Egyptian national autonomy that she has come to believe in, approaching Lord Cromer himself to appeal for British support for the education of Egyptian women. She chooses to "see" the Egyptian people, separating herself from her former complicity with the indifferent British colonizing machine.

By making herself open to all the possible experiences of her new life abroad, Anna is not penned in by the binaries of Western and Other, nor even by the binaries of male and female. Rather than being treated as a delicate English lady as in her other encounters with men, she meets Sharif on terms of her own devising, which allow her to forge not only a romantic but an intellectual connection with him. As King observes, Anna is Sharif's "true intellectual partner" as they share "key Saidean ideas that undergird the novel's political poetics" (144). Indeed, years earlier, Sharif had divorced his first wife after discovering their intellectual incompatibility. He narrates his thoughts at that time in a letter to his mother:

> I cannot live my life with a woman who has no key to my mind and who does not share my concerns. She cannot—will not—read anything. She shrugs off the grave problems of the day and asks if I think her new tablecloth is pretty. We are living in difficult times and it is not enough for a person to be interested in his home and his job—in his own personal life. I need my partner to be someone to whom I can turn, confident of her sympathy, believing her when she tells me I'm in the wrong, strengthened when she tells me I'm in the right. I want to love, and be loved back—but what I see is not love or companionship but a sort of transaction of convenience sanctioned by religion and society and I do not want it. (151)

Knowing she is deeply concerned over the "grave problems of the day" for Egyptian people, Sharif cherishes Anna, as the partner that she is to him in every way. As Layla describes, "Anna started to help him, to translate for him from the British newspapers, and to use her connections in England to bring him what news she could that had a bearing on life here" (373). Because Anna and Sharif are well matched in mind and spirit—and because Anna knows and expresses the strength of her own mind—neither Anna's race, religion, culture, and language nor her gender prove as real obstacles to their mental connection. In fact, Sharif is obliged to acknowledge to himself that he fell in love with Anna in spite of, and perhaps partly because of, her gender-bending ways: "As they travelled through the Sinai, he had laughed at himself—at the end of his time he would desire a man. A fair youngamrad, who rode with grace and skill, who raced him neck to neck—there were times when he would forget that his companion was a woman, she blended so well with the taciturn men, with the silence of the desert" (274). The homoerotic feelings Sharif describes here don't impede their relationship but, rather, help to solidify their intellectual bond as they work together to achieve goals within the typically masculine political arena of postcolonial nation-building.

Both characters seem rendered more whole—and more free—for such explorations of love, desire, and sexuality, which lead to their eventual marriage. For Anna, their sexual relationship arouses in her a sense of embodied female being she has never felt before. The morning after their wedding night she writes, "And now, today, I feel as if—I hardly know how to describe it, but it is as if my body had been absent and now it is present. As though I am for the first time present in my own body" (335). Anna links a deep, newly realized happiness to this bodily epiphany:

> I feel happiness—I could laugh aloud as I write the words—as surely as I would feel the warmth of a fire upon coming to it from a cold, damp night. And the oddest thing is that I am grown fond of my own limbs. The hands and feet that have served me these thirty years, the hair I have brushed unthinkingly each night—I feel a tenderness for them now as though they were cherished creatures in their own right. (350)

The body that has "served" Anna for all her years—she now serves it, cherishing a wholeness of being that she was never able to have within the confines of an indifferent British society. And this new physical awareness provides a true sense of peace to her formerly restless spirit: "And I am content. I am content just to be" (335).

In their non-traditional, interracial, cross-cultural relationship, Anna and Sharif are indeed experiencing something rare, liberating, and transgressive. Specifically the case of a white woman pursuing a "native" man was a cause for disgrace in Europe: "The sexual choices of white women were at issue; they are desired objects, but unruly desiring subjects as well" (Stoler 41). Anna's very identity, then, as a "desiring subject" is problematic, but her actions make her a dangerous transgressor of the British nation itself. Sharif, as an Arab man, isn't questioned for his actual desire for a white woman. As postcolonial scholar Ania Loomba asserts, Western ideology presumed that "darker races or non-Europeans were immoral, promiscuous, libidinous and always desired white people" (158). But Anna's audacity to identify and pursue her desires, particularly when the target of them is an non-white man, places her outside the realm of acceptable female behavior for a well-born British woman, in whom colonial "anxieties about female sexuality and racial purity" converge (Loomba 159). As Stoler articulates regarding an interplay of race, nationality, gender, and class, "Discourses of sexuality do more than define the distinctions of the bourgeois self; in identifying marginal members of the body politic, they have mapped the moral parameters of European nations" (7).

Embracing the freedom she finds there in the margins as a sexual woman, both desiring and desirous, Anna interrogates these "moral parameters," standing up to Lord Cromer himself in defense of her interracial union. While Spivak facetiously asserts, regarding colonial interference in traditional native culture, that "white men are saving brown women from brown men," in this case, white men, like the historical Lord Cromer as British controller-general of Egypt, can't even save white women from brown men. In that sense, Soueif revisits history and offers Anna's transgressive actions, particularly her sexuality, as a challenge to the British nation and empire at the turn of the twentieth century.

Conclusion

> My dear Sir Charles, I understand so much more now of what I used to hear you say. I have started to believe that what we are doing is denying that Egyptians have a "consciousness of themselves" . . . and that by doing so we settle any qualms of conscience as to our right to be here. So long as we believe that they are like pets or small children, we can remain here to "guide them" and help them "develop." But if we see that they are as fully conscious of themselves and their place in the world as we are, why then the honourable thing is to pack up and go.
>
> Anna, *The Map of Love*[9]

With this realization—following the lead of Sir Charles but only after she has seen for herself—Anna breaks the hold of the colonizer's indifference in her own life, recognizing the dehumanizing effects on both sides of treating others as beings less endowed with a right to exist freely. It is an enterprise with which she can no longer be complicit, an ideology she has never fully shared and must finally break with in order to achieve self-actualization—finding freedom, purpose, and peace—by fulfilling her desires. As Massad contends, "Desire, in Soueif's work, always exists in a context of politics, history, and geography, all of which are intermeshed and cannot be disentangled" (74). In that context, Anna strikes out, making herself a willing exile as she travels the map of the complicated new postcolonial world Said describes. And on that journey, Anna doesn't leave the most difficult philosophical questions and political tasks to the men. When Sharif asks his sister if she believes Anna is up to the task of marrying him, of sharing his challenging life, Layla says, "[O]f course it will not be easy for her, and if it had been anyone else I would say she would not be able to do it. But Anna is different. She has a big mind" (284).

By loving Sharif and partnering with him in the Egyptian anti-colonial movement—leaving behind her former life to embrace a new one—Anna performs her own political act; she makes history. She blurs the lines between the political and the domestic, between the public and the personal, between history and romance, rendering the lines themselves irrelevant in the sphere of her own life. Regarding the complex interplay of history, politics, and sexuality in the novel, Soueif reminds us, "[I]t's still desire that brings the characters together" (qtd. in Massad 84). And that personal realm of desire, as Davis asserts, does not serve "merely as an allegorical stand-in for politics." Rather, "Soueif's complex narrative structure explores the linkages between sexual politics and national and international politics" (Davis). The sexual and romantic center of the novel is not *mere* romance at all but the makings of an important reconsideration of colonial history itself.

In her own living Arab pastiche, Anna reinvents the harem, following her desires and creating and fulfilling her own fantasy, where Orientalist illusions give way to reality and where love and family share a space with the modern fight for an ancient nation. The novel opens with a family tree that stretches back to Sharif's ancestors in the eighteenth century, but everything hinges on Anna, from the narrative's romantic center and the family she creates to the novel itself as Soueif's "imagined recovery of ancestral history" (Wynne 65). Not just one family's history but history itself can be revisited—and revised—through Anna's journey from a privileged British woman, surrounded by indifference for those colonized by her nation, to becoming "that son." As it turns out, that son could only be a daughter.

NOTES

1. Soueif 281-82.
2. *Culture and Imperialism* 332.
3. In fact, we see Sharif comforting Anna over the historical Denshwai (or Dinshaway) incident, in which the British react to the accidental death of one of their officers during a pigeon hunt by arresting over fifty native Egyptians and cruelly punishing them. Four

were executed. As Rogan explains, this incident reinforced the efforts of Egyptian nationalism, and "Dinshaway was not forgotten nor were the British forgiven" (145-46). Upon hearing the fates of those convicted, Anna weeps and says, "I am ashamed." Sharif tells her, "Listen. You must not—ever—feel like this. This is not to do with being British. . . . The only way we can bear this is to make it work for us. To make sure it can never happen again. Never" (429).

4. Sharif's awareness of the trope of the harem in Orientalist texts is notable here. He jokingly identifies his place in such stereotypical stories as the "wicked Pasha," the powerful Arab man so masculine as to need a bevy of women to satisfy his insatiable sexual desires. Feminist consideration of the harem trope "conceptualizes the harem as a set of sites crucial to gender construction" (Booth 11). While a complete survey of the many insightful critiques of the harem trope is impossible here, I suggest Booth's anthology *Harem Histories: Envisioning Places and Living Spaces*, Joan Del Plato's *Multiple Wives, Multiple Pleasures: Representing the Harem, 1800-1875*, and Reina Lewis' *Rethinking Orientalism: Women, Travel and the Ottoman Empire*, to name just a few.
5. Anna's sense of exclusion from traveling within the male-dominated realm of the British colonies was appropriate. As David Goldberg asserts, "The colonies thus were male clubs of a kind, at once the laboratory, factory, and stable of white men's making, their fantasies forcibly serviced by the local populations, men and women of color alike. Colonization in effect was about power and to serve country, king (no doubt preferably), and God (undoubtedly masculinized)." The qualities associated with the feminine nature of white women exclude them from participating in the male fantasy of such enterprises, as Goldberg continues: "White women were seen as getting in the way of completing the 'rough' work colonization necessitated and its vast profits required, too squeamish in the face of the necessary violence, too soft and tearful before health and hellish standards, too sensitive even for the hardships of difficult administrative decision-making" (95). No doubt these stereotypes didn't always hold true when European women did venture into the colonies. However, by keeping women cordoned off

from these "hellish" realities, European men ensured a "squeamish" woman's empathetic capacity wouldn't interfere with the standard of apathy toward the colonized. Many of Anna's fellow British women are content to let their husbands, fathers, etc., shelter them from such violence, but Anna proves herself eager to leave the easy shelter of apathy behind.

6. As Amin Malak explains of another influence for Anna's writing in British literature, "Soueif's rendition of Anna's intelligently inquisitive sensibility revealed in journals, diaries and letters recalls the English literary tradition of epistolary fiction, especially Samuel Richardson's two eponymous novels *Pamela* and *Clarissa*" (157).
7. I distinguish Anna's desire to *see* Egypt for herself from the concept of the Western imperial gaze I discuss early in this essay. In the same way that Anna protects herself from the male gaze by concealing her gender, she makes efforts to remove herself from complicity with the problematic British imperial gaze. While Anna's initial curiosity regarding Arab culture originates with Orientalist portrayals such as the Lewis paintings, she allows all of her preconceptions to be refigured by her contact with the reality of Egyptian life. Anna's self-consciousness of her positioning is key here; she is aware that power dynamics make any effort to really know and understand the individuals one has power over a futile act (see upcoming quote from the novel regarding Anna's maidservant Emily). Moreover, when Anna turns her critical gaze toward, for example, the racism in her Cook guidebook, she willingly relinquishes any measure of power afforded her by the Western construction of the Arab. Anna takes many such steps in removing herself from participation with the British gaze upon the Other, each step reinforcing her willingness to give up the power the gaze endows the gazer. Anna also comes to feel protective of her new life, seeking to guard the culture of the harem from the gaze of her British friend Caroline. And, as I will consider in the next section, Anna's sister-in-law explains how Anna values their Arab culture with such innocence and eagerness that the family, in turn, comes to revalue their culture anew. Ultimately, what Soueif shows us is that these encounters with Arab culture and people write on Anna

more than she influences them. Having followed Anna's journey from the outset, we know that this is what she always wanted.

8. Loomba discusses the "potentially unhinging" experience of "going native," as famously represented in English literature through the character of Kurtz in Joseph Conrad's *Heart of Darkness* (136).
9. Soueif 247.

Works Cited

Amireh, Amal. "Between Complicity and Subversion: Body Politics in Palestinian National Narrative." *The South Atlantic Quarterly* 102.4 (2003): 747-72.

Booth, Marilyn. *Harem Histories: Envisioning Places and Living Spaces*. Durham, NC: Duke UP, 2010.

Burleigh, Nina. *Mirage: Napoleon's Scientists and the Unveiling of Egypt*. New York: HarperCollins, 2007.

Darraj, Susan Muaddi. "Narrating England and Egypt: The Hybrid Fiction of Ahdaf Soueif." *Studies in the Humanities* 30.1 (2003): 91-107.

Davis, Emily S. "Romance as Political Aesthetic in Ahdaf Soueif*'s The Map of Love*." *Genders* 45 (2007): n.p.

El Naga, Shereen Bou. "New Politics, Old Identities: Arab Women in (Their) English Words." *Agenda* 54 (2002): 60-73.

Goldberg, David Theo. "Racial Rule." *Relocating Postcolonialism*. Ed. Goldberg and Ato Quayson. Oxford: Blackwell, 2002. 82-102.

King, Katherine Callen. "Translating Heroism: Locating Edward Said on Ahdaf Soueif*'s The Map of Love*." *Edward Said: A Legacy of Emancipation and Representation*. Ed. Adel Iskandar and Hakem Rustom. 142-58. Berkeley, CA: U of California P, 2010.

Loomba, Ania. *Colonialism/Postcolonialism*. London: Routledge, 1998.

Malak, Amin. "Arab-Muslim Feminism and the Narrative of Hybridity: The Fiction of Ahdaf Soueif." *Alif: Journal of Comparative Poetics* 20 (2000): 140-83.

Massad, Joseph. "The Politics of Desire in the Writings of Ahdaf Soueif."*Journal of Palestine Studies* 28.4 (1999): 74-90.

McClintock, Anne. *Imperial Leather: Race, Gender, and Sexuality in the Colonial Contest*. New York: Routledge, 1995.

Rogan, Eugene. *The Arabs: A History*. New York: Basic Books, 2009.

Said, Edward. *Culture and Imperialism*. New York: Vintage, 1993.

_____ . *The Edward Said Reader*. Ed. Moustafa Bayoumi and Andrew Rubin. New York: Vintage, 2000.

Soueif, Ahdaf. *The Map of Love*. New York: Anchor, 2000.

Stoler, Ann Laura. *Race and the Education of Desire: Foucault's* History of Sexuality *and the Colonial Order of Things*. Durham, NC: Duke UP, 1995.

Wynne, Catherine. "Navigating the Mezzaterra: Home, Harem and the Hybrid Family in Ahdaf Soueif's *The Map of Love*."*Critical Survey* 18.2 (2006): 56-66.

From Post-colonial Vision of Nature to Ecocinema: A Study of Satyajit Ray's *Aranyer Din Ratri* and Goutam Ghose's *Abar Aranye*

AKAITAB MUKHERJEE & RAJNI SINGH

Ecocriticism is literary and cultural criticism from the environmentalist viewpoint. This critical approach evaluates texts in terms of how they depict the natural world, and the helpful or harmful effects on this environment by humans. Ecocritics prefer transformative discourse to understand the relationship between nature and human nature from multiple dimensions. This tendency makes ecocriticism overlap other disciplines. Hence, ecocriticism, when using the theoretical framework of postcolonialism, investigates the changes wrought on the environment during the colonial period, the effects of these changes on colonial subjects, and the approach of postcolonial governments to these issues. Cinema is an important medium that frequently documents environmental hazards and other issues related to environmental health, giving us the term "ecocinema," which deals with such issues as pollution and environmental justice. This genre includes all the sub-genres of cinema, including the documentary, the feature film, and the *avant-garde* film, to name a few. However, *Aranyer Din Ratri* (1970) by Satyajit Ray and Goutam Ghose's *Abar Aranye* (2003) highlight the relevance of the forest in Indian culture in a post-independent and globalised world. Thus, these two films have become a testament of the alliance between nature and post-independent Indians as well as Indians of the global village. This paper will explicate these two movies in the light of postcolonial ecocriticism and ecocinema.

Ecocriticism, an earth-centred approach to literary analysis, evaluates texts in terms of their coherence and usefulness as response to environmental crisis. It analyses the history of concepts such as "nature," to understand the cultural developments that have led to the present global ecological crisis (Waugh 530). Ecocritics seek to offer a transformative discourse in order to understand nature from multiple dimensions, and as a consequence it merges with other disciplines. This cross-fertilization with other discourses enables ecocriticism to analyze and criticize the world, and attention is increasingly given to the cultural processes and products in which, and through which, the complex negotiations of nature and culture take place (Gerrard4). Karla Armbruster and Kathleen Wallace's *Beyond Nature Writing: Expanding the Boundaries of Ecocriticism* proposes that the task of ecocriticism at this time is to expand boundaries and address wide spectrum of texts. This eclectic, interdisciplinary approach allows scope for redefining environmental themes. Michael P. Cohen says that ecocriticism should not limit itself to analyzing environmental narratives, but should also evaluate the nature of environmental narratives (Maricondi 7).

This tendency of crossing the theoretical terrain to fathom the relationship between nature and human beings from different perspectives makes ecocriticism amalgamate with other theories, including Marxism, feminism, and postcolonialism. Postcolonialism is the theoretical approach which involves the study of transformational resistance to unjust and unequal forms of political and cultural authority which extends back across the twentieth century and beyond (Waugh 340).Ecocriticism, using the theoretical framework of postcolonialism, investigates the transformation of environment in the colonized societies by colonial masters, its effects on the colonized subjects and recovery of environmental degradation in post-colonial or post-independent period. In this connection, existing documents which provide environmental policies and other sources are also surveyed. The combination of these two theories is well-suited to reconstruct an ecological history of the nation from the pre-colonial to the post-colonial period. Cinema, too, comes under the consideration of ecocritics because of its strategy of representing nature. Film is a deceptively transparent medium that creates the illusion of direct, immediate and objective access to reality. Ecocinema presents worldviews by showing how we inhabit the planet and might help account for current ecological crisis. The cinematic representation of nature is remarkable because using the techniques and the vocabularies of the medium, it can either reinforce or challenge ideologies regarding nature. The depiction of nature in film is conditioned by a number of factors, including the economics of the entertainment industry, cinematic technology, the objective of the film-maker, the prevailing concepts of nature, and the perceived tastes of the audience (Maricondi 8-9). Ecocinema makes audiences understand, in a non-hierarchical manner, that they are part of a planetary ecosphere. By virtue of representing the "real" world, films often create a world which is indeed virtual; hence ecocinema can offer alternative model of representing the nature. This educational and political agenda of ecocinema makes it distinct from environmentalist films where environmental issues are represented as merely another trivial case (Maricondi7).

Aranyer Din Ratri (1970) by Satyajit Ray and Goutam Ghose's *Abar Aranye* (2003) are especially notable examples of films that highlight the relevance of the forest in Indian culture in a post-independent and globalised world. These documents of contemporary forest cultures also recapitulate the kinship between nature and human society in pre-colonial, colonial and postcolonial times. They do so by giving account of ecological history, which is an amalgam of profligacy and prudence regarding both sustainable and exhaustive uses of natural resources. In pre-colonial times, the forests in India had been viewed as a retreat, a place for reading scriptures, self-searching, renunciation, and the quest for union with God, and thus it was coupled with spirituality (Ganguly 98). In *Ramayana* and *Mahabharata*, the forest has been represented as a place of exile for civilized people. In the "Ashramavasika Parva" section of *Mahabharata*, Dhritarashtra and Gandhari took *sannyasa* and lived a hermit's life in the forest. In *Rig-Veda*, the forest has been depicted as a place of *rishis,* or saints.

But this is not the unabridged representation of forests in Indian culture. Both in *Mahabharata* and *Ramayana,* the forest dwellers are portrayed as backward or demonic creatures. The dark and deep forests of these two epics are populated by animals and non-human creatures like *Nagas*, *Rakshasas* and *danavas*. There are also ample examples of destruction of forests in these two epics. The burning of Khandava Forest with all the creatures inhabiting it by Arjuna in order to establish Indraprastha, or contemporary Delhi, in *Mahabharata* is an example of discrimination. Buddhism and Jainism, on the other hand, played pivotal roles in designing social conventions that promoted prudent use of natural resources by bolstering traditions that encouraged protection of some animals, plants and other elements of nature. During Aryan (3000-1200 BC), Vedic (1200-500 BC), Mauryan (322-185 BC) and Gupta (320 BC-540 AD) periods, forests were worshipped. Since the time of Mauryan kings, state control over forest started, disregarding the bond between the forest and the tribal people (Gadvil and Guha 87). In the colonial period, environmental degradation of India was caused mainly by western imperialism, which was part of a European alteration of world ecology at that time. In the 1860s, Britain emerged as the leader of deforestation all over the globe, and they even destroyed the forests of their own country. In Ireland, South Africa, and the north-eastern United States, industries removed timber for shipbuilding, farming and iron-smelting. According to Madhav Gadgil and Ramachandra Guha, the destruction of forests was done by the British partly to symbolize political power. Alfred Cosby in his monograph on ecological imperialism asserts that Europeans brought with them complex of weeds, animals and diseases and demolished the flora and fauna and human societies of the colonized countries. The annihilation of native ecosystem and populations turned the colonized countries into "Neo-Europes." The transformation of ecological landscape in India was caused by the railways. Hugh Cleghorn, in his acclaimed book, *The Forests and Gardens of South India*, anatomizes this issue with precision. During colonialism, the first attempt to exert state monopoly over forest was Indian Forest Act of 1865 which was amended in 1878. It was a "Bill for confiscation instead of protection," according to the governor of Madras, "it was probably the same process which the Norman Kings adopted in England for their forest extension" (qtd. in Gadgil and Guha130). It was indeed a step towards destruction of tribal communities which were prohibited to kill animals and cut trees in the forests. Moreover, the large numbers of animals killed by the colonizers challenged the ecosystem of the forest. The consequence of enactment of this rule was the decline of various forms of artisanal industry. The use of the resources of nature, introduced by British, continued to operate after independence with modifications.

Satyajit Ray's *Aranyer Din Ratri* is an adaptation of Sunil Ganguly's novel with the same title. In this movie, four friends, Ashim, Hari, Sekhar and Sanjay, depart from Kolkata to get release from the vexed routines of their bounded lives. They go to Palamau to relish the wildness of the forest which can make them forget suffocating experience of the pent-up life in the city. These four young men were indicating that "they were in the mood to go haywire and follow to the letter the antics of untamed, hot-blooded rebels" (Bandyopadhyay147). The *Santhal* Pargana of Palamau appears as a setting which is a duty-free zone. Sheltering the urban young men from the hustle and bustle of metropolis, the forest allows them to relax and re-discover themselves. Ray shows the forest through the eyes of these four young men.

Chidananda Dasgupta says in *The Cinema of Satyajit Ray* that in his post-*Charulata* films, Ray embarks on the venture of searching the identity of the post-independent generation that "does not share with him the full value of the Indian Renaissance" (89). In this movie Ray tries to show how post-colonial hybrids see the forest. Bhabha predicts about the hybrids in his essay *The Third Space*:

> For me the importance of hybridity is not to be able to trace two original moments from which the third emerges, rather hybridity to me is the 'third space' which enabled other positions to emerge. This third space displaces the histories that constitute it, sets up new structures of authority, new political initiatives, which are inadequately understood through received wisdom. (qtd. Huddart 85)

In the rest of Ray's movies, he shows how these hybrids have occupied the place of ex-colonizer. The movie starts with the reading of *Palamou*, the travelogue authored by Sajibchandra Chattopadhyay (1834-1889).It was first serialized from 1880 to 1882 in the literary journal *Bangadarshan*. Through this travelogue Bengali *bhadralok* (elite) relished the primitive culture of *Santhals* and *Kols* of Palamau district. It was indeed first-hand account of experiences gathered by the author when he travelled in the interiors of *Santhal Pargana* in the late nineteenth century (Bandyopadhyay149). Like other self-conscious chroniclers, Sanjibchandra was also critical about the culture of the Bengali *bhadralok* of Kolkata from which he set out. The sarcastic tone of the author indicates that his documents are not the outcome of idle curiosity; rather they are serious sociological study.

Charles Tesson says that the title sequence of *Aranyer Din Ratri*, with the views of the forest through the letters of the title, is a pictorial language which utters in the film that we look nature through culture (Roberge 64). The dialectics of nature and culture has been well picturized by the director. Ashim says during the journey: "Foresters are beautiful in forests; children in mother's laps." This aphorism from *Palamou* illustrates the economy of the gaze of city-bred people. The movie shows that these men are incapable of understanding the forest, because their vision has been shaped by modern civilization. However, Sanjay reads selective sections of that nearly century-old travelogue which reflect their intention about forest. He reads the sections which elaborate on tribal women and country liquor. Sekhar appreciates those descriptions. The land appears barbaric, uncivilized. Their patriarchal vision interprets the land as "western society," since the society lacks the gender dichotomy. This ironical attitude puts down the cultural practices of the *Santhals* and simultaneously references to the English people indicate the snobbery of the urban elite and its hunger for western modernization.

Moreover, these are the same stereotypes that were part of colonial discourse and which formed the heart of colonial power. This discourse confirms the colonial authority, but here the place of the authority has been occupied by the native hybrids. However, according to them, it is a place of eternal youth. They do not try to see the forest, the tribal people and the problem of deforestation. There is a scene in which Sadashib Tripathi tells them about reduction of the number of animals from the forest. John Berger in his essay *Why Look at Animals?* says that because of industrialization, most of the animals are removed from daily life and these marginalized creatures are visible in the society as "human puppets" (qtd. in Garrard 139). The reduction of the number of animals is the symptom of deforestation. But they were hardly inquisitive about it. In the rest house, the wife of the gateman suffers from serious disease but they remain indifferent to it. When the gas station suddenly crops up in the middle of the wilderness of the forest and displays Caltex sign in English, it does not surprise the audience. It bespeaks that all third world landscapes bear the sign of economic and imperial exploitation (Ganguly 98). Ray shows the slavery of the colonial masters since two centuries could not stop the natives to mimic the ex-colonizer's cultural habits, assumptions, institutions and values. This parody makes them new imperial masters and patrons of the crypto-barbarian tribals in independent country. Ashis Nandy says that colonialism colonized minds in addition to bodies and it lured the colonized societies to alter their cultural priorities. He says: "The west is now everywhere, within the west and outside; in structures and in minds" (Nandy iii). The psychological impact of colonialism has been visible through the activities of these four young men in this cinema. The neurotic deployment of the word "hippie" shows the genealogical connection between the footloose *Calcutta s*and Hippies, who were their role-models. The forest reminds them of Johnny Weissmuller's familiar Tarzan cry and the scene of sunset in old Burt Lancaster movies. When Ashim goes to the balcony of Mr. Tripathy's house, it appears to him as "Juliet's Balcony." They graft for foreign cultural signifiers which are hopelessly incongruous. Pauline Kael rightly says about the film: "The subtext is perhaps the subtlest, most plangent study of the cultural tragedy of imperialism; the young men are self-parodies—clowns who ape the worst snobberies of the British" (qtd. Roberge 64).

The memory game in this movie is an interesting episode in which Ray shows disillusionment with the post-independence Indian generation. The game requires each of them to remember in proper sequence the names of famous people that others have invoked and then the player should add a new name. They recall the names of the people who belong to the East and the West: Rabindranath, Karl Marx, Cleopatra, Atulya Ghosh, Helen of Troy, Shakespeare, Mao Tse-tung, Don Bradman, Rani Rashmoni, Bobby Kennedy, Tek Chand Thakur, Napoleon and Mumtaz

Mahal. At the beginning Sekhar remembers Gandhi, Nehru, Azad. This rapid naming of person indicates their involvement with history and culture which comes out as hybrid. The amnesia which most of the people suffer in this game is an implicit hint of their tendency to forget their own past. It is obvious that people like them will forget the cultural inheritance and adopt the ideology of the colonizers. Therefore, the movie shows that the post-colonial era does not inaugurate the process of decolonization, but an unconscious imitation of colonial system.

The tribals in India developed a culture dependent on nature. They have been subject to repeated forms of exploitation and abuse since colonial times. Deforestation, urban sprawl and illegal seizure of lands has caused many tribals to become "ecological refugees." A few Indian films pertain to this issue, while others merely hyperbolize it. *Aranyer Din Ratri* Ray shows the changing scenario of Palamau district. It lacks the earlier exotic look of the travelogue and it is no more a remote village. Sanjibchandra, the narrator of *Palamou*, enjoyed the luxury of being carried to his destination by palanquin, but in this movie the four young men reach the rest house by taxi. There is the suggestion of communication through railways also. According to Sibaji Bandyopadhyay, this movie ties together two types of ideologies, primitivism and tourism. Discovering primitivism was the classic saga of the colonialists. When the colonial machinery needed help and support of the colonized, they made a cunning system of classification. The superiority of the upper-caste natives and their affinity with the colonial masters placed the tribal people or "primitives" on the periphery. Indian forest gained the status of "reserve-forest" because it became the museum of age-old beliefs and practices which were fast vanishing. Tourism, on the other hand, often equated with the concept of pilgrimage, redefines primitivism by commodifying primitives or tribals (Bandyopadhyay 153-55).

Thus, in Ray's film, the purpose of the four young men's expedition is to relish the wilderness and primitive life of the forest, which was indeed a mockery towards the cultures of poor *santhals*. The culture of the *santhals* appears to them prehistoric, because they deduce it from their hybrid culture. When Lokha, a *Santhal,* who belongs to this place, tries to sit beside Sekhar, he deliberately refuses to sit with lower caste villager. The rest-house is provided to those who have permission from the higher authority which indirectly points to the prohibition of local inhabitants to visit the place. Later Sekhar shoos away a couple of tribals who watch him bathe at the road side well and then he calls them "asabhya" or uncivilized. When they go to the liquor shop, Sekhar addresses the intoxicated tribal men as "chotolok" or lower caste people and immediately feels insecure because of their presence. The "santhal twist" and the juxtaposition of tribal and western culture of these young men, when they become drunk again, defames the tribal art form. When Sekhar meets Duli for the first time, he calls her "Miss India," which demonstrates the condescending attitude of urban people. Moreover, in this context, the word is charged with sexual implication. Later, Sekhar hires Duli and two of her companions to perform menial jobs for the men and he calls it "tribal welfare." This phrase mocks the government schemes which are ostensibly launched to improve the condition of the tribals.

Additionally, since the colonized are seen from a Eurocentric viewpoint that includes sexualized exoticism, sexuality is an integral part of the colonial discourse. From the perspective of colonialism, the word commerce includes exchange of both the merchandise and bodies of the colonized subjects. It is a strategy of economic and political trafficking. When Duli, the tribal woman, offers her body to Hari with the exchange of money, it demonstrates the continuation of the colonial commerce in independent country and that the new empire has inherited the position of the ex-colonizers. However, the *Santhals* and the *Kols* in the movie are not dependent on nature for their daily living and they have become labourers to earn daily wages. It is an evidence of changing ecosystem which has altered the ancient relationship between tribal people and nature. In Bihar *District Gazette*, published in 1961, there is abundant information regarding the daily life of tribal people of this district in ancient times. The forest offered a subsidiary living to the inhabitants of the place who used grass, reeds, bamboos and developed typical cottage industries like catechu manufacture, rope-making, cocoon rearing etc. Animal husbandry laid the way to dairy business also. Using cotton trees they created another cottage industry. G. Thompson, the revenue officer of the colonial period, observed that the place was famous for cotton weaving. The advent of mining at the end of colonial period and in the post-independence period changed the ecosystem of this area. This altered situation has been disclosed in Ray's movie.

The movie ends with the return of these four young men to their city, but they don't return unhurt or unchanged. Hari returns with bandage on his head that is a sign of what may happen to "civilized" society if "uncivilized" tribal people decide to strike back. Though this movie ends with a moral lesson to urban cynics, in his last movie *Agantuk (*1992), Satyajit Ray makes this message more clear. In this movie, the protagonist is Manmohan, a professional anthropologist, a Bengali double of Levi-Strauss and an alter-ego of Ray, who is an expert in structural anthropology. However, Manmohan declares in *Agantuk*: "civilized life, as in a city, is illusory. Tribal civilization is the real one," for they inherit their own language, art, religion, science, architecture and technology. *Aranyer Din Ratri* explicates the facade of urban life and in an implicit way holds the same suggestion.

Goutam Ghose's *Abar Arnye* (2003) is a sequel to *Aranyer Din Ratri*, though the director is hesitant to categorize the movie as such. In this film, the characters of Ray's film re-visit forest after thirty years. Here, Ghose chooses the forest of North Bengal rather than Palamau, which was the locale of Ray's film. In Ghose's movie Ashim, Hari and Sanjay go on the expedition. The movie could not include Sekhar, because Rabi Ghosh, who played the role of Sekhar, passed away in 1992. However, these three friends go on the trip with their families. In the course of the journey, they re-discover themselves. Human relations deepen in the exotic natural setting and the spirit of escape from the city becomes the crux of the movie. Ghose places the three young men and their families in a new social context and explores contemporary life-issues.

Ghose shows the domination of neo-colonialism in the new millennium in India and its consequences. He shows that political independence of the country cannot dismantle colonial power in all its forms. Long after independence, the nation is still mimicking political, cultural and economic models of colonizers. In another way, we can say that the developing economics or the third world remains incapable of developing an independent economic and political identity under the pressure of globalization. Ashim, as in earlier movie, compares nature with western cultural icons. Hence the sunset in the countryside appears to him as Turner's canvas and reminds him of cowboys. The plan of the trip makes Hari animated and he shouts like Johnny Wessimuller's Tarzan. Ashim's *bungalow* in the tea-garden which was established during the colonial period, continues the same maintenance that was introduced during colonial period, disregarding the poor condition of the tea business and the labourers. Though the beauty and serenity of the place enchants them and at the same time galvanizes them to recapitulate the colonial past and the oppression of the labourers during this period. The younger generation in the movie is ignorant about the culture of the country. Amrita, Ashim's daughter, who has spent long time in United States, is literally unenlightened about the culture of her own nation. Jishu, the son of Italian mother and Indian father, who teams up with these families, is also heedless about the

Indian culture. Amrita suffers from hyper-sensitivity after the uncanny experience of 9/11 attack. The pastoral setting of nature offers her tranquillity and it releases her from the violence which she experiences everyday through media. The break from everyday life and the exotic nature make them exercise different art forms to derive pleasure out of them, though none of them are connected with Indian culture.

The memory game which was used by Ray as psychological enquiry to understand the socio-cultural fabric has been used by Ghose also. In this memory game, new names are incorporated which indicate a change in cultural history. The names used in the memory game are: Charlie Chaplin, Che Guevara, Swami Vivekananda,, Jibananda Das, John Lenon, Bill Gates, Dalai Lama, Michael Madhusudan Dutt, Voltaire, Lalan Fakir, Osama Bin Laden, Satyajit Ray, Madonna, and Atul Prasad Sen. The names Bill Gates and Osama Bin Laden are very significant in this list, because they represent capitalism and terrorism respectively, which is a subplot of the movie. Aparna, who utters the name of Bobby Kennedy in the previous movie, mentions Laden's name here. Aparna's mention of Laden connotes the mushrooming of terror all over the world and its effects on people's mind. In the movie, the son of the manager of the tea-garden has been found playing with toy guns and videogames of war. It is the nadir of human civilization.

Apart from slight changes, the movie focuses on the trip like the prequel, until Amrita reaches tribal village which shows the condition of the aboriginal people in the new millennium. When Amrita falls in the river, the tribal people rescue her and take her to their village. There, she comes to know about their education system, daily life and rituals. She easily sees the difference between them and her urban life. However, her endeavour to help those poor tribals financially ends in disaster, for suddenly the police appear on the scene to arrest the leader of the community and bring Amrita back. The film also denotes the negligence and failure of the government to provide the minimum facilities to the tribals. The sudden raid in the forest and arrest without reason points to the violence of the state that mocks ideals like secularism and democracy upon which our constitution depends.

The changed ecosystem of the tribal people, caused by the environmental imperialism that was initiated during the colonial epoch, is also illustrated here. Rather than resolving the system, the government of independent India has made the condition worse. Ghose shows the condition in the aftermath of Bauxite mining in Dooars region. After the changed ecosystem how the inhabitants of the place adapt themselves to the consumer society is a subplot of the movie. He shows how environmental hazards affect the life of the tribal people. When the mining industry was closed, it created unrest in society, making the jobless young men agitated. Here "filiation" or the ancient heritage of the local inhabitants has been destroyed as it has been "affiliated" to capitalist society and has adopted their culture. This move from "filiation" to "affiliation" bespeaks hegemonic power of dominant imperial culture.

The film ends on the same tone as *Aranyer Din Ratri*. The urban visitors return to the city, but unlike the earlier film, here they receive a strong blow. They realize that they are unable to understand nature. When the police arrest the leader of the tribals, it infuriates Aparna, who calls other men "hypocrites." Ashim's aphorism in the prequel: "Foresters are beautiful in forests; children in mother's laps" becomes relevant in this context also. The tribals, whom Gadgil and Guha, categorize as "ecosystem people" because of their bonding with nature and direct access to natural resources, believe that they are a part of a community that includes nature and other animals. Through their religious beliefs, they remain connected with nature in such a way that they treat it as sacred and protect it. Thus, the locals venerate and protect the Himalayan peak of Nanda Devi and Talakaveri, from where the River Kaveri originates in the Western

Ghats. This time-worn tradition of protecting nature can play an important role in conserving India's heritage of biodiversity. The laxity of the government often makes these communities violent. North Bengal similarly experienced the Naxalite movement, beginning in Naxalbari in 1967, which later encouraged armed struggles against the state. At that time, Dooars also protested against ecological exploitation.

In this movie, Ghose suggests that proper development in these areas and deciphering the tribals' culture can solve this problem. In another film, *Shunyo Awanko* (2013), he shows how the irresponsibility of the government makes the poor villagers participate in the armed forces to save their forests and traditions. Ghose, as a humanist, thinks that development can restore the proper ecosystem of the tribals and can make them leave the path of war against the state. As an example of ecocinema, Ghose's film is quite unusual, for it talks less about pollution and the responses of societies to this threat. The intension of the film is to focus on the condition of the tribals, and this political agenda is a main feature of ecocinema. Through his appealing cinematography, Ghose tries to relocate our relationship with nature. In *Toward an Environmental Justice Ecocriticism*, T.V. Reed argues that the aesthetic appreciation of nature and representation of nature in advertising, film, photography and literature paradoxically veils the causes and effects of environmental degradation. But through his almost picture-postcard-type presentation of nature, Ghose shows that beauty is not mechanical reproduction and that it can heal the wounds of neurotics like Amrita. It makes us realize that human society cannot flourish unless natural system also flourishes (Maricondi15). Ghose holds the position of eco-Marxists, who believe that environmental problem cannot be alienated from social problems. He advocates decentralized society which will be derived from an anarchistic political tradition (Gerard 29). Ghose "recognized the priorness [sic] of an 'external' or 'first' nature, that gave birth to humankind. But humans then worked on this 'first' nature to produce a 'second' nature: the material creations of society plus its institutions, ideas and values" (qtd. in Gerrard 29), and his film becomes a critique of it. Thus, his aesthetic vision of nature is completely justified.

Aranyer Din Ratri and *Abar Aranye* thus give voice to marginalized counter-narratives, but both directors could not envision an affirmative future for tribals or for nature. Provocations from abstract forces like capitalism, materialism, and even modern western science make mainstream society overlook the significance of forests in Indian culture today. These two movies expose how socio-political hierarchies, as environmental justice scholars like Robert Bullard and Vandana Shiva theorize, are the cause of exploitation of both the "ecosystem people" and nature. The films help us discern the necessity to nurture and build compassionate, equable, responsible relationships among humans in all societies. C.A. Bowers, in *Educating for Ecojustice and Community*, proposes to reform education which can assist to solve the problems of environmental challenges and can conserve traditions essential to communities. "Eco-justice pedagogy," suggested by Bowers, can make the larger sections of society understand the environmental jeremiad and marginalization of tribals, and solve issues related to them.

Works Cited

Act Zero [Shunyo Awanko]. Perf. Priyanshu Chatterjee, Konkona Sensharma, Priyanka Bose, Soumitra Chatterjee. Dir. Goutam Ghose. Kolkata: Rose Valley, 2013. Film.

Ashcroft, Bill, and Gareth Griffiths and Helen Tiffin. *Post-Colonial Studies: The Key Concepts.* New York: Routledge, 2007.

Bandyopadhyay, Sibaji. *Sibaji Bandyopadhyay Reader: An Anthology of Essays.* Delhi: Worldview, 2012.

Bihar. *Palamau.* Patna: The Superintendent Secretariat Press, 1961.

Cooper, Darius. *The Cinema of Satyajit Ray: Between Tradition and Modernity*. New York: Cambridge UP, 2000.

Das Gupta, Chidananda. *The Cinema of Satyajit Ray*. New Delhi: National Book Trust, 1994.

Days and Nights in the Forest [Aranyer Din Ratri].Dir. Satyajit Ray. Perf. Soumitra Chatterjee, Subhendu Chatterjee, Shamit Bhanja, Sharmila Tagore. Kolkata: Priya Films, 1970. Film.

Gadgil, Madhav and Ramachandra Guha. *The Use and Abuse of Nature*. New Delhi: Oxford UP, 2013.

Ganguly, Suranjan. *Satyajit Ray: In Search of the Modern*. New Delhi: Penguin Books, 2011.

Garrard, Greg. *Ecocriticism*. New York: Routledge, 2004.

Ghosal, Somnath. "Precolonial and Colonial Forest Culture in Presidency of Bengal." *Journal of Studies in Human Geography* 5.1 (2011). humangeographies.org.ro/articles/51/5_1_11_8_ghosal.pdf

In the Forest . . . again [Abar Aranye].Dir. Goutam Ghose. Perf. Sharmila Tagore, Shamit Bhanja, Soumitra Chatterjee, Rupa Ganguly, Jishu Sengupta, Swaswata Chatterjee. Kolkata: Rainbow and T. Sarkar, 2003.Film.

Jha, Sourish. "Radical Politics and Environmentalism against Taungya in Dooars." *Economic & Political Weekly* 47: 1 (2012): 112-118.

Maricondi, Paula Willoquet. Ed. *Framing the World: Explorations in Ecocriticism and Film*. New York: U of Virginia Press, 2010.

Nandy, Ashis. *Exiled at Home*. New Delhi: Oxford UP, 2005.

Roberge, Gaston. *Satyajit Ray: Essays (1970-2005)*. New Delhi: Manohar, 2007.

Robinson, Andrew. *Satyajit Ray: The Inner Eye*. New York: I.B. Tauris, 2004.

Saran, Renu. *History of Indian Cinema*. New Delhi: Diamond Books, 2012.

The Stranger [Agantuk]. Dir. Satyajit Ray. Perf. Utpal Dutt, Mamata Shankar, Dipankar Dey,

Dhritiman Chatterjee. Kolkata: National Film Development Corporation of India, 1992.

Waugh, Patricia. *An Oxford Guide to Literary Theory and Criticism*. New York: Oxford, 2005.

Fantasy as Narrative Device in Postcolonial Fictional Writings

SANTWANA HALDAR

Broadly speaking, the postcolonial condition is a concept that seeks emancipation from all types of subjugation—racial, gender-based and culture-based. The native mode of storytelling that included fantastic events as parts of life was undermined by the elite in colonized countries who, under the influence of the colonial culture, wholeheartedly embraced the British mode of realistic fiction. Postcolonial trend, in its attempt to emancipate native culture from colonial subjugation, turned to Fantasy as a possible source for fiction writing and the postcolonial writers of fiction began to use fantasy "as a method of producing intensified images of reality"[1]. The present article intends to discuss how Salman Rushdie, the eminent postcolonial Indian writer in English as well as the owner of Booker's Booker, and Manoj Das, another postcolonial Indian writer, a Padma recipient for his English stories, used fantasy in their fictional writings and challenged the realistic mode of narration popularized by the colonial power as the only possible way of rendering reality.

It is pertinent in this context to have a view of the use of fantasy in Latin American literature that has been famous as 'magic realism' in the literary world. Broadly speaking, the Latin American writers (to be specific, the fictional writings of Ricardo Palma, Louis Borges, Alejo Carpentier and Gabriel Garcia Marquez) denounced the false claim of socialist realism that detailed descriptions of social ills in a particular region can express the essence of that region. These writers profusely used elements taken from folk tales, legends and fables in their stories with realistic setting; they did so not for a stunt but for presenting reality from the perspectives of those persons whose cultural presuppositions were different from the presuppositions of Western bourgeois society. Though the Latin American countries were free from Spanish rule in eighteenth century, freedom from foreign control was a complex and time-taking process for the region. During the first decades of the nineteenth century Latin American literature as a self-conscious activity emerged as a result of the independence process. The founders of nation and literature were often the same in Latin America and one of the most compelling tasks confronting Latin American intellectuals after independence was the projection of a past. They tuned to the common people's quasi-medieval belief in miracles and sought to project the past through fantasy. With an analysis of the two competing tendencies in early twentieth century Latin American literature—one preoccupied with formal experimentation and the other allied to political movements—a Latin American critic Roberto Gonzalez Echevarria observes that those tendencies helped to develop a unique blending of fantasy and reality in Latin American fictional writings. To quote Echevarria, "The meeting of the two would yield, in Spanish America, a tendency that has been known as "magical realism," but also as the expression of Latin American "marvelous reality." In all this, in the broadest of terms, one could still see the dichotomy between civilization and barbarism, the urban and the rural, the coastal and the jungle—in short, the uneasy coexistence of the modern and the pre modern in Latin America"[2]. It is the blending of fantasy and modern themes that brought this coexistence of 'civilization' and 'barbarism,' because belief in fantasy had been associated with the rural, the unscientific and also the uncivilized 'other' in colonial mind which was recognized as 'civilized.' For the Latin American writers in general, use of fantasy in fiction was a part of 'inventing the past,' a past that had existed before the arrival of the colonizers. The Indian postcolonial writers of fiction also felt an urge to turn to the past in search of new devices and some of them consciously used fantasy as a device which was different from the western device of realistic narration and which had its roots in Indian folktales and epics.

In *Midnight's Children,* Rushdie presents the time of turmoil in the Indian subcontinent in the decades preceding and following the Partition and the Independence. The device of fantasy used in the novel helped the writer create an encompassing vision of the times of political upheaval, popular upsurge and chaos in the name of development. He faced the problem of rendering the 'present' which according to him could not be rendered in the mode of realistic narration. To quote from the section 'All India Radio' in the novel *Midnight's Children'*: "Reality is a question of perspective; the further you get from the past, the more concrete and plausible it seems—but as you approach the present, it inevitably seems more and more incredible. Suppose yourself in a large cinema, sitting at first in the back row, and gradually moving up, row by row, until your nose is almost pressed against the screen. Gradually the stars' faces dissolve into dancing grain; tiny details assume grotesque proportions; the illusion dissolves—or rather, it becomes clear that illusion itself is reality" (165-66). With the use of the metaphor of cinema the writer justifies the use of fantasy: just as in cinema hall closeness to the screen offers a grotesque view of real pictures, so also details assume grotesque proportions when rendered through the writer's close observation. In the beginning of the novel the narrator Saleem Sinai also seeks to justify "a commingling of the improbable and the mundane" as he has to consume "such an excess of intertwined lives events miracles places rumours" (9). The European claim of discovering the Orient—as if the ignorance of the Europeans obliterated the very existence of the region—is ridiculed by Rushdie in a way that shows his hold on the language of fantasy. Saleem's description of the change in his grandfather's vision after his five years' stay in Germany for higher studies starts in an ironic way, revealing his grudge against colonial practice of brain-washing: "Heidelberg, in which along with medicine and politics, he learned that India—like radium—had been 'discovered' by the Europeans; even Oscar was filled with admiration for Vasco da Gama, and this was what finally separated Aadam Aziz from his friends, this belief of theirs that he was somehow the invention of their ancestors" (11). And as he portrays Aziz physically, he embraces fantasy, describing his nose as "comparable only to the trunk of the elephant-headed god Ganesha" (13). "There it was, reflected in the water, undulating like a mad plantain in the centre of his face. . .It would have dominated less dramatic faces than his easily; even on him, it is what one sees first and remembers longest. 'A cyranose,' Ilse Lubin said, and Oscar added, 'A proboscissimus.' Ingrid announced, 'You could cross a river on that nose" (13).Doctor Aziz's patriotic zeal as well as his optimism is rendered through exaggeration. He is said to have contacted a highly dangerous form of 'optimism,' a "virulent disease (that) had been breaking out all over India" (39). This 'disease' refers to the Quit India Movement in 1942 when most of the people in the Indian subcontinent were optimistic in regard to freedom. Besides such exaggerated description there is fabrication of facts as when the narrator describes the age of the boatman Tai: "Nobody could remember when Tai had been young. He had been plying the same boat, standing in the same hunched position, across the Dal and Nageen lakes . . . forever. As far as anyone knew. He lived somewhere in the insanitary bowels of the old wooden house quarter and his wife grew lotus roots and other curios vegetables on one of the many 'floating gardens/ lilting on the surface of the spring and summer water. Tai himself cheerfully admitted he had no idea of his age. Neither did his wife—he was, she said, already leathery when they married" (14). Despite the use of metaphorical language the mundane reality—the utter poverty of the boatman's family and their marginalized existence—is expressed with a force that could not be done in the language of realistic narration. Blending of fantasy and mundane reality thus creates an encompassing vision of reality.

Rushdie's imagination was let loose—one may recall in this context the dictionary meaning of fantasy as 'a creation of the unrestricted imagination'—when he describes the simultaneous birth of the Indian nation and of Saleeem Sinai. The ominous sign of the cry of "the monster in the streets" at the time of birth creates an eerie atmosphere: "And beneath the roar of the monster there are two more yells, cries, bellows, the howls of children arriving in the world, their unavailing protests mingling with the din of independence which hangs saffron-and-green in the night sky—'A moment comes which comes but rarely in the history, when we step out from the old to the new. . .'while in a room with saffron-and-green carpet (Ahmed Sinai's wife gave birth to a son on the stroke of midnight). . .as Jawaharlal Nehru told the Assembly Hall, 'We end to-day a period of ill-fortune,' as conch-shells blared out the news of freedom, it was on my account that my father cried out too, because the falling chair shattered his toe" (116-17).Here is an attempt to bring parallelism between the destinies of the individuals and those of the new born nation through juxtaposition of the realistic and the fantastic. The novel is full of such parallelism: the events of the year 1956 such as the Suez crisis, the launching of the Five-year plans by Nehru and the language riots are some of the examples. While President Nasser "sank ships at Suez, thus slowing down the movements of the world by obliging it to travel around the Cape of Good Hope" (150), Saleem's sister the Brass Monkey developed the curious habit of setting fire to shoes, trying thereby to impede others' progress. When Ahmed Sinai and Dr. Narikar were playing chess and were arguing for and against President Nasser, "At the same time Jawaharlal Nehru was consulting astrologers about the country's Five Year Plan, in order to avoid another Karamstan" (158). When the tropical summer grew strange fruits and exotic flowers, and "unease was in the air," "Language marchers demanded the partition of the state of Bombay along linguistic boundaries. . .Heat, gnawing at the mind's divisions between fantasy and reality, made anything seem possible" (167). Through the use of such complex technique of juxtaposition the writer seriously attempts to reveal the multi-layered and complex reality of the socio-political life of the Indian subcontinent and also relates it to the world outside.

The narrator of the novel claims that among the midnight's children there were infants with powers of transmutation, flight, prophecy and wizardry; but among them the narrator himself, Saleem, and Shiva having been born on the stroke of midnight, were specially gifted. Referring to the characters in the epics the narrator describes Shiva's gifts of war: he had the power of Rama who could draw the 'undrawable bow,' of Arjuna and Bhima, of the ancient prowess of Kurus and Pandavas united. And Saleem had the greatest talent of looking into the hearts and minds of men. A deliberate subversion of the moral standard of the epics is noted in Saleem's observation: "But it is in Kali-Yuga; the children of the hour of darkness were born, I'm afraid, in the midst of the age of darkness; so that although we find it easy to be brilliant, we were always confused about being good" (200). Rushdie makes it clear through Saleem that his turning to the Indian epics and sometimes to the fables and folktales has nothing to do with the sublime moral structure of those epics and fables. He is interested only in narrative device and hence he makes experiments through the subversion of myths and through juxtaposition of the ancient and the recent. While the epics and the folktales made liberal use for the fantastic to establish a moral order, Rushdie uses the fantastic—the apparently unbelievable and chaotic happenings—only to unveil the facets of reality which are so many in number that the reality itself appears blurred in the process. The immense variety of life-experiences in India—it's great and little traditions with their respective visions of reality—is indeed difficult to be portrayed, particularly in the postcolonial context. Hence it is necessary to make experiments with different devices and Rushdie's experiment in *Midnight's Children* has been successful.

One of the foremost bilingual authors writing in English and Odiya in postcolonial India, Manoj Das is particularly noted for a touch of fantasy and surprise in his fictional writings set either in rural or in urban India. The celebrated British novelist Graham Greene compared his stories with R.K. Narayan's and found in the former "an added mystery" which refers, obviously, to the elements of fantasy and spiritual experience in them which differentiate Das's narrative mode from the realistic mode of writing that established itself in colonial India, proclaiming a strong deviation from the 'once upon a time ambience' of the tales that had so long prevailed. Fantasy used in Das's stories has close similarities with the fantasy used in Indian fairly tales, folk tales and fables such as *Panchatantra,* though the moral teaching is replaced by a broadening of sensibilities that touches spirituality. Use of fantasy in Manoj Das's fiction may broadly be divided into three categories: a) pure fantasy in which realistic backdrop is not used; b) stories with a rural and historical backdrop in which fantasy is used as the characters' felt experiences; c)stories with an urban setting in which fantastic element is used in the form of dream/hallucination. All these categories of fantastic elements in his stories highlight the basic truths of human life. Take, for example, his story 'The Dusky Horizon' in which Das explores the origin of legends and shows how the folk tales are related to the psychological truth, revealing thereby his deviation from the popular trend of socialist realism. The narrator of the story starts with an innocent query of "Where do the butterflies go during the storm?" followed by a comment that "it was rather strange that storms, birds and dead leaves should tackle my memory while I read a fairy tale" (*Selected Fiction,*202). The gist of the fairy tale which the narrator was reading is given towards the end of the story: it is about a sweet, little girl who lived alone on a hill top and whose beneficent influence changed an ogre into a charming lad with whom the girl disappeared. The fairy tale reminds the narrator of an incident in his childhood when he stayed in some remote rural part of eastern India. The incident has the shape of a realistic story set in a village in colonial India. It is the story of three rural boys, the narrator and his two companions, who came in contact with a newcomer in the village—a beautiful orphan girl accompanied by her grandfather, a physician. The physician, who had been driven away from the village fifty years ago for marrying a Christian nurse, came to settle in his village with his granddaughter after the sad demise of his wife, son and daughter-in-law. The three boys were much surprised to see the girl with spectacles wearing a frock, as they had not been habituated to see a girl in such attire. Their first impulse was to humiliate and harass the girl and they even went to the extent of aiming stones at the girl's spectacles. Thanks to the girl's lack of fear and her magnanimity, their plan was foiled and the 'ogre' in them was replaced with a lover's mind. The boys even readily agreed to her proposal of visiting the 'peacock hill' at the outskirt of the village which was infamous as an abode of ogre. On their return journey from the hill after sunset, they encountered a severe rainfall and storm and the girl having lost her specs became almost blind, trying hard to find her way clasping the narrator's hand. But climbing down with the use of one hand being impossible the narrator soon freed his hand from hers and when the three boys at last managed to reach the base, the girl was nowhere. Later her dead body was found in a pit and she was buried at that place. After many a year, when the narrator lost all connections with his village, he read the fairy tale written by some 'Butterfly' and was immediately reminded of the girl. After investigation he recognized the author as one of his two friends in the village. Later the other friend was also recognized who now became a hermit and made a small shrine on the hill where the girl had been buried. The narrator weeps at this revelation and his suppressed sense of sin for being an instrument in the girl's accidental death comes out. He laments that he could not expiate while his two friends were doing penance in their own ways, one recreating the girl as a charming heroine and the other worshipping her. The writer friend tells him that the narrator is doing penance through shedding his tears. This psychologically realistic account is powerful enough to affect the readers' mind focusing on the old physician's utter loneliness and the repentance of three village boys who were responsible for the girl's death and who, after so many years are unable to forgive themselves for letting the girl die. Both the fairy tale and the realistic account carry the message of the possibility of man's progress in consciousness: the fairy tale carries the message that beneficent influence can change an ogre into a lover and the realistic account highlights how the girl's beneficent influence changes the boys' behavior. The inclusion of the fairy tale in the story clarifies Das's view that a fairy tale has the capacity to reveal some basic truths in life through its distinct images and powerful symbols and as such a fairy tale can also serve the purpose of a realistic story in a more effective way. In the story Das also investigates the origin of the legend of an ogre in the peacock hill: it is possible that some woodcutters saw a column of smoke coiling up above a clump of trees and discovered a stranger there, who might very well be a fugitive from the law; the stranger might be huddling over a fire and his eyes must have reflected the flames, thereby giving an impression that they spouted sparks; his scream, combined with the howling wind, must have sounded eerie and blood-curdling, leading the superstitious woodcutters to believe that the stranger was an ogre. With this analysis of the origin of the legend of an ogre, Das uses 'ogre' as the symbol of the dark region of human mind, a region pervaded by ignorance, greed, intolerance and jealousy all of which may be eradicated through proper understanding and love which alone ensure man's progress in consciousness. The girl's description of the faint presence of her mother's ghost in a photograph in which the girl was held by her grandfather and her lament that the ghost's image completely faded out when she grew up to distinguish between natural and supernatural, also highlights the orphan girl's intense desire to see her dead mother.

In his story 'Farewell to a Ghost,' Manoj Das presents the ghost of a girl, who, according to the legend, had been the illegitimate daughter of a 'Sahib' by a tribal woman and who had been living in a villa left by the colonial masters for hundred years as a member of the neighborhood. The village boys dared to steal glimpses of the lonely loving one and the villagers never forgot to offer her a meal at the time of feast. A problem arose when the villa had to be destroyed. No one could even think of leaving the girl homeless. The problem was solved at last when a priest was called and a ritual was arranged to evacuate the villa and the ghost was settled on a tall palm tree at the outskirt of the village. The villagers offered her gifts and food and bade her adieu with burdened hearts. 'The Crocodile's Lady' is a unique story by Manoj Das in which a representative of the civilized western society was spell bound after he could gauge the rural Indian's deep faith in God, in ghosts and in fantastic events such as a young girl's elopement with a crocodile. The setting is a remote village in colonized India and the interviewer was Dr. Batstone, a distinguished sociologist from the west. He was simply amazed by the presence of two dozen villagers sitting in front of him and observing him with curiosity. He asked them, through the interpreter, if they believed in God and in ghosts. As they were not used to such interrogations, they failed to give prompt answer allowing the European conjecture about the percentage of believers among the Indian rural. Soon the head pandit's commentary removed all his doubts. The pandit explained how the ghost of his distant relative, whom he described as his own cousin, continued to disturb him at night and forced him to spend for the ritual of his annual *shraddha* ceremony and yet he felt that all the ghosts were not as bad as that one. The European understood that the question of whether they believed in ghost had no meaning at all, as for them ghosts were as real as the living persons. The pandit's argument against raising the question of faith in God was more forceful: "And Sahib, isn't the issue of believing in God or not quite absurd? Is God moneylender or pawnbroker that the question of trust should arise? He created the earth, he brought us down here, he will take us away elsewhere, he will bring us here again." (*Selected Fiction*: 20). The European understood that for them God was the only reality and that they could not even dream of a doubt in God's existence. Dr. Batstone was finally spell bound when he listened to the old woman's account of how she had been taken by the crocodile in a deep pit at the confluence of two rivers, miles to the north of their village, and how they lived there as husband and wife for ten years. She talked for nearly an hour and a half, describing how she could change her into a crocodile after reciting a 'mantra' and again could change her into human being through the same device. She fondly remembered her crocodile husband's love for her and lamented that when she had come to attend her mother in her death bed, the anxious crocodile risked climbing the embankment in search of her only to be killed by the villagers. The villagers believed in this story and they also believed that no crocodile would attack the villagers as a girl from that village had once married a member of their species. But Dr. Batstone hoped to get a different story from the old woman who had been a widow at the age of four and it was likely that in her youth she might have stayed with some man of her liking. The woman's mesmerizing description revealed her utter distress to the sociologist who maintained silence after the visit. Years later, he wrote in a letter to the narrator that he had been under the spell of a 'mantra' for a brief time. His silence is suggestive of his understanding of the marginalized old woman: the experience of her love which was the only reality in her wretched life compelled her to convert her experience into a legend and this conversion enabled her to survive with the help of the villagers. Thus Manoj Das's experiments with fantasy enabled him to reveal the hidden reality beneath the surface in a subtle way.

Both Salman Rushdie and Manoj Das used fantasy as narrative device and challenged thereby the realistic mode of narration imposed by colonialism. Rushdie chose a vast background for *Midnight's Children* and projected grandiosely the 'macro-reality' of national concerns. He deals with a situation where truth is manufactured; in this situation fantasy is used as a device of tracing and uncovering what is hidden. Manoj Das, on the other hand, deals with common situations, often set in rural India, and he is hardly concerned with political or national issues. His use of fantasy helps him to render the happenings in life from the perspective of the believers. It also helps him to transcend the mundane reality.

NOTES

1. Salman Rushdie's observation in Hoffenden, John (ed.) *Novelists in Interview,* London; Methuen; 1985, p.246
2. Introduction to Echeverria, Roberto Gonzalez, ed. *Latin American Short Stories,* Oxford University Press; 1997

Works Cited

Das, Manoj: *Selected Fiction,* New Delhi; Penguin; 2001

Rushdie, Salman: *Midnight's Children,* London; Picador; 1982

___. *Imaginary Homelands*. London: Vintage, 2010.

Voice of the Subaltern: A Case Study of Khaleed Hosseini's *The Kite Runner* and *A Thousand Splendid Suns*

PRIYANKA LAMBA

Today, the definition of subaltern has changed from what it used to be in the past. Originally, it simply meant "having a subordinate position"; in the present global scenario, subaltern can refer to a variety of people who stand aloof from the rest by certain yardsticks. For example, there are people segregated on the basis of colour, ethnic roots, number and sex. Khaleed Hosseini, as an Afghani Diaspora in the US, is giving voice to the subaltern in and as the terror-stricken Afghanistan. Through his novels *The Kite Runner* and *A Thousand Splendid Suns*, Hosseini makes audible all those who have been confined to the muted zones of public as well as private spheres for long, under the politics of terror which is political, ethnic, patriarchal, external and domestic.

The Kite Runner is a novel brimming over with details of traditional Afghan culture, ethnic and religious schism of the Afghan society, tumultuous history of civil war and foreign invasions and the travails of immigrant Afghans in the US. All these issues form the backdrop of the story of Amir, the narrator, who seeks redemption for the betrayal of his friend Hassan. Amir and Hassan belong to two opposite ends of the ethnic hierarchy within Afghanistan. Amir being a Pashtun enjoys every social advantage whereas Hassan being a Hazara is merely a servant and is regarded inferior.

It becomes pertinent to discuss, in brief, some aspects of ethnic hierarchy in Afghanistan from historical perspective. Afghanistan is an ethnically diverse country. The Pashtun are the largest ethnic group making up around 40% of Afghanistan's population. They are Sunnis and speak Pashto. They are the members of the upper class and dominate the politics, society and economy of the country. They are often accused of persecuting minorities—especially Hazaras. The Hazaras are the third largest ethnic group of Afghanistan. They are mostly Shi'a Muslims and speak Farsi. The Sunni prejudices against the Shi'a drove the Hazaras to barren dry mountains of Central Afghanistan (the Hazarajat). In 1891 Amir Dost Mohammad, the king of Afghanistan, started attacking Hazarajat which resulted in the destruction of Hazara tribal system and the enslavement of Hazaras to be sold in the Kabul bazaar. The kings kept Hazaras as "Kaniz," "Gulam Bacha" and "Gulam." Shah Amanullah in 1929 outlawed slavery but the old practices of Hazaras still persisted. In Afghanistan, socio-political status is correlated with ethnicity. So, being on the lowest rung of social hierarchy, the Hazaras are on the lowest economic rung too. In towns like Kabul, they labour as servants (nokhar or muzdur), cooks, drivers, maids and gardeners in high society households.

In the novel *The Kite Runner*, the narrator Amir is the son of a wealthy, well-respected philanthropist Pashtun businessman known to the reader as "baba." He lives in a palatial house in Wazir Akbar Khan district of Kabul. He grows up with Hassan, son of Ali, his father's servant. Ali and Hassan are Hazaras. The two boys had lost their mothers and were breastfed by the same nursemaid, and therefore, "A brotherhood between people who had fed from the same breast, a kinship that not even time could break" (10) existed between Amir and Hassan. The boys grew up together and Amir says, "we were kids who had learned to crawl together . . . my entire childhood seems like one long lazy summer day with Hassan" (22). Despite this kinship, the class divisions and ethnic divide existed in Baba's house. Amir lived in a "mansion" and Hassan in a "mud shack where he had been born, where he'd lived his entire life" (5). Ali is a servant in the house and does cooking, cleaning and other mundane things, whereas Amir has all the opportunities like education, comfort etc. Ali raises his son Hassan to be a personal servant to Amir because, "Hassan would grow up illiterate like Ali and most Hazaras, had been decided the minute he had been born, perhaps even the moment he had been conceived . . . what use did a servant have for the written word" (24). Commenting further on this discrimination Amir says, "Ali prepared my breakfast . . . while I ate and complained about homework, Hassan made my bed, polished my shoes, ironed my outfit, and packed my books and pencils" (23). This discrimination existed because it had the religious and historical sanction—"Because history isn't easy to overcome. Neither is religion. In the end, I was a Pashtun and he was a Hazara. I was Sunni and he was Shi'a and nothing was ever going to change that, nothing" (22).Probably, this is why even Hassan didn't question Amir's superiority and didn't mind when Amir played with him only when no one else was around, and why he was not included in the games Amir played with the kids of his father's friends. In fact, Hassan so strongly identifies himself as a servant that years later, when he relocates to Baba's house, he stays in the hut and does the household chores. He has no entitlement to the house. He dies defending the house because he is a loyal servant of Amir and Baba. Hassan's staying out of the house is similar to the physical positioning of the bastard child Mariam outside the human society of Herat in the novel *A Thousand Splendid Suns*.

This staying out of the society is symbolical of the isolation and, alienation of Hazara community and women in the patriarchal Pashtun dominated Afghanistan. Hosseini himself said, "I would like the readers to walk away the sense of empathy for Afghans and more specifically for Afghan women on whom the effects of war and extremism have been devastating." Mariam's life is a saga of pain, suffering and humiliation and her life reflects the life of thousands of Afghani women who have endured despite the odds. She is "a harami who is like an insect, a scurrying cockroach" living out of the boundaries of the city "removed, detached" (8), all alone with her mother Nana. Like any bastard girl child, she "never had legitimate claim to things other people had, things such as love family, home, acceptance." Her father's legitimate children had ice creams while harami Mariam would have "stories of ice cream" (6). Once she made an attempt to be in the society and visited her father Jalal house, but was not allowed to enter the house and ended up "sleeping on the street like a stray dog" (35). This one attempt to get recognized, to get accepted lands her in a brutal world of marriage. Her mother Nana could not bear the shock of Mariam's going to her father and committed suicide. Jalal made a great show of caring about her and married off 15-year old Mariam to a Kabul-based much older shoe-maker, Rasheed. He was a piggy brute of a man who said it embarrassed him, "to see a man who has lost control of his wife" (63).

Through Mariam's married life the writer shows what life is like for women in Afghani society. There, "a woman's face is her husband's business only" (63) and they are valued only for reproduction. Mariam is forced to wear a burqa and she is not allowed to go out anywhere without Rasheed. Once she has suffered a series of miscarriages, Mariam's marriage becomes a prison, "she was afraid, she lived in fear of his shifting moods . . . his insistence on resolving mundane things . . . with punches, slaps and kicks." Her life had become a "systematic business of being beaten" (89). This marginalization of women symbolizes the exclusion of the underprivileged by the powerful and their use of violence as a tool to gag their voice for a respectable life. In *The Kite Runner,* Assef's rape of Hassan after the kite flying tournament has no lust involved, rather it is an act to show his ethnic superiority and dominance. Justifying himself, he tells his friends, "It's just a Hazara . . . there's nothing sinful about teaching a lesson to a disrespectful donkey" (66). Amir too tries to console himself and play down his act of betrayal by telling his conscience that, "He was just a Hazara, wasn't he?" This event of kite flying is central to the novel as the title suggests. The social status of Amir and Hassan decides the role played by them in kite flying. Amir being the Pashtun has the control over the kite whereas Hassan being the Hazara can only assist Amir. Amir claims the victory and Hassan runs to catch the rival kite but only to bring it back to Amir as a trophy of his achievement saying, "for you, a thousand times over." Unfortunately, he runs into an alley where Hassan is surrounded by Assef and his friends. Since the blue kite represents Hassan's loyalty towards Amir, he refuses to give up the kite. Assef exacts his revenge by raping Hassan. Amir witnesses this but doesn't stand up for his friend Hassan. He sees, "the look of the sacrificial lamb" (66) on Hassan's face. He flees from the scene but this scar of betrayal and sin gets engraved on his soul and haunts him till the end of the novel. This mutilation of the subalterns' selfhood is conflated with the external devastation of Afghanistan under militancy. The kite flying becomes a symbolic manifestation of Afghanistan's turbulent history which is marked with bloodshed and carnage. In this scene, young Afghan boys challenge and encounter their rivals in the way as their elder counterparts meet their rivals on the warfronts. Kiteflyer's desperate attempts to capture his adversary's kite almost resemble the fighting between the Afghan government and mujahedeen guerrilla factions. Their young hands are cut and stained with blood when ground glass coating of the kite string sears through their flesh. The blood stains in their hands symbolically hint at the history of the nation tainted by blood and violence.

The political and civil disturbance in Afghanistan parallels the brutality and horror of the domestic life of Mariam as "On

April 17, 1978, the year Mariam turned nineteen, a man named Mir Akhbar Khyber was found murdered . . . and his supporters were blaming the murder on President Daoud Khan's Government . . . On April 27 Air Force Colonel Abdul Qader reported that . . . Rebel MIGs had attacked the Presidential Palace . . . Daoud Khan had been killed . . . and now our watan will be known as the Democratic Republic of Afghanistan . . . a glorious era in the history of our country is afoot. A new Afghanistan is born" (88-92). The second protagonist of the novel, Laila is born on the night of April coup of 1978 "DOWN THE STREET, as the night lit up in sudden flashes of red and yellow, an exhausted Fariba had propped herself up on her elbows . . . . At her bedside, the elderly midwife, Wajima, watched as Fariba's husband and sons passed around the infant" (92-93). Thus, Hosseini has paralleled the life history of his female protagonists with the national history because nowhere in the world has been the condition of women and minorities so much dependent on that of nations as has been in Afghanistan. The ups and downs in the political identity of Afghanistan have manifested in the empowerment and disempowerment of women and minority communities.

In TSS, the Soviet occupation rules Laila's childhood and the writer has depicted the optimism of the people of Kabul under the communists in the chapter titled 'Kabul, Spring, 1987.' Under the Soviets, "it's good time to be a woman in Afghanistan . . . the government had sponsored literacy classes for all women . . . women were studying law, medicine and engineering" (121). Along with this is strengthening of the Mujahedeen because the Pashtuns saw the communist decrees to liberate women as an insult to their centuries-old tradition. And as Laila turned fourteen, the nation's history also took a turn—the Russians were ousted by the Mujahedeens and they turned from idealized freedom fighters to oppressors: "it was dizzy how quickly everything unraveled. The leadership council was formed prematurely. It elected Rabbani president. The other factions cried nepotism. . . .

Hekmatyar, who had been excluded, was incensed. The Mujahedeen, armed to the teeth, but lacking a common enemy, had found the enemy in each other" (154-55).The romance between Laila and Tariq is overshadowed by this brutal reality when like thousands of Afghans, Tariq and his family flee to Peshawar. A devastating tragedy happens to Laila—her parents die, her house is destroyed and she is pregnant with Tariq's child. This tragedy brings Laila to the home of Rasheed and Mariam, where she is made to make a horrific choice of marrying Rasheed to escape the fate of hundreds of orphan Afghan women who have "no food, no water . . . bullets and rockets flying everywhere . . . she'd be abducted, raped or tossed into some roadside ditch with her throat slit" (192). After her marriage, Laila gives birth to Tariq's daughter Aziza. Rasheed is unhappy and suspicious and more abusive towards his wives. The common people of Afghanistan had to bear the brunt of the civil war among the warlords with the old enmity between Pashtuns and Hazaras taking an ugly turn and again the women becoming the worst targets of this ethnic violence:

> In June of that year, 1992, there was heavy fighting in West Kabul between the Pashtun forces of the warlord Sayyaf and the Hazaras of the Wahdat faction. . . . . Laila heard that Pashtun militiamen were attacking Hazara households, breaking in and shooting entire families, execution style, and that Hazaras were retaliating by abducting Pashtun civilians, raping Pashtun girls, shelling Pashtun neighborhoods, and killing indiscriminately. Every day, bodies were found tied to trees, sometimes burned beyond recognition. Often, they'd been shot in the head, had had their eyes gouged out, their tongues cut out. (159)

The same kind of ethnic intolerance is echoed by Assef in *The Kite Runner* when he talks of sharing his vision with President Daoud Khan to efface the Hazaras from the land of Pashtuns i.e. Afghanistan like Hitler did in Germany. He says, "Afghanistan is the land of Pashtuns . . . We are the true Afghans, the pure Afghans, not this flat nose here. His people pollute our homeland, our watan. They dirty our blood . . . Too late for Hitler But not for us . . . I'll ask the President . . . to rid Afghanistan of all the dirty kasseef Hazaras" (35-36). So Hosseini, by weaving historical events within the fabric of his fictional narrative, uncovers the social truths of Afghani society and talks at length about the fate of the marginalized that have to "endure the hardships of life, the slight of men, the disdain of society" (4).

As Afghanistan's history took another worse turn in September 1996 with the coming of the Taliban, there were great upheavals in the life of Mariam and Laila. The descriptions of the ensuing violence (some physical, but most often mental) that visited upon Laila and Mariam as women Hassan, his wife Farzana, his son Sohrab as Hazaras, and the people of Afghanistan in general, are presented in a straightforward manner. The attitude of the Taliban toward women, as Mariam says, "Like a compass needle that points north, a man's accusing finger always finds a woman, always" (9). Hosseini has an unerring ear for just the right phrase, the exact descriptive words to evoke both the reality and the deeper meaning of a particular scene. One example of this is the description of how Laila endures a cesarean section in a Taliban hospital without anesthesia: "[The female doctor] bent over Laila. Laila's eyes snapped open. Then her mouth opened. She held like this, held, shivering. The cords in her neck stretched, sweat dripping from her face her fingers crushing Mariam's. Mariam would always admire Laila for how much time passed before she screamed" (260).

The situation of Laila and Mariam becomes worse as Rasheed's shop is burnt down and he has to do odd jobs not suited to his temperament. Aziza has to be sent to an orphanage to save the family from starvation. When no longer able to bear Rasheed's torture, and to save Laila's life, Mariam kills him. This killing of the oppressor leads to her brutal public execution by the Taliban. The novel shows how the Hazaras suffered greatly under the Taliban which was dominated by the ethnic Pashtuns. The Taliban had Hazarajat totally isolated from the rest of the world going so far as not allowing the United Nations to deliver food to the province. There was a large scale human right abuse, particularly after the capture of Hazara Sharif in 1998, when after a massive ethnic killing of some 8000 civilians, the Taliban openly declared that Hazaras will be targeted because they are not Muslims, "they are Shi'a, they are Kaffir."Similar persecution is echoed in the novel also. After Rahim Khan left for Peshawar, the Taliban came to claim the house from the Hazaras and shot dead Hassan and his wife. No one in the neighbourhood came to their rescue because nobody "was going to risk anything for a pair of Hazara servants" (193). Combining his guilt and grief, Amir describes Hassan's death as "Hassan slumps to the asphalt, his life of unrequited loyalty drifting from him like the windblown kites he used to chase" (192).Assef, the Talib, takes pride in describing what he calls "ethnic cleansing" (249). He says that Afghanistan is like "a beautiful mansion littered with garbage and someone has to take out this garbage" (.249), and in 1998 in Mazar-e-Sharif, they cleared the garbage: "Door to door we went, calling for the men and the boys. We'd shoot them right there in front of their families, let them see . . . who they were, where they belonged . . . I'd sweep the barrel of my machine gun around the room and fire and fire until the smoke blinded me and . . . let the bullets fly, free of guilt and remorse, knowing you are virtuous, good and decent, knowing you're doing God's work, it's breath taking" (242). This genocide of Hazaras can very well be compared with what happened to Jews in Germany during World War II, and to the Tutsis in Rwanda in 1992.

Thus through these two novels, Hosseini draws attention to the deprivation, injustice and alienation that the subalterns in a society have to put up with. The alert eye of the artist in him perceives inequities with anguish and questions the imbalances in the society with courage. He strongly urges for standing against age-old prejudices of the mighty and rich who take pride in their superiority. And it is this urge that makes Amir come back from America to the Taliban-ruled Afghanistan to pay the retribution for the betrayal of Ali and Hassan by saving Sohrab from the Taliban. In order to atone for his sins and his father's betrayal Amir has to rescue Sohrab, the living embodiment of Hassan. Assef agrees to relinquish him but only for a price—by cruelly beating Amir. He is badly hurt in his fight with Assef but he feels he is purged of his sin and feels "healed." But this healing is not complete redemption. However, Amir is saved when Sohrab uses his sling shot to shoot out Assef's left eye—fulfilling the threat Hassan had made many years before. To redeem himself completely, Amir must break the old shackles of discrimination by giving Sohrab an equal opportunity at success and happiness. A transformed Amir takes Sohrab to US and tries to restore his dignity as a human being. He tells his father-in-law, "You will never again refer to him as 'Hazara Boy.' He has a name and it's Sohrab" (315).The story comes to a full circle and Amir forgives himself and runs the kite for Sohrab just as Hassan ran his last kite for Amir half a century before. Like Hassan, he truthfully repeats his words, "for you, a thousand times over" and he is finally seen running with humanity and freedom in his heart. Similarly, instead of fear, Mariam's stoic suffering initiates a better future for Laila, who is finally reunited with Tariq. Once free from the domestic terrorism, she goes back to Mariam's native village Gul Daman where she receives the video-copy of the movie along with a pile of money "her share of inheritance what was rightfully hers along" and a letter written by Jalal (a documentary proof of him being her father).All these things purged Mariam of the sin of being a harami and proves that "it is the creator of Harami who are culpable, not the harami whose only sin is being born harami" (4).

Khaleed Hosseini, thus explores in his novels, the dynamics of oppression and, its manifestation in human relationships, with the full sanction it enjoys in the society he describes. Through systematic exposure of false distinctions that perpetuate systems of domination, he challenges the marginalization and exclusion of the underprivileged and raises the consciousness of people to have an equality-oriented humanist perspective towards the subalterns, as "there is always a way to be good again"

Works Cited

Hosseini, Khaled. *The Kite Runner.* London: Bloomsbury, 2004.

___. *A Thousand Splendid Suns.* London: Bloomsbury, 2007.

Sublimation of the Subaltern: A Glimpse of Malayalam Dalit Literature

SAKUNTHALA A.I.

The term "subaltern" is conceptually derived from the work of the Italian Marxist intellectual, Antonio Gramsci, who identified the social groups who are excluded from a society's established structures of political representation. The common theoretical position is that subaltern is the social group which is socially, politically and geographically outside the hegemonic power structure of the colony/colonial homeland. This is a term that is now regularly used in history, anthropology, sociology and literary criticism to denote the dispossessed, the marginalized and those outside the hegemonic power structure of the ruling class.

Since the concepts of subalternity and marginality refer to the unequal power equations that stratify societies into pyramidal structures of opposite groups, these terms obviously inform post-colonial theory. "In post-colonial theory, the term 'subaltern' describes the lower classes and the social groups who are at the margins of a society—a subaltern is a person rendered without human agency, by his or her social status" (Young 32).This unjust system of classification created a great, unbridgeable divide between the privileged and the deprived. The apex of power retained the limited but the powerful groups which became the centre of authority. The powerless multitudes were pushed to the periphery of the lowest levels of the social ladder. The male, the rich, the superior castes, the colonial masters and the racial whites thus occupied the coveted space of power and authority, while the woman, the poor, the untouchables, the colonized natives and the coloured races were marginalized.

Presently, subaltern is generally used in India synonymously with the term Dalit, with scholars especially focusing their attention on the oppressive structures of caste in the Indian context, which has divided people as superiors and inferiors, touchables and untouchables, upper castes and lower castes. Thus, "The subordination and subjection that marks the life of Dalits in India bring them into the contours of a particularly contextual assembly of subalternity" (Guha7).The term subaltern has an added significance in India, which as a British colony experienced subaltern status with its people being subjected to subordination based on class, caste and gender. Thus, the extent of hopelessness was compounded by the fact that the so-called lower castes were doubly dispossessed and marginalized.

Many social reformers and protesters have tried to bring equality and thus we have many movements fighting for the rights of the marginalized groups. Their resistance to the phallocentric social structure and their attempts at critiquing or deconstructing are the very logical reactions to the centuries old process of planned dehumanization. The voices of the subaltern, freshly raised, rising from the soil, highlight disturbing issues. Subaltern literature or Dalit literature is the expression of these people who were unjustly deprived, humiliated, ill-treated and oppressed.

Sree Narayana Guru, the greatest philosopher-seer-poet of Kerala, was a religious as well as a social reformer. When these two roles meet in some rare prophetic personalities, their impact is not limited only to the society around them, but is felt by the entire mankind. Guru was the great iconoclast who transformed the caste-ridden Kerala into an abode of self-respecting individuals with the feelings of equality and fraternity.

This paper focusses on the attempts Guru made to eradicate the evil practice of caste that was prevalent in Kerala. He accomplished this feat through his literary works, the consecration of idols, and by his most famous dictum *"Ask not, Say not, Think not Caste,* "which was a direct ultimatum to the custodians of casteism. The study also proposes to examine how Kumaran Asan, an ardent disciple of Guru and one of the triumvirates of Malayalam poetry, initiated a revolution in literature by writing repeatedly about the dehumanizing experiences of the individuals who have been deprived of the fundamental human dignity. Guru and Kumaran Asan, through their spiritual, social and literary efforts, aimed at *the sublimation of the subaltern* by a reconditioning and recasting of the minds of both the oppressor and the oppressed.

Medieval feudal society in Kerala was caste-centered. The *Chaturvarna system* reigned supreme, and society was cleft into Savarnas and Avarnas. The Avarnas—the subalterns—were exploited socially, culturally, educationally and economically, and were forced to live in shame as the deprived and the destitute. Both the temples of learning and the temples of gods were shut to them. They were labelled untouchables and were not allowed to walk on the roads meant for the upper castes.

It was in this dangerous social set-up that a spiritual catalyst with the message of holistic realism, a common man telling simple truths and propagating practical propositions, a divine human without pretensions, penetrating into the human essence with arrows of spiritual-material power, and unfolding a cosmic vision of universal oneness and individual excellence, made his entry. Sree Narayana Guru fought against all sorts of discrimination, including the oppression of untouchability. He devised a well-defined programme to save society from such decadence by making each person aware of the inner strength that could help them understand and respond positively to their problems. The emergence of Guru on the spiritual and social front electrified the entire society in general and the downtrodden in particular.

In fact, the progressive movements in Malayalam literature originated from him.

Guru's endeavour was to evolve a new culture, a synthesis of the old and the new, a smooth transfer from outdated ideas to progressive modernism. And he achieved this social miracle within a short span of forty years. He had metamorphosed the depressed castes of Kerala from prostate subhuman status to educated citizenry with dignity, self-respect and economic power. A radical change in sentiment, intellect and perspective was ushered in, introducing unity and harmony where rancour and dissention had prevailed. Poverty and ignorance were replaced with prosperity and erudition. This impetus brought out the literary, artistic and academic talents hidden in the depressed people, and opened before them the way for growth and prosperity for which sky was the limit.

Guru decided that the elimination of social inequality between the oppressor and the oppressed, the tormentor and the tormented in a caste-ridden society lies only in the restructuring of minds beyond the reach of caste practices. Realizing that the caste system is the root of all evils in society and is the weapon formed by the upper castes to suppress the lower castes, Guru declared that the entire human race belongs to one *jati*. He made people aware of this and exhorted them to root out caste and pave the way for liberty, equality and fraternity. The essence of his philosophy is in three major assertions: *"One Caste, One Religion, One God for Man," "Ask not, Say not, Think not Caste," "Whatever be the religion of a man, it is enough if it makes him virtuous."*These gospels shook the social conscience of Kerala 100 years ago, but it is equally relevant in the modern ages the best antidote for communal disharmony and religious fundamentalism.

One of Guru's cardinal aims was the spiritual upliftment of the people of Kerala. The caste system was so wildly practised in Kerala that the lower community people were denied entry into temples. Even gods were segregated, and the Dalits were not allowed to worship *sattwik* gods. They were allowed to worship only inferior local deities like Madan, Marutha, Chathan and Yakshi. These restrictions actually affected the intellectual capacity and quality of mind of the common man. Guru exhorted them to exclude the mischievous and malevolent forces of nature from the sphere of worship, and to do away with the self-destructing customs and dogmas practiced by society out of sheer ignorance even though in the name of god.

Since religion, which should have been a solace and support to people, had become an instrument of tribulation, by raising barriers and imposing restrictions in the name of caste, the saint in Guru turned a revolutionary. As temples were the main culprits in keeping people divided, subjecting them to oppression and misery, he started his relentless war by launching a unique and novel method of using the same institutions as vehicles of social change to integrate, to guide and to resurrect them.

Guru started his revolutionary mission with the consecration of Siva Temple at Aruvippuram, when he, an Avarna, picked up a stone from the river Neyyar, stood in meditation for hours, then placed it on an altar as *Sivalingam.* Historically, this action was the beginning of a major rebellion against Indian orthodoxy. This was an assertion of the fundamental right of man to worship the deity of his choice and the death knell to priestly authority. The small stanza which he wrote on the walls of the newly constructed temple was not "*Ohm Namahsivaya,*"—the Panchaksharimanthra to worship Lord Siva—but a declaration of equality and fraternity, an eye-opener to the custodians of casteism:

Jaathibhedam-mathadvesham	This is a model abode breaking barriers
Ethumillathesarvarum	where all men shall live as brothers
Sodarathvenavazhunna	without caste distinctions
Mathrukasthanamamithu	and religious rivalries

The installation and consecration of the temple at Aruvippuram became a milestone in the history of India's spiritual emancipation. This was a direct challenge to the caste-ridden tradition of India that had resulted in the idea of a common man, an "untouchable," who had no claim to priestly tradition or the installation of a temple, which was the monopoly of the Brahmins. Though a religious renovation, the temple at Aruvippuram became a part of the social revolution of India in general and Kerala in particular.

Progress demands self-confidence and self-assertion. Under the yoke of caste, there was no way for the underprivileged to progress in life. Guru realized that only education can make these crippled souls aware of their rights and potentialities and induce in them the strength and confidence to compete with the privileged classes. The modern education pioneered by the British missionaries had started creating ripples in the existing evil practices. Guru's movement turned into a tempest of revolution as he started educational institutions attached to temples which empowered the low-caste beneficiaries with literacy. He advised the people to make use of education as a tool to liberate themselves from the superstitious traditions, a means for economic independence, and a weapon to fight social injustice.

The downtrodden people breathed a fresh spirit of freedom and found a source of inspiration in his dictum: "*Education for Liberation*."The very fact that he consecrated Sarada Devi temple—Sarada being another name for Saraswathi, goddess of learning—at the religious headquarters, Sivagiri, shows the importance he attached to education. Guru also stressed the importance of imparting education to women. It should be noted that 55 years before the UN Declaration of Emancipation of Discrimination against Women, Guru had understood that liberation of any society can be complete only if women, too, are educated.

Sree Narayana Guru wrote many books, about 63 of which are now available. These books can be categorized into five sections: (1) Devotional Songs (2) Philosophical Books (3) Books of Proclamations (4) Translations and (5) Prose. *Darsanamala* (A Garland of Vision of the Absolute), *Atmopadesa-sathakam* (One hundred Verses of Self Instruction), *Advaita Dipika (*Lamp of Non-dual Wisdom), *Anukampa Dasakam* (Ten Verses of Mercy), *Arivu* (Epistemology of Gnosis), *Cit-Jada-Cintanam* (Reverie on Consciousness and Matter), *Pindanandi (*Pre-natal Gratitude, *Daiva Dasakam (*Ten Verses to God), *Janani Navaratna Manjari* (Nine-jewelled Bouquet to Mother), and *Kundalini Pattu* (The Song of the Kundalini Power) are some of Guru's popular books. These works are incomparable for their haunting melody, sublime concepts, and mystic experiences.

In *Darsanamala*, the concept of the absolute is elucidated in one hundred verses, divided into ten darsanas of ten verses each. Into this ten-fold container is distilled Guru's vision of life. *Atmopadesa Satakam* could be considered as the representative of his philosophy. The verses in this book are written in simple Malayalam, but the depth of the philosophy contained in it is immeasurable. *Daiva Dasakam* is a prayer written by Guru, having ten verses which are very simple, but when we search for the meaning and attempt to interpret, we see that it is the essence of Vedantic philosophy given in a capsule form for the use of common people. Those from any caste, creed, religion, and region can use this prayer, which has become a universal prayer after the Gayatri Mantra.

If the state of Kerala now stands first in literacy, it is the ultimate result of the massive educational projects launched by Sree Narayana Guru. If untouchability has become a thing of the past in Kerala, Guru's temples are the inspiration behind it. If conflicts and confrontations in the name of religion are minimal in Kerala, the credit goes to Guru's Gospels of Unity. Guru's impact was not limited to his own contributions; he had encouraged, supported and guided a number of his close followers, some of whom became the leading lights of the literary era in which they lived. In the upsurge of the silent, bloodless revolution set in motion by Sree Narayana Guru, Kumaran Asan emerged as the greatest literary luminary of his time.

Kumaran Asan, the most ardent disciple of Guru fully imbibed to the core the lofty ideals propounded by his master and wielded the mighty power of his pen to deal with the burning questions of those times. The works of Asan, a social reformer and humanist, strongly attempted to demolish the caste system, social oppression and orthodoxy in a way which was unprecedented before.

Asan revolutionized Malayalam literature in the twentieth century by repeatedly writing about those destitutes who were yoked under the dehumanizing caste system which denied them even the fundamental human rights. In an age, when learning was denied to the low-castes, Asan born as a low-caste Ezhava, stepped out of the barriers of the traditional convictions and conventions which discriminated man against man and earned a reputation far surpassing that of his contemporaries. It must be mentioned here that Kumaran Asan was the only poet who was given the honorific title of *Mahakavi* (great poet) without writing a single *Mahakaavya* (great epic). The essential difference between Asan and many others was that while most others wrote to display their erudition, Asan wrote with a specific purpose—to educate, to enlighten and to guide because of his strict adherence to the words of Guru "*Education for Liberation*." Asan's poems, rendered for the first time in Malayalam literature the essence of the subaltern who possessed a higher moral authority than the oppressors.

Asan's major poetic works like *Nalini, Veena Poovu, Leela, Chandala Bhikshuki, Duravastha, Chinthavishtayaya Sita, and Karuna* indeed deal with the theme of love, but not at the carnal or sensuous level. Instead, he describes love in its spiritual aspect. Asan's *Duravastha* (1922) occupies a unique position among his works as it has shaken the social conscience of Kerala. In *Duravastha,* based on the Muslim Revolt of Malabar (1921), Asan reveals his revolutionary zeal by skillfully tearing down the barriers of orthodoxy and casteism and consummates the dictum of Guru "*One Caste, One Religion, One God for Man.*"Savithri, a Brahmin woman disregards the dictates of the caste-bound society by marrying Chathan, a lower-caste untouchable, after he had given her refuge when her family home was destroyed in the revolt. This event was unimaginable in the social circumstances of those days when the Brahmins considered the lower castes as untouchables and it was incendiary material in the eyes of the orthodoxy. The much acclaimed exhortation in the poem: "*Mattuvinchattangaleswayam/ Allenkilmattumathukaleeningale than*" (If you do not voluntarily change the irrational traditions and practices, you will simply be wiped out by them) was the timely warning—a clarion call for social revolution. In these lines we see in him not only a revolutionary poet, but a great prophet too.

One should note with special attention that in this poem, the heroine Savithri recognizes the significance of education and undertakes and succeeds in converting an almost illiterate Chathan into a literate person. Savithri's attempts to teach Chathan reflect Guru's advice "*Education for Liberation.*" The poignancy of feeling, the vehement criticism of the social system as displayed in this work has stirred the people in Kerala more than any of his other works. This poem which questioned the orthodox Indian society can be seen as revolutionary as the Muslim revolt of Malabar.

In *Chandalabhikshuki*, which also focusses on the untouchability prevalent in the state, we find the greatest tirade against the caste system and the most powerful exhortation for eradicating it. It was a period when the lower caste people would not even come close to the higher caste people lest they should pollute them. They would not touch any item meant for the higher caste people. Public wells were not to be used by lower castes and so on. The message of the poem has gone a long way to stem the growing tide of this social evil in Kerala.

A Buddhist monk, Ananda asks for water from a low-caste woman, Mathangi. She wonders: "*How dost thou take water from me, an outcaste, who may not touch thee without contamination?*" Ananda replied: "*My sister, I ask not thy caste, I ask thee for water to drink.*" The chandala girl was overjoyed and she gave the Bhikshu water to drink. Mathangi undergoes a conversion and finally becomes a Buddhist nun. When King Prasenajit came to remonstrate with Lord Buddha about the inclusion of a chandala as his follower, Buddha demonstrated the futility of caste distinctions by the following reasoning: "Is the chandala woman's body infertile to the Brahmin seed? Is the sacred thread or the tuft or the mark of forehead/ An adjunct of birth? /Does the Brahmin get his learning without being tutored?"

His poignant words that a Brahmin does not descend from the sky nor from the wind, nor does he arise piercing the earth, and that the Brahmin is brought forth from the womb of a woman in exactly the same way as a chandala, so how can they be regarded as belonging to a different species?—these sentiments in fact provoked the Brahminical orthodoxy. The poem concludes with the words of Lord Buddha that all humanity has only one caste and Love is universal. The poem trumpeted the process of eradication of the caste system, paving the way for "one caste for the whole humanity," which was in perfect accordance with the advice Guru gave to the society. By making a Buddhist bhikshu accept drinking water from a chandala girl, Asan sends a not-so-subtle message against this detested practice. The divine and the deprived are sustained by the same air and water which are the two major constituents of all beings—the very same argument Guru raised before Mahatma Gandhi during their historical meeting at Sivagiri in 1924.

The poem *Karuna* is also based on Buddhist lore, and the poet wants to convey the message as expounded by Guru, that beauty of flesh is transitory whereas the only eternal thing is the beauty of the soul. Vasavadutta, a very attractive prostitute of the city of Madura waits for Upagupta, one of the committed missionaries of Buddha. Finally, he comes to her, but only in the last phase of her life, when she is awaiting her death, with her limbs, nose and ears cut off, as she was convicted for murder. She dies in peace and tranquility after listening to the words of Upagupta. The last lines of Karuna are: "*Salutations to thee, O Upagupta; without getting lost in nirvana,/come back again to serve the world/Mother Earth today needs more of such sons as you /whose compassion reaches the lowliest and lost.*" While presenting Upagupta as the redeemer of Vasavadutta, Asan probably had in his mind the image of Guru as the greatest redeemer of mankind from the irrational caste-ridden society.

The spark of human desire for emancipation and self-dignity was there deep in the hearts of the subdued and the subjugated, but hidden and muted by retrogressive convictions and conventions. It was this hidden spark that Sree Narayana Guru and Kumaran Asan ignited, through their Gospels and revolutionary writings which eventually became the propelling force for the social, literary and spiritual upward mobility of the downtrodden. It was after the democratic and egalitarian writings of these two great masters as also of others, who convincingly articulated the sources and modes of caste oppression, that modern Dalit writing as a distinct genre began to emerge in Malayalam literature. It was a new voice, fresh and pure, with strong commitment to usher in a classless and casteless society where the creative faculties of human beings would blossom without hindrance.

Apart from Kumaran Asan, Poikayil Yohannan, also known as Kumaraguru, was a contemporary of Kumaran Asan and was an activist, preacher and poet. His most famous line *Kanunneeloraksharavum, entevamsathintethayi* (Gone without a trace, every scrawl of my race) is probably the most authentic statement by a Dalit writer. Pandit Karuppan was another great Dalit poet of the period. His *Jatikkummi* is a social satire against untouchability and caste Hindus.

The revolutionary aspect of Dali literature is fuelled by the great poet Changampuzha Krishna Pillai, who always depicted truth of harsh social realities. His famous poem *Vazhakkula* narrates the story of Malayan, a Dalit peasant who plants a plantain in front of his hut. He and his family attend to the plant with great care, and his children get excited about the fruit. The dreams of the poor family are dashed, however, when the landlord asks Malayan to submit the fruit as a tribute. The poem ends ona revolutionary note: "*Ithinokkeprathikaramcheyyathadangumo / pathithare Ningal than pinmurakkar? (*Oh depressed! For all these, there would be a vendetta/ from your own generations to come).

Edassery Govindan Nair, another great poet of the period, wrote poems which carried the spirit of the times. In his poem *Panimudakkam*, when the factory owners exploit the workers by denying them their due wages, the poet urges them: "*Kuzhivettimoodukavedanakal/ kuthikolkasaktiyilekkunammal."* (Let's bury our pains/ And leap forward to strength). The final couplet of his famous poem *Puthan Kalavum Arivalum,* which gives a touching rendition of the plight of Dalit tenants in society, underlines the need for self-conscious and collective struggle which the tenants should undertake to advance in life: "*AdhikaramKoyyannamadyam,/ AthinumelekkatePonnaryan*." (Let's first reap the power to shape our destiny/ Then the golden harvest in the fields).

Protagonists from the marginalized society, who were hitherto absent from the mainstream literature, thus began to march tumultuously across the borders of silence, due to the activities of the progressive Literary Movement and the resultant Jeeval Sahitya Sangam. These movements reflected the aspirations of the unrepresented class. The oppressed were thus given a voice.

Thakazhi Sivasankara Pillai's *Randidangazh*i and *Thottiyude Makan* also deal with the Dalit predicament. Written by a veteran in the field of drama, Thoppil Bhasi's *Ningalenne Communistakki*, with its powerful dialogues and revolutionary songs, fanned the fire of Dalit rebellion against oppression, and the landlords shuddered in fear of the shaking of their very foundations. Ayyappa Paniker's *Kudumpapuranam*, K. Sachidandan's *Pulayappattu* and Kadammanitta Ramakrishnan's *Kurathy* are all examples of powerful literary expressions of the dissatisfaction and discontent of the downtrodden.

The eighties and nineties saw a host of Dalit poets bursting onto the scene, like Raghavan Atholi, S. Joseph, M.B. Manoj, M.R. Renukumar, Narayan, C.K. Janu, and Kaviyoor Murali, to name a few. Modern Dalit writings challenge the literary canons of dominant groups and turn our attention to the neglected and marginalized aspects of experience, vision, and language, forcing society to refashion its tools for empowerment. These writers break the rules of language propriety, balance, restraint and decency, by using words which the Savarna poetics would consider uncouth or rustic. Writers like S. Joseph, Narayan, T.K.C. Vaduthala, and others often retrieve from oblivion words and phrases seldom used in mainstream literature, but which are very much a part of lived reality. All these subaltern writers have carved a niche for themselves and have been instrumental in establishing Dalit literature as a distinct literary entity.

The beginning of Dalit literature was powerful: an unleashing of experiential pangs, an opening up of concealed traumas and angst, a reclamation of negated self and assertion of identity. In an age, when even decent words were not allowed to be pronounced by the subalterns, these earlier writers' assertion of identity and self-respect was an act of subversion in the eyes of the so-called upper castes, who for centuries had refused to acknowledge such individuality. This literary endeavor not only challenges the Savarna poetics by creating a different poetics, language, sensibility and cultural paradigm, but also heralds a new search beyond the colour of skin, a disclosure of the inside and the outside.

The potential energy inherent in the Dalits, dragged behind an invisible identity, was unleashed in a typhoon of change, which in fact transformed Kerala—the lunatic asylum—into God's own country. Sree Narayana Guru and Kumaran Asan, through their spiritual, social and literary efforts, accomplished this feat, *the sublimation of the subaltern*, by reconditioning and recasting the minds of both the oppressor and the oppressed.

Works Cited

Guha, Ranjit, ed. *Subaltern Studies: Writings on South Asian History and Society*. New Delhi: Oxford, 1982.

Young, Robert J.C. *Post-Colonialism: A Very Short Introduction*. New York: Oxford, 2003.

Postmodern Strategies in Writing by Amitav Ghosh: The Case of *The Calcutta Chromosome*

PIER PAOLO PICIUCCO

"This guy's decided to re-write the history books." Amitav Ghosh

In recent times, Indian novels in English have suffered quite a bizarre fate: their being read, analysed and marked as postcolonial fictional works, while it has in some cases overstated their distinctive traits, has also had the effect of restricting the scholarly approach to them and limiting their reading to a specific perspective. Amitav Ghosh, Indian postcolonial novelist, author of the diaspora, interpreter of Subaltern Studies as well as postmodern voice, is a case in point. A leading Indian exponent of the contemporary international literary scene, Ghosh has distinguished himself for, among other reasons, being a writer sensitive enough to capture all the stimula that a misty contemporaneity offers, and to express them in a complex array of works that reflect the contradictions, challenges, ambiguities and conflicts that our global society copiously produces. My intention here is to stress how Ghosh's fiction mirrors many of the key elements of postmodern writing. In order to do so, I will focus my attention on his 1995 novel *The Calcutta Chromosome* to suggest analogies with a recognized masterpiece of postmodern literature, A.S. Byatt's 1990 novel *Possession.*

The Calcutta Chromosome is indeed an ingenious and innovative work of art, and Ghosh's reviewers and critics have not underestimated such aspects. The plot vividly combines the stories of a number of brilliantly sketched out characters, scattered over a period of time ranging from the end of the nineteenth century to an imminent future. By and large, we may select three main time units in which the action takes place:

1. **Past**: A period of time from the last decades of the 1800s up to the 1930s. The setting is generally India, with most scenes set in Calcutta. A key protagonist is real-life British bacteriologist Ronald Ross who gained fame for (supposedly) discovering the link between the anopheles mosquito and malarial infection.
2. **Present**: Since the novel was published in 1995, "present" time is in line with the technological developments and general circumstances of this decade. Events in the novel occur in a limited but crucial period of time, which spans a few weeks up to 21 August 1995. Half of the story takes place in New York, half in Calcutta and its surroundings. The protagonist is the Bengali clerk Murugan.
3. **Future**: There are no hints to a specific period of time in the whole novel. We may reasonably presume that the action takes place within the first two decades of the 21st century, more or less our present. The location is New York, and the protagonist is Antar, an Egyptian computer archivist.

We may add a fourth time unit. I would refer to it as either a "future beyond" or as a totally "out-of-time" period. This is the time dimension of the narrating voice, which reports the events occurring in the future in the past tense. The *incipit* of the novel, for instance, is set in the future but narrated in the past tense. This time unit, in which no event whatsoever occurs, is the one from which the narrator tells the whole (hi)story and should therefore be considered a privileged point of view.

Before shifting to further considerations, it would be worthwhile to focus our attention on the most piquant and innovative time section: the future. *The Calcutta Chromosome* has fascinated the critics, so much so that every one has felt compelled to define it, to attach tags to it, or simply to place it within an acknowledged literary canon: labels such as "mystery novel,"[1] "mystery thriller,"[2] "philosophical novel,"[3] "scientific thriller a metaphorical whodunit,"[4] "experimental work,"[5] "anthropologic detective-story"[6] are evidence of a feverish quest for categorization that has possessed critics in much the same way, ironically, as the novel's fictional characters. Curiously enough, not even the contributors of Wikipedia have kept their critical creativeness under restraint and have given in to this temptation: "medical thriller"[7] is the label chosen to refer to the novel. This variegated critical response attests to the multifacetedness of the novel, as well as to critics' creativity. However, it is rather bizarre that rarely have critics called this fictional work a "historiographic metafiction," the famous label adopted by Linda Hutcheon to describe texts, such as the novel under scrutiny, that are part of postmodern literary production. I believe this expression to be particularly suitable for Ghosh's novel, especially if we take into account that the Canadian academic stresses that such so-called historiographic metafictions are "obsessed with the question of how we can come to know the past today."[8]

In keeping with Hutcheon's theory, *The Calcutta Chromosome* in fact challenges the traditional notion of a water-proof past, isolated and uncontaminated from possible re-writings and re-presentations. Written six years before Ghosh's *The Calcutta Chromosome*, Hutcheon's *The Politics of Postmodernism* theorizes that

> postmodern fiction stresses . . . the tensions that exist, on the one hand, between the pastness (and absence) of the past and the presentness (and presence) of the present, and on the other, between the actual events of the past and the historian's act of processing them into facts.[9]

A.S. Byatt's *Possession* also clearly addresses such issue: the void of the past is completed with the present's fullness, a strategy similar to that employed by Amitav Ghosh in *The Calcutta*

Chromosome. The Indian novelist's crafty and innovative variation on Hutcheon's canon however consists in his broadening the time dimensions on which the plot is unravelled from two to three parallel time units, and enlarging the extent of his *pastiche* to a re-organization of the science-fiction genre. This also explains how Ghosh's novel manages to present a totally irreverent historical point of view, at least if read against a traditional approach to historical report, by subverting the natural laws of time.

Amitav Ghosh moves with the ease and the freedom of an anarchist back and forth through time and space units. He jollily sacrifices them by proposing a new concept of plot unit, independent of historical rigour. Contrasting the assessed norms of reason, which would prescribe that a certain past event has consequences on the present, which will further influence future mechanisms, the novelist deconstructs history by writing a story which arises in the future and has repercussions on the present and the past; once the farthest point has been reached, the narrative circles viciously backward and is eventually extinguished at the genesis. Future is both the starting point and the end of a cycle; it has control over past and present, in that it possesses the kind of power that technology employs over the weak and the powerless. Amitav Ghosh seems to indicate that in order to keep control over both past and present, one has to control the future: or, alternatively, the act of re-writing both the past and the present is possible in the future because of its technological supremacy. This is why, although both past and present are largely set against the background of Calcutta, the future can be as far away as New York. More precisely, the stage on which future scenes are essentially represented is Antar's extremely fast AVA computer. The AVA system with its breathtaking potentialities is in fact the element which most relevantly distinguishes future from present. Were it not for the striking innovations of the AVA, Antar could almost be an ordinary everyman of the present. The state of perfection which machines have reached takes them at least to the same level as men. The AVA treats Antar as any human being would: it is amused to talk to him (in the "appropriate rural dialect of the Nile Delta"[10]), it watches and hears him, it answers him back if ordered to shut up, it causes reductions in his pay if he is idle at work. It is not the stage of the 'rebellion of the machines' because they still live harmoniously and peacefully with men, but on conditions which—at that point—are no longer decided and imposed entirely by man. The man/computer relationship is now of the *au-pair* kind. Actually, Ghosh depicts the computer in its most humanised traits, since the AVA is always referred to with the feminine pronoun 'she' and not by a neutral 'it'; besides, we know that it works "with a bizzarrely human smugness" (7). On the other hand, the novelist shows how the human mind may be assimilated to a computer. Antar's ideas are focussed like images on a computer screen when we read that "the image grew clearer in Antar's mind" (18). Therefore, the future is the stage where man and computer reduce their differences to the very least, and the powerful AVA system metaphorically comprises all those elements that enable Antar to have an advantaged point of view. Discourses about power-control and supremacy acquire great significance in the context of *The Calcutta Chromosome*, and the literary background posited by Hutcheon is once again fundamental for a full understanding of such a situation: narrative representation at the time of postmodernism "is a historical and a political act,"[11] and Amitav Ghosh strikes us as acutely aware of the former as well as of the latter.

Similar to what happens in A.S. Byatt's *Possession*, the reader of *The Calcutta Chromosome* is left to believe that the plot originates after a fortuitous discovery occurred to the protagonist: in the first case, Roland Mitchell unintentionally discovers two unknown letters by the English poet Ash, while in the second case, due to a system malfunction, Antar finds the remnants of an ID card on his screen. Excited by their findings, Roland and Antar—both of them living on the margins of society—naively imagine that such discoveries may represent a turning point in their lives and transform their dull routine to a state of ferment, while they remain unaware that this episode simply entangles them in a mechanism whose contours they completely ignore. Although they picture themselves as the protagonists of a new plot, they are actually manoeuvred by that same plot. In other words, they are both possessed by a feverish drive which leads them into a blind research rather emerging as self-conscious agents of a frantic investigation.

Antar soon discovers that the retrieved document belongs to Murugan, a colleague of his who disappeared in Calcutta in August 1995. The whole story puzzles and enthrals the Egyptian clerk who, at his own risk, tries to unearth the mystery revolving around this case of missing person. Murugan, on his part, had gone to Calcutta in order to conduct personal investigations on Sir Ronald Ross—who in 1906 received the Nobel prize for his discovery of the life-cycle of the malaria parasite—convinced that the latter's research had been side-tracked by an occult organisation. The plot can be roughly summarised as 'Antar searching for Murugan searching for Ross.' At this juncture, the genius of Amitav Ghosh is twofold: first, he skilfully involves in a feverish and reciprocal inquiry a host of complementary characters, each of them concerned in his/her own puzzle to solve. Secondly, he clones different replicas of past events which he disseminates both in the present and in the future. Thanks to this technique, Ghosh creates intersections of time units, thus 'magically' connecting the future with the present and/or with the past. The novel abounds in cyclic repetitive patterns; the reader more than once feels that the narrated event has already happened in the future or in the past. In the following paragraphs, such a systematic approach (and tendency) in narration will be discussed.

To start with, it may be useful to file the cases into two distinct groups: the first one will simply list recurring episodes, whereas the second will reckon the repeating instances related to a particular character. An example of the first sort is that of the pigeons. We first come across them while following Elijah Farley's research on malaria. Farley was one of the scientists who had worked on the malaria project in the same Calcutta laboratory, which will later become the theatre of Ronald Ross's discovery. His theory was along the same lines of Laveran's, whose results dated back to 1860 but which were then rejected by the majority of the scientific world. By chance Farley noticed that his researches were actually manipulated by his assistant, Lutchman, and the laboratory sweeper-woman, Mangala; it was as if they wanted to keep the bacteriologist away from a certain truth as they provided him with wrong proofs for his research. At the scientist's vehement reaction, they simply gave in and revealed Laveran's parasite on a slide smeared with the fresh blood of a pigeon affected by *halterdium,* a bird version of malaria. That was the test which most clearly evidenced the searched for information. The same species of birds also feature in the present time when Murugan, summarising this story to Urmila, throws a stone at a group of pigeons exclaiming: "'I wouldn't be surprised at all' he said, 'if there were a couple of descendants of Lutchman's flock up there'" (166). A pigeon, finally, is the link with the future as well. While Antar is at home ready to work at his computer,

> something shot up out of the airshaft and began to knock furiously on the glass windowpane. Antar recoiled, throwing his arms up: it was a pigeon, flapping against the glass. Its beady red eyes fixed on him for an instant, and then it was gone. (196)

The emphasis on repetitive instances related to a particular character is still more significant. A web of information not only creates correspondences among different incidents but also among different characters living in separate time sections: this technique leaves the reader with the sensation that, being the affinities or combinations so plentiful, one is facing various levels of 'double' cases. In this sense we should also register how this aspect characterises A.S. Byatt's *Possession* as well, where a romantic thread connects two distinct plots unravelling during the Victorian age and the present time. The secret romance between Randolph Henry Ash and Christabel LaMotte has a commanding influence over the lives of Roland Michell and Maud Bailey who, almost despite themselves, seem to carry on from where the two Victorian lovers had left. The equivalence between the two love-stories is further validated by an element of secrecy and sense of guilt, because the two men are respectively married and engaged. In simple terms, Roland mirrors Randolph Ash in the same way as Maud replicates Christabel LaMotte. These sets of analogies across different time ages or—as we shall soon see—different countries should be directly associated with the postmodern cultural milieu. Steven Connor is assertive as he claims that "postmodernist fiction is ontological,"[12] and stresses how crucial the issue of identity is in this literary context.

Like A.S. Byatt's *Possession*, Ghosh's *The Calcutta Chromosome* creates an impressive net of mirror-like situations among different sets of characters. We may start by taking into account the remarkable analogy between Lutchman and Lucky, a friend of Tara, Antar's neighbour. Their similitude is not merely a noun assonance. Lutchman's peculiar physical mark is that

> his left hand was missing a thumb. It doesn't seem to have made any difference to his manual skills. He was probably born that way, because his index finger seems to have re-trained itself to do the thumb's job. (210)

On the other hand, we might say, Lucky does some cleaning in Tara's flat. There is an evident allusion to Lutchman as he is described in the following way: "Lucky was notoriously clumsy, always dropping trays and spilling tea: 'all thumbs' as Tara often said." (185). A similitude of this kind therefore not only connects past with future, but leaves the reader with the legitimate doubt that Lucky is playing a role analogous to Lutchman's.

There are also a number of elements that seem to suggest that Murugan is able to establish an impressive work of links with every and each male character of the novel, with a handful of alter-ego situations dispersed all along the plot. Not only are episodes cloned, but so are identities. The parallelism with Antar is sketched out as soon as they meet: the narrating voice reports that "they were about the same age, Antar estimated; both in their early forties" (41). Both of them suffer a reduction of salary because entangled in their own researches. Yet, most important of all, they share some relevant affinities with Ronald Ross. Like his two future counterparts, while implicated in his successful three years' research, Sir Ronald Ross is "about to hit his mid-life crisis" (45). Very soon, as the narration flows, the reader learns that the three protagonists had contracted malaria.

Involved in a personal challenge within the breathless process of investigations, the male triad sometimes misses important clues. In this respect, they very much resemble Grigson, a linguist who first discovered Lutchman's double nature. In terms of the succession of events, he provides an anticipation to Murugan: he is a busybody, a meddler, but a guileless, somehow an instinctive, trouble-seeker, too engrossed in his ingenious discovering to notice other remarkable but evident cues. The following passage provides evidence of those common traits:

> So Grigson gives him a smile, and says, speaking to him in his own dialect: "So your name is really Laakhan isn't it? Isn't that how they say it where you're from?"
>
> The minute he says that word, Lutchman's face goes into rigor mortis. But Grigson doesn't notice; he's busy congratulating himself on his infallible ear. (79)

The most important issue is the solving of a linguistic enigma; Grigson does not go beyond that point and, say, wonders why a man disguises himself under a wrong identity. Consequently, he puts his life at severe risk. His behaviour also places him on the same wavelength as Ronald Ross, who had just been described by Murugan in such terms:

> there's this one guy who's doing world-class science, and who's caught up in what he's doing he hardly notices whether there's anything happening around him—and there is, there's a lot happening around him, only the stupid son-of-a-bitch is such a fucking genius he doesn't know. (75)

Murugan is obviously a genius himself; yet, Amitav Ghosh uses a kind of thrift in depicting him as an extraordinary character. At most, while dealing with Urmila's private considerations, he hints that "he wasn't like anyone she knew" (182).

In addition, Murugan is associated with Phulboni, the old and celebrated Bengali writer, whom we find intent on giving a very elaborate speech, fascinating and poetical in its eloquence, but also spiced with what may seem an excessively rhetorical tone. Addressing himself somewhat mysteriously to the silence of the city (Calcutta), he invokes this enigmatic figure with the unmistakable tone of a plea, an act of devotion which seems out of place:

> The time of the crossing is at hand, I know, and that is why I am here now, standing in front of you: to beg—to appeal to the mistress of silence, that most secret deities, to give me what she has so long denied: to show herself to me. (27)

This scene can be easily juxtaposed to the episode occurring in the final section of the novel when Murugan kneels at Urmila's feet. In Phulboni's case, the figure is just symbolically feminine, whereas she becomes a real woman with Murugan. In the case of the writer, then, his devotion is directed at an identity which metaphorically personifies Calcutta, which, by the way, happens to be the curious nickname Murugan uses to address himself to Urmila.

Finally, Murugan disappears just like Farley. Moreover, while in the case of the American bacteriologist he was last seen at Sealdah Railway station, Murugan's traces are lost while he is going to the same railway station by taxi.

As far as female characters are concerned, the topic becomes more and more complex. At the beginning, the plot portrays Antar in a future landscape. He soon comes across two women; Maria, a Guyanese clerk in a Chelsea used-clothes store, and Tara, an Indian emigrant looking for a job. When first described, they provide a good study in contrast:

> Tara was small and bird-like, with a fine-boned beak of a nose. She was youngish—in her thirties, Antar reckoned—a good deal younger than Maria: he guessed at once that she was from India: the connection was obvious really, because Maria was a Guyanese of Indian origin and he knew she still had relatives there.
>
> The two women made an interesting contrast, although they seemed very easy with each other. Maria was tall, stately, and unfailingly well-dressed, although she barely made minimum wage, Tara on the other hand seemed so uncomfortable in Western clothes that it was clear she'd just arrived: the first time she came to Penn Station she was wearing a loose white shirt that hung halfway down to her knees and a pair of trousers that flapped limply above her ankles. (14-15)

Almost immediately after this description, the scene skips to the present time. The leading character here is Murugan who accidentally meets two women: Sonali Das, a renowned socialite, and Urmila Roy, a young reporter working for the *Calcutta* magazine. Compare their first description with the one just quoted:

> Taken by surprise, Murugan looked up and down the glass-fronted hall. It was still empty. Then he noticed two women running up the stairs. They came pelting into the hall and stood by the door, wip-

> ing the rain from their hair and shaking it off their sarees. One of them was in her mid-twenties, a thin aquiline woman with a fine-boned face, dressed in a limp, rather bedraggled saree. The other was taller and older, in the beginnings of a youthful middle age, darkly handsome and quite elegant, in a black cotton saree. (21-22)

The analogy between the two scenes, although set in different time units, is too evident to be ignored. If it further enhances the theory of a likely mixture and contamination of the two male protagonists, it prefigures a similar condition for the female characters. More specifically, the analogies between Tara and Urmila are intensified as the plot unfolds. On 20th August 1995, Murugan perpetrates his researches on his own for quite a considerably long time. The first time he actually has a partner in his investigations occurs when Urmila steps in. Their alliance is symbolically sealed under a summer storm with a sexual relationship. Ghosh, at any rate, is subtle enough to describe the entire amorous scene by placing it within an 'as if' area, a sort of virtual reality, an unrestrainable lust which remains unresolved between desire and consummation. As soon as the next scene appears, the reader is projected into Antar's New York flat. He is thinking of a time when he witnessed the damages a pouring rain was causing to Tara's flat, left unguarded with open windows. He has now helped her in searching for a job; she is grateful to him and ready to offer her assistance, as he now feels feverish. They seem genuinely and reciprocally affectionately tied. The reader has a vague sensation that a tender feeling has been established between the two of them. A sort of alliance is therefore secured. There are, anyway, some odd elements that the novelist introduces at this juncture in the narrative. In a couple of circumstances Tara appears as a mysterious figure: the first time is when Antar catches Lucky prostrated at her feet (her explanations of the fact seem an excuse rather than a convincing clarification). The second time is during the telephone conversation: she first tells him that his previous message was mysterious and then hints that in case he needs her she can be next to him in a moment. This fact somehow stuns Antar as she is now working and quite far away from him. The first accident, in particular, can be linked to similar events which portrays a woman revered by a man (I am referring to the already debated cases of the mistress of the silence and Urmila) but has a correspondence with a past episode of which Farley is the witness: "On the floor, by the divan, clustered around the woman [Mangala]'s feet, were some half dozen people in various attitudes of supplication, some touching her feet, others lying prostrated." (125)

The connection is overt and the critic M. Adhikari is keen in stressing it: "It cannot escape the notice of the readers that the majority of the female characters are christened after the Great Mother archetype. Mangala, Tara, Urmila, Maria are the ideological representatives of the Great Mother."[13]

This issue leads to a crucial point: if the reader can accept the similitude between Tara and Urmila, both of them being 'allied' to Antar and Murugan, he/she is not equally ready to welcome the news of Tara being part of an occult organisation. Her role would be utterly ambiguous. If the two final chapters once more represent the situation of the likely continuity of Urmila through Tara, that, nonetheless, does not solve all the puzzles for the critics. "One moment they are all rushing to the station in 1995, with Urmila saying that she would save them and take them across, the next moment we find Antar hearing voices, finding resemblance between Tara and Urmila and Maria and Sonali, talking to him, as if they were all with him in his room."[14]

Subash Chandra's doubts are made still more evident as she approaches the closing lines. Following, she discusses Tara and Maria's appearance in the end wearing saris: "Who are these women? Are they Sonali and Urmila? They were the ones who were with Murugan. Or are they Tara and Maria, as they appear to be. But they are living in New York, Tara living in the same building as Antar. But then how come Tara and Maria are wearing sarees."[15]

There are few doubts, however, that the mayhem around all these characters is a deliberate choice of the novelist. A possible explanation for the conundrum revolving around the strange connections among female characters, as well as for many other mysteries which the novel seems to leave unresolved, is originated and solved through the character of Murugan, who, as previously discussed, displays an impressive set of links with all the other male characters of the novel. He has a similar variety of time-links: he has a virtual life in the future but also some virtual connections with the past. For instance, when talking about Ronald Ross, he insists on saying:

> This guy's decided he's going to re-write the history books. He wants everyone to know the story like he's going to tell it; he's not about to leave any of it up for grabs, not a single minute if he can help it. He's figured on a guy like me coming along some day and I'm happy to oblige. (44)

In addition, Murugan, the agent of future and the fulcrum in this novel, is the sole character who possesses the right connections to both science and what he names "counter-science" (88) as well as to the West and to India. That is the central enigma of the plot: if on one hand scientists were painstakingly carrying on their research work in order to cure malaria, they did find—that is Murugan's amazing but disturbing discovery—a strong reaction from an occult organisation working in order to side-track the course of medical studies. The Bengali clerk postulates the theory that the occult society carries on this program in order to reach a further, grander result: immortality. The opposition becomes a challenge and a clash too, when some dead bodies are left on the ground. Some characters, frightened, flee, thus avoiding any risk. The "Other Mind" (31), as Murugan calls this clandestine order, works on a parallel stage; rather than looking for solutions in the scientific domain, it directs its efforts towards a mystical field. Mangala, the sweeper-woman who is at the head of such an organisation, is "not in this because she wants to be a scientist. She's in this because she thinks she is a god" (208). Biologists versus gods, that is the essence of the conflict: if the former work by method and reason, the latter counter with faith and 'sixth sense.' What is most striking of Murugan, and what makes him a breed apart among the characters of *The Calcutta Chromosome*, is that his mind is perfectly able to switch from one domain to another, without losing the control of the situation. His intelligence allows him to grasp all the scientific principles and details which would be largely incomprehensible to a mind not trained in medical studies; on the other hand, whenever clues are out of his range, he fills in the blanks by using his intuition, a process, it must be stressed, that never fails him. The three following passages bear testimony of how often the term 'guess' is used in his idiom:

> 'The Calcutta chromosome,' said Murugan. 'That's my name for what she was working towards.'
>
> 'Now I'm really lost,' said Urmila. 'I've lived here all my life ad I've never heard of this thing you're talking about.'
>
> 'And who knows if you ever will?' said Murugan. 'Or whether I will. Or whether it exists or has ever existed. At this point in time it's still all *guess*work on my part.' (203, italics mine)
>
> I'm just *guessing* wildly here, okay? (204, italics mine)
>
> It's my *guess* that by about 1897 Mangala had run into a dead end, and she'd come to the conclusion that the existent strains of malaria wouldn't let her go any further. (208, italics mine)

Murugan therefore is also the bridge between science and counter-science. That is why the chain of interpersonal transfers from Mangala to Mrs. Aratounian, to Urmila way up to Tara undergoes a mutation halfway along its course. To start with, Mangala is quite a terrifying character. As M. Adhikari aptly underscores: "No Indian reader can overlook the idea that Mangala is one of the names of Goddess Kali"[16] and the correspondence with the terrible Goddess is reinforced in the scene where she appears to Farley with a knife in one hand and a decapitated bleeding pigeon in the other one. Mrs. Aratounian still somehow adheres to that model; when Sonali spies her doing her experiments, she is still a rather dreadful figure. The change occurs with Urmila who, being on Murugan's side, is no longer a terrible figure. Urmila is still modelled on the archetypal Great Mother but, as the critic G.C. Pande underlines, that is a representation of woman "as the embodiment of spiritual power, of light and love or pure bliss,"[17] which finds his favourite example in Savitri. Tara, of course, is modelled along the same lines of Urmila's. The dichotomy present in the nature of the archetypal Great Mother cannot be better formulated than in Jung's own words. See how precisely Ghosh's female characters adhere to Jung's classification:

> The qualities associated with it [the Great Mother] are maternal solicitude and sympathy; the magic authority of the female; the wisdom and spiritual exaltation that transcend reason; any helpful instinct or impulse; all that is benign, all that cherishes and sustains, that fosters growth and fertility. The place of magic transformation and rebirth, together with the underworld and its inhabitants, are presided over by the mother. On the negative side, the mother archetype may connote anything secret, hidden, dark; the abyss, the world of the dead, anything that devours, seduces and poisons, that is terrifying and inescapable like fate.[18]

Like the Kali myth they incarnate, Mangala and Mrs. Aratounian are not seen in connection with any man; incidentally, their being modelled on the terrible Kali goddess creates further associations with the city of Calcutta, whose name reveals a devotional attitude towards the Hindu goddess. On a parallel route, Urmila and Tara, even though still unmarried, can be considered very close to Murugan and Antar and their role as protectors is a further confirmation of their mythical heritage. Finally, as far as the open ending of the novel with the intersection between Tara and Urmila is concerned, their individual symbolic representation may be evaluated in relation to the locus of their action. Urmila plays on a Calcutta stage; therefore her role as protector of her man can be quite naturally ascribed to an influence of a Savitri-kind myth. On the other hand, Tara, whose action takes place in New York and who is portrayed as a sort of a virtual female character offering warmth and shelter to Antar, is similar to the Christian typology of angels. She does not quite differ from the celestial images we have seen in the movies of Wim Wenders. In sum, Murugan would appear as a go-between both from a Kali to a Savitri-based model, in that he bridges science with counter-science, and from a Savitri to an angelic model, in that he is able to link East with West.

In conclusion, *The Calcutta Chromosome*, a brilliant cocktail of genres, perspectives and characters, deals with a painstaking search for identity. In his mental journey to 1995 and to the past, the Egyptian Antar does not only unravel a mystery about a scientific/mystical case, but also investigates his own roots. His search for a mystery in the past and the unsuspected discovery of a key to his own self mirrors the situation that Byatt represents in *Possession*, where Maud Bailey is equally astonished to learn that she has connections with Christabel LaMotte: possibly, it is the discovery about her linkage to the passionate Victorian poetess that enables her to change from a somewhat frigid, and cerebral scholar, to an uninhibited and loving woman. The fascinating feature of both these novels lies in their protagonists' total lack of deliberation regarding the search of identity.

NOTES

1. Babli Gupta, "Enigma as Ontology in *The Calcutta Chromosome*," in *The Novels of Amitav Ghosh*, edited by R.K. Dhawan, Delhi, Prestige, 1998, p. 206.

2. Meenakshi Mukherjee, "Spine Chiller," in *India Today*, 15 May 1996, p. 163.
3. Madhumalati Adhikari, "The Continuity of Life, Mission and Mystery in *The Calcutta Chromosome*," in *The Novels of Amitav Ghosh*, edited by R.K. Dhawan, Delhi, Prestige, 1998, p. 233.
4. S. Prasannarajan, "An Echo of Eco," in *Biblio*, Vol. 2 N° 4, May 1996, pp. 10-11.
5. Tapan K. Ghosh, "A Journey to The Unknown: A Quest for Immortality in *The Calcutta Chromosome*," in *The Novels of Amitav Ghosh*, edited by R.K. Dhawan, Delhi, Prestige, 1998, p. 249.
6. John Thieme, "The Discoverer Discovered", in *Amitav Ghosh. A Critical Companion*, edited by Tabish Khair, Delhi, Permanent Black, 2003, p. 132.
7. http://en.wikipedia.org/wiki/The_Calcutta_Chromosome [July 2012]
8. Linda Hutcheon, *The Politics of Postmodernism*, London, Routledge, 1989 (2001), p. 47.
9. Linda Hutcheon, *The Politics of Postmodernism*, London, Routledge, 1989 (2001), p. 73.
10. Amitav Ghosh, *The Calcutta Chromosome*, Delhi, Dayal, p.11.
11. Linda Hutcheon, *The Politics of Postmodernism*, London, Routledge, 1989 (2001), p. 51.
12. Steven Connor, *The Cambridge Companion to Postmodernism*, Cambridge, Cambridge University Press, 2004, p. 66.
13. M. Adhikari, "Female Empowerment in Amitav Ghosh's *The Calcutta Chromosome*," in *Indian Fiction of the Nineties*, edited by R.S. Pathak, Delhi, Creative, 1997, p. 197.
14. Indira Bhatt, "Disappearances and Discovery: a Study of *The Calcutta Chromosome*," in *The Novels of Amitav Ghosh*, edited by R.K. Dhawan, Delhi, Prestige, 1998, p. 240.
15. Subash Chandra, "*The Calcutta Chromosome*: a Postmodernist Text," in *The Novels of Amitav Ghosh*, edited by R.K. Dhawan, Delhi, Prestige, 1998, p. 268.
16. M. Adhikari, "Female Empowerment in Amitav Ghosh's *The Calcutta Chromosome*," in *Indian Fiction of the Nineties*, edited by R.S. Pathak, Delhi, Creative, 1997, p. 230.

17. G. C. Pande, "The Image of Woman in Indian Tradition: Some Reflections," in *Women Images* edited by Jain and Mahan, Jaipur, Rawat Publications, 1996, p. 44.
18. Carl G. Jung, *Collected Works*, transl. R.F.C. Hull (Princeton University Press, 1953-79), vol. 9, pt. 1, p. 82.

Discourses of Resistance and Protest: A Reading of the Autobiographies of Nomadic Writers in G.N. Devy's *Painted Words*

PARVATHI V. & K. BALRAJ

Where the mind is without fear and the head is held high;
Where knowledge is free
Where the world has not been broken up into fragments;
By narrow domestic walls. (35)

Rabindranath Tagore

We are living in the 21st century and the world has advanced to a great extent, yet the gulf between the "*haves*" and the "*have not's*" has not been filled till today. The above quoted lines of Tagore aptly fit in the case of life led by the tribal people in our country, for even after six decades of Independence, they actually live in fear and despair. India has been the land of tribes since times immemorial and every tribe has a unique history and culture. The Adivasi people, who are also called indigenous, native and aboriginal are known for their nomadic lifestyle and have been continuously exploited on account of lack of social equality, education, citizenship rights, cultural and political privileges. Tribals possess a rich resource of oral narratives in the form of songs, tales, riddles, etc. Adivasis were deprived of written scripts for centuries. In fact, Adivasi literature in India came to light only from the 19th century. With the initiation of the government to provide a formal education to tribes, they became aware of their society, levels of deprivation and depiction of their miserable life in the mainstream literature.

This consciousness prompted people from denotified and nomadic Communities to write about different aspects of their long suffering. Their writings, now being translated into English and published in various journals, deal with the realities of life and depict the problems faced by Adivasis and assume the form of protest against the processes and phenomena of degradation, deprivation and dehumanization. One such anthology of tribal writings is *Painted Words*.

Ganesh Narayandas Devy, the editor of *Painted Words*, was born in 1950 and worked as a professor of English at Maharaja Sayajirao University, Baroda, retiring in 1996 to dedicate his life fully to tribal development. His close association with tribal communities in Gujarat enabled him to comprehend the problems of tribes and provoked him to fight for them. He is one of the stalwarts of Indian tribal literature, social activist and an adoring scholar who stands for tribal autonomy and development. In his works, he tries to depict how Indian tribal people are censored and deceived by the elite in the so called democratic nation. Devy, along with tribal activists such as Mahasweta Devi, Kishore Kale, Laxman Mane, Atmaram Rathod and Laxman Gaikwad, addresses the crucial problems that Indian tribals face in writing about their communities.

Of the writings included in Devy's edited volume, the excerpts from autobiographies by four eminent writers express experiences of the problems Adivasis have faced in both colonial and postcolonial times, including the authors' own lifetime. They present various modes of resistance to social norms, and thematize the expediency of self-representation and the need to find a voice to counter the limitations of marginalization. These four autobiographies of nomadic writers selected for our study are:

Koletyeche Por (Kolhati Child) written in Marathi (1994) by Kishore Shantabai Kale was translated into "*Against All Odds*" *(2000)* by Sandhya Pandey.

Upara (Master-less child) written in Marathi (1980) by Laxman Mane was translated into "The Outsider" (1997) by A.K. Kamat.

Tanda (A Group) written in Marathi by Atmaram Kaniram Rathod was translated into "*The Camp*" by D.T. Nandan Pawar.

Uchalya (A Pilferer) written in Marathi (1987) by Laxman Gaikwad was translated into "The *Branded*" *(1997)* by P.A. Kolharkar.

Social Oppression

The autobiographies of Kishore Kale, Mane, Atmaram and Gaikwad represent *social oppression* in the life of tribal people in India who have always been ill-treated and segregated from the mainstream society. They have been suffering for ages. They are considered to be socially inferior and this discrimination is responsible for their social backwardness. They are even deprived of the basic human rights and in the scale of hierarchy, these people occupy the lowest rung. Isolation from the mainstream Indian culture, economic, social, political and educational backwardness compared to non-tribal or its counterparts, superstition among tribal people and instability of family life due to frequent changes of spouses are some of the issues discussed by these writers.

In *Against All Odds*, Kishore narrates his resistance to all odds that he faced in society and he portrays himself as 'Kisrya' in this work, which is writer's pet name. Here, the protagonist acts according to his mistress's commands and demands because of the social hierarchy and economic deprivation. Rambha Maushi says:

> 'Kisrya, hook up my blouse for me.' . . .
> 'Ay, you monkey. . .
> Just go and see. . .
> If not, I'll be in trouble.' (178)

A young Kolhati boy 'Kisrya' did not get any respect from his superiors and others because he was born in a tribal community, which was deprived of material prosperity and equal opportunity. The community is not defined as a particular group falling under any hierarchy, even though they are in real life forced to follow caste hierarchy under which they were at the lower level in social order. Castes were predominantly hailed in the colonial period and people were compelled to reveal their identity. Kishore belongs to a lower community especially an entertaining (tamasha dancer) community. One can find that the central character is only a robot and an obedient worker with no personal preferences. The tamasha, which used to be a form of traditional folk dance, has today worsened to a kind of prostitution growing up in an environment where such dealings were made daily. Kishore witnesses the misery of such a life and his expressions reveal its impact on him.

Similarly, in *The Outsider,* Mane also represents a similar resistance towards the disrespect and plight that he faced at a wedding. He says: "Whenever a guest of honour arrived, someone from the bridegroom's family would say, 'Hey! Where are the musicians?" (204). They earn their living doing odd jobs like working as musicians or slaves in Karne's restaurant or selling news papers. Mane gives a disturbing account of the life of the nomadic tribe called 'Kaikadi.' Mane came up the hard way in life. He was exposed to the university education and to the discourse of social justice in his college days. Anand Mahanand gives an account of how these tribal people are oppressed. He delineates the agony of Laxman Mane's mother: "Even a dog's life has a certain dignity, but not ours" (43). Anand's narrative presents the shocking reality of this community which lives under a social stigma and suffers gross atrocities. It highlights the poverty, illiteracy and inhuman living conditions of this community.

Psychological Subjugation

Many psychologists agree that social oppression in turn leads to psychological subjugation. Kale, Mane, Atmaram and Gaikwad demonstrate the lived problems of Indian tribes such as atrocities, discrimination and violation of rights which have ultimately led these people to be mentally weak and oppressed. They are so victimized that it results in self destructive activities. Kale writes that this marginalization has inculcated in them a strong sense of insecurity. It was observed from my study that failure, experienced by the tribal children in the school resulted in a strong sense of insecurity. Similarly, fear of failure, and lack of ambition among tribal children were the major impediments in their way of education.

> Why didn't my mother let me live with her?
> Was I not her son?
> A million tormenting questions raced through my mind.
> I thought I would go mad. (182)

Kishore is abandoned by his mother because they belong to the tamasha dancer community. They earn their living by performing dances and by entertaining people. So, the boys are left at their grand parents' house. The narrator undergoes series of questions when he compares himself with the well established elite society. His resistance is unimaginable as depicted in these words:

> Poor motherless child' . . .
> 'What harm has he done'?
> These people lived on the earnings of his mother, and now they treat him like an animal. (181)

Abandoned by his mother, Kishore lives with his grandparents. He undergoes hardships and many torments in the inner self. The lines depict how the protagonist was ill-treated and suffered hardships in his childhood.

Laxman Gaikwad comes from a tribal community called Uchalya which literally means 'Pilferer' *The Branded* is about his experience in life as an individual from a branded community. People from this community were branded as criminals, thieves, dacoits and so on. A careful reading of these lines reveals the impact of caste system on the minds of tribal people. The inferiority complex made Gaikwad tongue-tied. Here the protagonist feels that he may be insulted among a large gathering of his own village people. Gaikwad says: "I had said I would make a speech. . . I was afraid even to pass by the village sarpanch and patel. Now the very thought of making a speech before them made me tongue tied" (239).

The humiliation they faced even from the police is expressed in these lines.

> Dada begged, 'Please don't. I'm only going to Jawali'
> The policeman questioned him further:
> 'You bastard. . . Somebody from your gang took it.' (250)

The central character is depicted as a school going boy and he is from the community of pilferers. Due to economic inconsistency, Adivasis' life was wrongly projected. It branded them as criminals because they were doubted by the policemen and the mainstream society and under suspicion these people were kept in jails where they were brutalized. The narrator depicts how the policeman behaves with the civilian and forces him to an act of stealing things otherwise he would be suspected without any reason and kept in jails for years together:

> Anna said, 'You are a school going boy. If you're caught by the police, you will be removed from school. Your name will go down in the police records as a thief.' (249)

The narrator also depicts the daily routine of his people which includes reporting to police station. While going to another village, they have to carry a certificate from the nearest police station and report it in other village.

Economic Deprivation and Political Repression

Next issue being discussed in this context is economic deprivation and political repression. The tribals suffer from the menace of economic oppression. It is a pity that this trend continues even today. They are targeted and subjected to both economic discrimination and social exclusion. extreme poverty, inability to afford the necessities of education, inadequacy of financial assistance for meeting the cost of boarding, lodging, books, etc. In *Against All Odds,* Kishore tries to compare the assessment of the life of these people by the mainstream society as slaves because they are working under them. 'Kisrya' is doubtful about it because he has come from a lower tribal community.

In 'The *Camp*,' Atmaram gives the background of a political set up in the year 1963-1972; a new crop of leaders began to grow rapidly in the Yavatmal district in Maharashtra. There was a true leadership wave among vagabonds, beggars, bankrupts and cheats. Scheming scoundrels began to pretend as political leaders, with their *khadi* robes and joined the political bandwagon. In the world of power politics, every body has to fight to secure his or her rights. If some of them secure their rights by fighting against the power brokers, their next generation must continue the fight to retain them.

> 'Gave the money to Neeta?' he thundered. . .
>
> 'Was it your money?
>
> My money? Does it not belong to the community? Who is Neeta? (219)

The cunning Sanawatji quickly read the crowd's mood. He roared at Atmaram. Atmaram could no longer tolerate Sanawatji's hypocritical sermons, especially when he was disrespected in front of his own acquaintances. Atmaram could not protest and shows his inability in asserting himself.

Educational Backwardness

Tribal people are deprived of educational opportunities due to various reasons like extreme poverty, inability to afford the expenditure of education, inadequacy of financial assistance, polygamy, nomadic life style and so on. Kishore Kale narrates his experience that he is identified as Kolhati boy rather than any normal student: "Nobody at school made friends with me. For days I kept to myself, quietly attending classes and then going home . . .others teased them and called them names for befriending me and soon they too kept away" (186).

Teachers were indifferent towards this community and they felt that they were doing a great favour to this community by imparting education. Mahanand also opines the same and emphasizes Mane's words in his book: "All the pupils started teasing me in the way the hens do when a strange chick intrudes upon their privacy" (42). Mane describes how the mainstream society children would ill-treat the children from a lower community when they were studying: "I feared that if we stopped here and we were spotted by other kids from our school, we'd be laughed at and made fun of" (199).

In India, these social practices are rigid and Mane tries to give an account of fear from his own classmates and hides himself from them because they would tease him in the name of his community and tries to find another route to reach his home. Anand Mahanand confirms the teachers' indifference towards these students from lower community who are given no importance when it comes to providing them education. Although, there are absolute rights given by the constitution in India, these people lag behind in availing of opportunities.

> Even the teacher would not take it easy. He would say: "You funny guy! Do nomadic beggars go to school? [. . . .] If they study, who will weave out baskets? Nothing doing!
>
> My school was moving on the donkey's back. (42)

Mane tries to project the problem that he faced because his family moved from one place to another and he had to change schools frequently. But he never gave up and did all kinds of odd jobs such as selling bread or cleaning dishes and continues his studies. He was also supported by some of his friends and teachers. Thus he managed to complete his school and joined college. While in college, he worked in the library as a part time employee but his services were terminated because he attended a protest rally. The book is a revealing account of the Kaikadi community. It reflects the misery and hardships of the people in the twentieth century. They do not have a permanent roof over their heads, no permanent source of income to meet their basic needs, no education to establish their identity and live in inhuman conditions.

In conclusion, we submit that these writers have created a world of their own and fear to allow strangers from the mainstream society to mingle with them because they have been deceived by them in the course of history. Kishore, Mane, Gaikwad and Atmaram have led an unhappy life and experienced fear, disgust and anxiety right from the beginning of their childhood as a result of long-standing prejudice. They have witnessed unpleasant events and conditions which they cannot even share with anybody in the society. Although they are educationally backward, they are able to view things in the right perspective and depict the realities that have affected them and many other writers.

Their anguish and agony is clearly deep. They reveal that in spite of positive policies and allocation of considerable funds given by the government, there is no improvement in the lives of Adivasis even after six decades of independence. Their autobiographies offer the honest experiences of the denotified communities, and they have clearly depicted the long-lasting suffering of these groups. They arouse compassion and sympathy in us because they are deprived of basic amenities that high society takes for granted for itself. We should feel remorse for being uncaring and unaware of the sufferings caused to our own fellow beings. There is a hope that these writings would certainly change the perception of intellectuals about tribals, and that nomadic writers would soon be called Indian writers.

Works Cited

Devy, Ganesh N. *Painted Words: An Anthology of Tribal Literature*, New Delhi: Penguin, 2002.

Mahanand, Anand. *Tribal Literature in India* Hyderabad: Publications Unit, CIEFL, 2005.

Tagore, Rabindranath. *Gitanjali* New Delhi: Rupa, 2002.

Cultural Conflict in Jhumpa Lahiri's *The Lowland*

SHRADDHA TRIPATHI

The postcolonial movement brought the diasporic phenomenon into sharp focus as it picked up momentum in the wake of decolonization. Almost all the postcolonial theorists like Edward Said, Homi Bhabha, Gloria Anzaldua, Stuart Hall, James Clifford, Paul Gilroy, Rey Chow, Arjun Appadurai, Theodor Adorno, Gilles Deleuze, Felix Guattari et al have, therefore, deliberated on the formation and continuation of diasporas in the fast globalizing world.

The reason for this fascination for the diaspora is the important issue of identity. First underlined in the context of newly-freed nations, the notion was quickly taken up to describe the condition of any minority group pitted against a majority based on different colour, race, sex, etc. In the case of the immigrants in any society, their identity is threatened by the culture of the host country. Besides, "The trajectory of a migrant follows the pattern of location, dislocation and relocation, each one of these phases being liminal rather than sharply defined ones. The process of acculturation is a slow one-sided (the minority seeking integration with the majority) one and is not without a sense of loss and exile. It is also not a clear transformation; it gives rise to hybridity marking different stages of acculturation" (Malik156). Jhumpa Lahiri, the Pulitzer award-winner novelist, has brought out these postcolonial concerns of identity and culture beautifully in her novel *The Lowland*.

Born and brought up in UK and USA, Lahiri is known for her insight into the life of the Indian immigrant community. Her parents were from India who shifted later to England where she was born. However, they relocated themselves in Rhode Island, America. It is here that Jhumpa grew up and had her education. Her initial contacts with India were through periodic visits of her parents to West Bengal. Her first collection of short stories titled *Interpreter of Maladies* focused on the immigrant experience besides dealing with the lives of some Indian characters in Indian setting. This anthology brought her the coveted Pulitzer Prize. Later, she published another collection of short stories titled *Unaccustomed Earth* and a novel *The Namesake*. In all these books, she examined different aspects of the lives of people who travelled from India to the 'land of promise,' viz., America, in search of livelihood or pursuit of higher studies. It is rightly said that "Her [Jhumpa Lahiri's] work has primarily focused on first and second-generation Bengali immigrants, exploring themes of exile, isolation, and assimilation. Lahiri's insight into the psychology of relationships, aging, maturity, and loss is remarkable" (Batra 2011: 50-51).

Needless to say, in such stories, the Indian background of the immigrants is examined minutely. Most of them are adults at the time of shifting to America, where they settle down for the rest of their lives. They have interaction with the American community, which was once upon a time a group of settlers themselves who travelled from different parts of Europe towards the close of the fifteenth century. The interface presents problems mainly due to different cultural backgrounds of these two communities. Even though in the three fictional works which Jhumpa produced, the major theme is diasporic experience, there is still a lot to say on this account and therefore, in *The Lowland* too, she sticks to this theme, even as she devotes considerable space to the background of the Indian characters—as a family back in Calcutta.

The story is set in the Tollygunge area of Calcutta. To begin with, the reader is introduced to two brothers—Subhash and Udayan. Subhash is elder to Udayan by fifteen months. They are inseparably attached to each other. The two ponds in the vicinity of their house symbolize these two brothers. When these get filled up with water during the rainy season, they appear as a single oblong pond, but when the summer sets in, the water evaporates and the ponds appear as two smaller and separate entities. In the same way, the two brothers are alike and yet different in their aptitude and mindset. As they grow up, they prove their brilliance in studies. While Udayan is interested in Physics, Subhash is at home in Chemistry. However, both of them have interest in electrical devices and they keep on conducting minor experiments and mending electrical gadgets at home. Later, Subhash gets a scholarship to study Physics abroad and he moves out to USA.

As a college student in India, Udayan gets involved in the underground Naxalite movement. This movement which began in 1960s takes its name from Naxalbari, a village where the landless labourers took up arms against the landlords. The ideology at the back of it was identified as radical Marxism as enunciated by Chairman Mao-Tse Tung of China and it favoured violent overthrow of government which was viewed as a capitalist adjunct. Udayan became a staunch supporter of the movement. He would take part in secret conclaves of the party, distribute subversive material and help in the organization of violent acts meant to challenge the state.

Around the same time, Udayan gets attracted towards Gauri. Her house was near his college and her brother Manash became Udayan's friend. Thus, Gauri comes into contact with Udayan and is also drawn towards the Naxalite movement. After sometime, Udayan is killed by the police in a fake encounter. Subhash comes to India to take part in the final rites of his brother. It is here that he thinks seriously about re-settling Udayan's wife Gauri. Much against the wishes of his parents, he marries Gauri and takes her to the United States to usher her into a new life. (186). He believes that she would be able to forget Udayan's tragedy and settle down to a new life in America.

But things happen in a different way. Gauri is able to relate to him physically but not emotionally. Later, this physical union does not remain Subhash-specific. She takes a number of lovers but with none of them she develops any emotional bonding. Then, it is either her teaching or the romancing as a time-pass to which she devotes herself fully. She becomes an emotional bankrupt. After many years, when her daughter has grown into a young woman and given birth to a girl, named Meghna, she visits them, not for any rapprochement but for getting divorce papers signed by Subhash. That shows her rigidity. However, her past attachment with her dead husband asserts itself and she goes to Calcutta as if on a pilgrimage, but comes back empty-handed. The visit is a failure.

How she absorbs the American culture and gives up the much-touted Indian emotionalism speaks volumes about the clash between two cultures. That brings us to the question of cultural difference and a shock which is faced by the diasporic people in any part of the world. The culture shock, as the anthropologist Kalervo Oberg defines it, is the psychological disorientation experienced by people who suddenly enter radically different cultural environments to live and work. "Culture shock is precipitated by the anxiety that results from losing all our familiar signs and symbols of social intercourse."

Upon entering a new society, the culture shock takes time to wane which could vary from a few weeks to some years or decades, and in some cases, it may not dissipate at all. In case of Indians migrating to the West, it takes a long time to go and even then, it is a mixed culture which they evolve, after fine-tuning the cultural traits of the host country to their taste. As to why it happens, it can be safely argued that India, being an old civilization, has a very deep impact on its people. Our culture is high on ritualism and symbolism. No day in the calendar goes without the mention of some ritual or the other. However, subtlety and refinement are the hallmarks of Jhumpa's approach so that the reader hardly feels the existence of culture shock. But the cultural difference is surely marked by the characters. Thus, we see in *The Lowland*, rather a slow demolition of the cultural barrier in Gauri. She does subscribe, in course of time, to American culture, and become fiercely individualistic person, and yet something of the old culture remains in her which takes her back to Calcutta towards the close of the story.

The novel does throw subtle hints of cultural difference, as Knopf review states, "The middle section of *The Lowland* presents a particularly arid stretch. We know the basic outlines of the assimilation story: the confusion about American customs, the unstaunchable (sic) loneliness, the sense of having made a horrible mistake in coming to this brash, cocky country. In "The Lowland," though, the characters are even more inert to their new home, trapped as they are in their own impenetrable depression."

Now, before taking up the area of cultural difference which is the main burden of this paper, let me briefly explore the meaning of culture. The English word culture is a participial form of the Latin verb *colere*, which means, variously, to "till," "foster," "care for," "pay attention to, "honor," or "worship." The central idea encompasses all that we value in our life at the collective level. Generally, when we talk of culture in the anthropological sense, we mean the way of life of a particular people or society. It includes the manner in which they eat, dress and live. It also means their customs, rituals, taboos and fetishes, beliefs and values. Culture is the key to understand how they would behave in a particular situation at the collective or individual level.

The meaning of culture "that dominated usage from the seventeenth to the early twentieth centuries (and the definition that Eliot sought to defend) centered around the development of the highest and most "sacred" elements of society" (Snoeberger 3).The contemporary theories of culture like cultural materialism do not contest our understanding of culture as enunciated here, rather these seek to point out the practices of common people which are ignored due to the elitist bias in our understanding. Generally, we have been trained to think of only the elite in a society as the upholders of culture. Scholars like Mathew Arnold and T.S. Eliot have viewed culture in this way, but the post-Marx approach tips the balance in favour of the common people. The Marxist view of culture is as "superstructure which is determined ultimately by the economic 'base' or 'structure.' According to them, whatever the textuality of history, a culture and its literary products are always conditioned by the material forces and relations of production in the relevant historical era" (Malik 138).

It goes without saying that while noting the cultural manifestation of a particular people, like the Indian diaspora in America in the present case, we are guided by practices indulged in at the level of people like Subhash and Gauri. They were ordinary people who travelled from India to settle in the United States. Taking up the cultural difference between Indians and Americans, which is the theme of this paper, we find that the writer betrays it at many places even as she devotes much of the space in this novel to the life in India itself.

As Subhash migrates to the US, he encounters many new things which influence his lifestyle. Upon reaching America, the first thing that appeals to him is the beautiful area of Rhode Island, which the human hand had beautified further. Looking at the steel piles of the two bridges stretching across the bay, he felt mesmerized. "The symmetrical rise and fall of the Newport Bridge, recently completed, had arched portals and cables that would light up at night. [. . .] End to end, he was told, the wires of all the suspended cables would span just over eight thousand miles. It was the distance between America and India; the distance that now separated him from his family" (65). He liked the lighthouse with three windows "like three buttons on the placket of a shirt" and felt he had discovered the most beautiful place on earth" (ibid). On cloudy days, "at intervals, the sound of a foghorn pierced the air, as conch shells were blown in Calcutta to ward off evil" (38). The difference was clear: while in the land left behind, they propitiated the gods to do things for them; in America, they depended upon their own efforts!

Not only the place looked different from what he was accustomed to seeing in India—the two lowland ponds back in Calcutta—but also the people and their lifestyle. The difference in the two cultures was to cast its shadow on his whole life: "Subhash could not fathom the extremes of his life: coming from a city with so little space for humans, arriving in a place where there was still so much of it to spare" (243). The over-populous India is clearly contrasted here with the sparsely populated America. India is also a land of unique characteristics and contradictions. Subhash felt it was difficult to explain the Indian situation at times, like when it came to politics about which his American friend Richard wanted to know, Subhash didn't know how to describe India's fractious politics, its complicated society, to an American. He said it was an ancient place that was also young, stills struggling to know itself" (41).

Gauri's experience of the difference talks about some other dimensions. The cold in Rhode Island was "severe in the mornings, the windowpanes like sheets of ice when she touched them, milky with frost" (129). When she went to the class room, she noted that the student sitting next to her was "wearing long silver earrings, a gauzy blouse, a skirt that stopped at her knees. Her body was unencumbered by the yards of silk material that Gauri wrapped and pleated and tucked every morning into a petticoat. These were the saris she'd worn since she stopped wearing frocks, at fifteen. What she'd worn while married to Udayan, and what she continued to wear now" (134).

It was in Rhode Island that Subhash met Holly, the pretty American woman, somewhat older than him, with whom he was to share the bed for many days. It was the lady's son Joshua playing at the beach who caught his eye and then became the means to reach the mother. She worked as a nurse at a small hospital in East Greenwich. She had been living separately from her husband for some time. Subhash found that she too was interested in sea-birds. She asked him about India and he told her that his married brother Udayan and his wife stayed with his parents. Now this is a system followed in India and not in America. "He knew that it was impossible for Holly, probably for any American woman, to imagine that life" (67).

They started meeting regularly at the beach. One day, when she invited Subhash to her home, he could not say no, even though he knew that "she was American, and that she was probably ten years older than he was" (68).Upon reaching there, he observed that it was a sequestered house. Other houses in the vicinity were also hardly inhabited as these were vacation-homes of rich people. How could a woman live with her son and a dog in this far-off lonely area—the question flummoxed him. "He marveled at the self-sufficient nature of her life. And he was also slightly nervous for her, living alone in such a remote plate, without bothering to lock her door. There was no one to help her, apart from the babysitter who looked after Joshua while she worked. Though her parents were alive, thought they lived nearby, in another part of Rhode Island, they had not come to take care of her" (72). This was indeed puzzling for him because it showed a cultural trait that was totally alien for an Indian.

One Friday evening, when he went to see Holly, Joshua was not there. He came to know that every Friday, he went to spend some time with his father. After taking dinner, the natural instincts worked and they were bedded. Though Subhash was a little hesitant, Holly did not care for any scruples in sexual matters. As he was about to leave, Holly asked him suggestively, "Should I let you know, the next time Joshua goes over to his father's?" (73).It was the American way, as he could see, very different from the Indian way!

Jhumpa Lahiri examines the American family life vis-à-vis Indian. When Holly asked Subhash if he was close to his father, Subhash was drawn into thinking for a while. The picture of Joshua riding his father's shoulder came to his mind. His father was not that loving but like all Indian parents, he was certainly "a consistent one" (76).Lahiri, as a keen observer of immigrant life, also probes the inter-racial marriages. Prof. Narsimhan and his American wife present the picture of a happy couple. That perhaps is the ideal of a globalized culture, as Lahiri seems to suggest. Again, Americans desist from poking their nose in others' affairs; the concept of privacy is sacrosanct there. When Gauri and Subhash attend a party at Prof. Narsimhans,' he is apprehensive about questions being asked about his marriage to Gauri, but contrary to his speculation, "No one questioned that Gauri was his wife, or that he was soon to be the father of her child. The group wished them well, and they were sent off with an assortment of objects" (139). Had they been in India, their past and present would have been shredded to bits!

Subhash considered for a while marrying Holly but her age, her child and the fact of her being technically the wife of another person were the dissuading factors. Little did he know that destiny would throw him into an almost similar situation! While Subhash should be credited for sticking to Indian cultural norms in trying hard to keep his allegiance to Gauri after he had married her, it is Gauri who deviates from her obligations as a wedded wife. She presents the example of acculturation of an immigrant. It begins with her fascination for American way of dressing. The yards of silk sari were indeed difficult to hold as Gauri was in an advanced stage of pregnancy. She liked the way American girls dressed themselves. So, one fine day, she scissored her sarees, petticoats and blouses and switched to the American dresses and hairstyle, without discussing the matter with Subhash. Later, when the child Bela was born, she wanted a baby-sitter for her, even though Subhash did not approve of it. He wanted to bring up the child in the Indian way—under the care of her parents, but it was clear that Gauri had imbibed American craze for individuality and was in no mood to compromise.

That Gauri is Americanized is also borne out by her fascination for a man in the 50's whom she chances upon seeing and then starts waiting for him even though nothing comes out of it. In contrast, Subhash stays faithful for a long time after Gauri has left him. She envisions life without any kind of encumbrance—daughter or husband: "Time to speculate that [taking up a doctoral program], without Bela or Subhash, her life might be a different thing" (174). She was indeed "disoriented by the sense of freedom, devouring the sensation as a beggar devours food" (174). It was this American individuality which propelled her to walk out on her husband after 12 years of wedded life to enjoy sexual liberty: "Sometimes she juggled lovers, and at other times, for extended periods, there was no one. She'd grown fond of some of these men, remaining friendly with them" (237). She even developed lesbian relationship with Lorna! Again it was something not so common and definitely not approved of in India.

If Gauri, born in India, could be so free, her daughter Bela, born and brought up in the liberal environs of America, was bound to be freer. She too enjoyed sex with all and sundry but did not commit to anyone all her life—picture of a typical American youth. However, she "swims against the materialist current in America and feels impressed by an 18th century cult preaching celibacy and simple life, though she amends the celibacy injunction herself later on. That is her take on radicalism of her father joined to free-wheeling lifestyle of her mother. She has steely determination like her mother and refuses to have any truck with the father of her child" (Batra 2014: 221)

On the Indian side, the picture is dismal. The way Udayan loses his life and Subhash migrates to USA along with Gauri, their mother, who lived all her life in India is a shattered person. As Khaleej Times review notes, "After the death of Subhash's father, his mother, who is going senile, starts to clean the detritus of the two ponds with her bare hands—the rotten waste she surfaces symbolic of her and her husband's dashed ambitions and hopes of living in a joint family with their sons and families, the modern indestructible plastic refuse uncovered, of the negligence by her sons." This is the other side of the picture—a picture of the home left behind by the immigrant and it is indeed a pathetic picture because emotions are rather strongly felt in India.

Indian culture is ancient and is well-ingested in the people through a rigorous and subtle accultural process, referred to normally as instilling *sanskar* by the family and that goes on throughout life. We see Ashoke and Ashima in *The Namesake*, who maintain their ties, howsoever tenuous, with India throughout with the latter vowing to straddle the two continents regularly after her husband's death. In *The Lowland* too, we find Subhash duly going to Calcutta to take part in the final rites of his dead brother Udayan. Gauri, even though substantially Americanized during her long stay in America, also has an urge to visit Calcutta to feel connected with the spirit of her late husband. This speaks volumes about the impact of her original Indian culture which has not totally been wiped out. She has been transformed but "The transformation cannot be viewed in terms of black and white, for they [the immigrants] inhabit a liminal space of constant contestation and appropriation of culture of the adopted country of their parents. In any process of acculturation, the possibility of change exists at all moments of life, so we get hybrid characters rather than pure subjectivities" (Batra 2011: 68).

We can conclude with the observation that despite all our talk of globalization sought to be achieved through common trade practices, cultural conflict between two societies is a hard reality that cannot be glossed over. Economics plays its part but even at the back of it, these are the beliefs, and values which always guide actions in the materialist world. Cultural conflict is something which even the most liberal of religions have failed to resolve and it is something that is to stay, maybe, forever.

Works Cited

Batra, Jagdish. *Jhumpa Lahiri's The Namesake: A Critical Study*. New Delhi: Prestige, 2011.

___. "Exploring the Dark Recesses of Mind in Jhumpa Lahiri's The Lowland: Insights and Illuminations," *The Fiction of Jhumpa Lahiri: A Critical Response*. Ed. Suman Bala. New Delhi: Khosla, 2014.

Das, Nigamananda. *Dynamics of Culture and Diaspora in Jhumpa Lahiri*. New Delhi: Adhyayan, 2010.

Lahiri, Jhumpa. *The Namesake*. New Delhi: HarperCollins, 2003.

___. *The Lowland*. NOIDA, India: Random House, 2013.

Malik, R.S. & Jagdish Batra. *A New Approach to Literary Theory and Criticism*. New Delhi: Atlantic, 2014.

Knopf Review. 24 Sept. 2013. 15 Jan. 2014. http://www. washingtonpost.com/entertainment/books/review-the-lowland-by-jhumpa-lahiri/2013/09/24/7b9dcbca-2005-11e3-8459-657e0c72fec8_ story.html

Snoeberger, Mark A. 'More Notes Towards the Definition of Culture.'<http://www.dbts.edu/pdf/macp/2008/Snoeberger,%20More%20Notes%20Towards%20the%20Definition%20of%20Culture.pdf>

Shehan Karunatilaka's *Chinaman: The Legend of Pradeep Mathew* A Critical Response

SUSHIL GUPTA

'The style is too rambling, the thesis unclear, and the language falls into the formal and vulgar . . . in places it is interesting, in places it is rubbish . . . the author goes off the topic a lot . . . brimming with cockeyed theories . . . anti-patriotic rantings of a drunk . . . gutter journalism at its worst . . . the story, like the man himself, seemed to forget its point . . . a book that rambles and has no conclusion . . . it was strange to share his warped thoughts and guess at which bits he made up.'

I could have written any one of those comments. But what do you do when the author anticipates you and disarms you with such self-deprecatory remarks, uttered through various characters, scattered all over the text? Well, you join in his humour.

At the outset a conundrum is placed as the epigraph: 'If a liar tells you he is lying, is he telling the truth?' That sets the tone of the narrative. Much that follows is a blend of truth and lies which defy sifting. Real personalities hobnob with phantasms and historical milestones meld into make-believe happenings. These Pirandellian ambiguities keep the tale oscillating between what is real and what is made up.

Let's begin with the title. A 'pony-tailed Chinaman' is a Sinhalese expression for someone gullible. The said oriental will believe anything. Chinaman is also the name of a ball delivered by a left-arm bowler turning in or away from the batsman; a lethal delivery. 'Is this a story about a pony-tailed Chinaman bowler? Or a tale to go tell a pony-tailed Chinaman?' As it turns out it is a bit of both. Like the wedding guest in Coleridge's lyrical ballad we are under the spell of the greybeard loon and cannot choose but hear his improbable tale.

The novel falls in the genre of quest-centred tales: a search for the Holy Grail or the El Dorado. A much feted sports journalist, W.G. Karunasena, assigns himself the task of making documentaries on outstanding cricketers of Sri Lanka. He is fascinated with Pradeep Mathew's achievements as a bowler. As he probes into records he discovers they are blanked out with an uncanny deliberation. That goads him into unravelling Mathew's mystery 'on the pitch and off it' as the mission of his life. A fortuitous cache of footage of matches in which Mathew had figured and interviews with people who had anything to do with him help him in piecing together the man.

Mathew appears as a maverick both as a man and as a cricketer. He was ambidextrous: bowled left-arm spin and right-arm pace; opened batting as well as bowling; could mimic any bowler; his repertoire included the flipper, the googly, the leaper, the floater, the darter, the lissa, and above all the double-bounce ball that spun twice; walked when he snicked and didn't appeal on a bounce catch, much against the wishes of the management; called the Skipper a prick and the Captain a cunt; moody, immature and foolish; wrote poems to his girlfriend; blackmailed the MD of SLBCC; masqueraded as another player in many a match; didn't listen to the coach—said he had his own; got into a brawl in a pub; and then disappeared without a trace. WG's dogged pursuit to trace him forms the skeleton of the plot.

The skeleton is fleshed out with anecdotes, eccentric characters, unscrupulous politicians, gifted sportsmen, ambitious maidens, homosexual pedophiles, corruption in polity and sports, assassinations and match-fixing, cricketing controversies like chucking and sledging, arcane calculation of Duckworth-Lewis on a rain-shortened play, long power-cuts, ruminations on life's ironies, and all this peppered with witticisms and wise-cracks galore. Historical landmarks provide the backdrop for the unfolding of events: the long drawn out civil war, Sri Lanka winning the World Cup in 1996, an assault on the Indian Prime Minister for sending the Peace Keeping Force et al.

In the midst of all this hurly-burly is silhouetted the portrait of a marriage. WG, a Tamil sports journalist who slides into alcoholism, is married to Shiela, a Burgher whom he had seduced away from her boyfriend. They have a son, Garfield, named after the West-Indian cricketer Sobers, not the cat of the comics. WG's character is defined by his relations with his wife, his son, his friend and neighbour, his weakness for drinks, his brilliant career as a sports journalist, and above all, his obsession with spotlighting the genius of Pradeep Mathew.

Following in the footsteps of Omar Khayyam, he extols the virtues of liquor as a great anodyne to the distressed soul. 'Alcohol has enhanced my life and the world I inhabit. It has given me insight, jocularity, and escape. I would not be who I am without it.' 'Alcohol strips my mind of noise and helps turn my thoughts to words. It keeps me smiling and guarantees me a dreamless sleep. It stops me from thinking of things that thought cannot cure.' It takes its toll though. The doctor shows him a 'yellow card' which means that 'if I behave myself, I may not have to miss any games.'

In a first person narrative whatever else may happen to the protagonist he cannot write, 'and then I died.' But this is more or less what happens here. At the end of chapter three "Close of Play," he writes: 'Mark my words, as a writer and a lover of sports. This story shall be finished. It is indeed possible to score a late goal in extra time, to land a knockout at the end of the 12th, to hit a six off the final ball. And I, W.G. Karunasena, husband of Sheila, father of Garfield, champion of Pradeep Sivanathan Mathew, am, without doubt, the man to do it.'

In the next chapter "Follow On," we learn that he is dead and his posthumous script is doing the rounds of the publishers with little prospect of success. The first person narrative continues with the sports journalist replaced by his musician son who, eight years later, takes upon himself to continue the mission of his father to find Mathew. Earlier we had the father's perspective on his good-for-nothing son, 'lazy useless fucker'; now in a role reversal we have the son who has done exceedingly well in life, 'I have nothing to do and plenty of money to do it with,' commenting on his father, 'The Thathi I knew was a foul-mouthed, argumentative prick.'

The search and the mystery, the leit-motifs of the novel, continue. It takes Garfield to a small town Pukekohe in New Zealand, where he has short-listed thirty-two probable Pradeep Mathews. As he goes about meeting all those characters, a string of delightful cameos surfaces. But the success eludes him. He is on the verge of giving up. 'What more can I do other than head home, clean up the book, and try and get it into print? I don't think Lankan publishers are all that picky about books that ramble and have no conclusion.'

"Last Over," however, is yet to be played. More deprecatory comments about the contents and the style of the book follow: 'The book is gutter journalism at its worst' and 'antipatriotic rantings of a drunk'. The dialogue between Garfield and a potential publisher is hilarious. The book is taken to shreds. 'Get rid of the unbelievable stories.' She mentions one of the more believable parts of my father's book. 'That is 100 percent bullshit.' 'One more thing. The Ending.' 'What about it?' 'To put it bluntly, it sucks.' During this near farcical tête-à-tête, a compromise formula emerges. 'Cricket non-fiction is a small market. But true fiction on the other hand. . . .'

'What's true fiction?' He raises the question like Jesting Pilate two millennia ago, and like him wouldn't stay for an answer. Fiction is aptly defined, elsewhere, as a lie that tells the truth. Come to think of it the entire corpus of literature, mythology, scriptures and history can be slotted in this category.

The upshot is that all the names in the book are either altered or deleted or concocted including that of the author, the protagonist and the title. 'Can we finalize the title? *The Book That No One Will Read*. Boring. *Revenge of the Chinaman*. Sounds like a Bruce Lee. *Shades of Brown*. What? *Konde Bandapu Cheena*. A pony-tailed Chinaman. . . '

The probable names for the main character are considered and dismissed: '*Vinothan Karnain*? Nope. *Charlie Jeganathan*? Nope. *Sanjeewa Amarasinghe*? Can't be a Sinhala name. *Juarangpathy Jeyarajasingham*? Sounds stupid. *Pradeep Mathew*? Who's that? I don't know. I just. . . . Try it.'

So that's that.

Shehan Karunatilaka's *Chinaman* resembles the canvases of Pieter Bruegel that are crowded with ordinary folk engaged in day-to-day activities of life. So much seems to be happening on the scene that one is tempted to go over the details with a magnifying glass. The exercise yields a rare connoisseur's delight.

Work Cited

Shehan Karunatilaka, *Chinaman: The Legend of Pradeep Mathew*, Random House India, 2011, 395 pp., Rs. 499

Postcolonial Ecological Concerns in Indian English Fiction

JAGDISH BATRA

Literature has always been engaged with different moods of nature. It has sung of its beauty, freshness and tranquility that have had a salubrious influence on humans. At the same time, it has sung of the sublime and terrifying moods of nature which humbled man and showed him his place in the universe. This is a truism that applies to the most ancient form of literature, viz., poetry which developed in all societies of the world.

Culture was supported by science. So, far from correcting the imbalance for future generations, the sharp focus on psychology in modern literature further distanced it from the physical world. The political crises in Europe that followed the First World War had a deep impact on individual mind and so literature turned from colourful pageant of nature to a functional art form, shorn of all trappings with the microscope zooming in on the human psyche only. The tussle has remained intractable so that in these postmodern times, we look upon this relationship as an ambivalent nature/culture binary or nature/humanity binary in which neither term is to be preferred to the other. This being the case, it is quite 'natural' or 'in order' to admit nature as an independent entity. As it favoured a re-look at the representation of history and culture of the colonial times by the colonizers, the postcolonial criticism has also turned towards examining the injustice to nature meted out by the colonizers. A strand of postcolonialism is rightly named as postcolonial eco-criticism.

At the same time, empirical evidence shows that the actual consequences of giving a raw deal to nature have been very serious for mankind. The phenomenon of global warming leading to a hole in the ozone layer around the globe, melting glaciers, rising sea levels, climatic catastrophes being felt all around in the world are too glaring to be glossed over. It is more than clear to man that he can neglect nature at his own peril only. Consequently, literary scholars have once again focussed their attention on nature. Postcolonial eco-criticism also favours studying the role of indigenous structures of power as also international neo-imperial structures in political moves that destroy natural habitat and divest its inhabitants including not only humans but also insects, birds and animals of their habitation and life support.

Turning to the Indian point of view, the Vedantist school of philosophy debunks the distinction between the animate and the inanimate world, for it believes all creation to be imbued with a cosmic consciousness. In fact, to believe that nature is only *jad* or inanimate entity would be a gross undervaluation. It is only so long as we have not gone beyond the immediate sensual experience. Not to talk of the organic world of vegetation all around us, even a pebble shows life in the form of plutons and electrons hidden inside every atom of it. How can one explain the order of movement of these tiny bits without lending credence to some sort of intelligence governing this natural phenomenon. This orderliness is a hint enough of the underlying intelligence and of an ethics or code of conduct informing operations in nature. That nature revolts and retaliates, if it is tempered with beyond a certain limit, is no new knowledge for mankind. Add to this the insight that nature too has whims like a human being: with its sudden tectonic movements, it can make man run like a panic-stricken mouse.

Indian culture, therefore, emphasizes respectful attitude to nature. From seeking God's blessings on all natural elements in the Vedic *Shantipath*[1] to god Hanuman's supplication to *Sanjeevani* herb to donate its leaves for Laxman's life, instances supporting the aforesaid view are not lacking in our ancient books. There is no doubt that Indian cultural and religious practices have had a holistic view of world in which all elements are linked to all other elements, even as we cannot gloss over the contemporary degradation in cultural practices due to the gulf between preaching and practice.

In postcolonial Indian English literature, the normal tendency has been to follow the trends in Western literature even as the basic tenets of postmodernism lend legitimacy to the native and local elements. Whatever the case, there is consolation in finding nature being treated differently from the purely scientific-intellectual standpoint, which itself has mercifully seen its weaknesses in having mercilessly ravaged nature all along and brought the world close to an ecological disaster.

While surveying Indian English Literature for marking its links with nature, what strikes at first instance is that in poetry, the concern with nature is at its utmost, which is justified, considering that poetry is the first genre that enchanted humanity at the dawn of civilization. Drama, on the other hand, seems totally bereft of this engagement but then Indian English drama is not so rich either. Let us, then, analyze some contemporary fictional texts—a genre that is presently the most voluminous—to find out the attitude towards nature.

As we undertake this exercise to focus on place, land, niche, home, habitat, etc., our main concern is to discover the writer's point of view with regard to nature. Is it just to provide a background and give a sense of physical context to what is denoted by the term 'pen-picture' in literature so that the reader feels that he is viewing a scene through the mental eye? Is nature portrayed as an independent entity out there just as the existentialists speak of 'being-there' in its own right? Does it have any impact on humans living in its lap like the symbiotic relationship between the mother and child? Are the values expressed in the work consistent with what is termed as 'eco-ethics' or sound ecological principles? Also, is there some fresh thinking on ways to tackle the suicidal destruction of nature that mankind has been indulging in? Does the literary work seek to re-mould our aesthetic appreciation of nature—of what we consider as scenic or sublime etc.?

II

In Indian English Fiction, the ecological concerns have always been there in various degrees. In early fictional writing, as in Raja Rao's *Kanthapura,* the villagers venerate the river Kanchammaas the Hindus all over India worship the Ganga. In R.K. Narayan's Malgudi-centric fiction, we find the benevolent influence of the river Sarayu on different characters. There is mention of the retreat across the river, of jungle-tribes living in hills, etc. all of which makes it a mysterious place imbued with the spirit of the place. Later in Kamala Markandaya's novels we see the evil impact of urbanization. The love for one's inherited land is integral to any environmental discourse. In her novel, *Nectar in a Sieve*, industrialization and drought—as onslaughts of man and nature—combine to pauperize Nathan. Being old, he is unable to take to any other trade and is forced to migrate to city with his wife and they turn to beggary!

In fiction, the use of names of flora and fauna is done sometimes to symbolize human condition which shows the ecological concern of the author. At other places, such description becomes necessary to the context of the narrative. In novels by Arundhati Roy, Anita Desai, Kiran Desai and many others, one finds that the description of local culture and lifestyle cannot be complete without reference to birds, insects, animals and even vegetation.

Arundhati Roy, an author-turned-activist has passionately championed the cause of ecology. With Vandana Shiva and Medha Patkar, she fought against the proposed Narmada dam project. In her celebrated novel *The God of Small Things* (1997), one finds nature in its pristine glory in the form of the free-flowing river Meenachal. The beauty of the landscape attracts the attention of the writer and the river Meenachal, seen through child's eyes—as the entire novel's point of view—evokes a beautiful picture in the reader's mind: "It was warm, the water green like reapplied silk. With fish in it. With the sky and trees in it. And at night, the broken yellow moon in it" (123). But modernization changes things. Over a period of time, we find the change in culture with modern trappings of life changing public attitude: "Years later when Rahel returned, it greeted her with a ghastly skull's smile, with holes where teeth had been and a limp hand raised from a hospital bed. . . . Despite the fact that it was June, and raining, the river was no more than a swollen drain now" (124).

The river had lost its pristine beauty and it "smelled of shit and pesticides brought with World Bank loans. Most of the fish had died. The ones that survived suffered from fin-rot and had broken out in boils" (13) .The River is full of plastic bags, weeds and untreated factory effluents. The novel gives a vivid description of harmful effects of modernization on animals. A temple elephant dies when it comes into contact with a high tension electric wire but Chacko is indifferent to this news. On the other hand, a puppy follows Estha when he returns after twenty-three years to Ayemenem and tries to show his intimacy but Estha is indifferent towards him.

The theme of degradation of natural habitat due to urbanization and industrialization is not new. We have seen tragedies on a gigantic scale in the form of the Bhopal Gas Tragedy in which the American multinational Union Carbide took all the earnings when the going was good but when, due to the poor upkeep of machinery, the lethal gas leaked out killing some 2500 people and maiming for life a large number of people, the company simply shut the door on the people including its employees. The hapless people were taken for a ride not only by the MNC but also by their own government which colluded with the multinational. A graphic account of the tragedy that life had become for the people is given by Indra Sinha in his novel *Animal's People*. The protagonist, a 19-year old boy, cannot stand up; he has to walk on all fours due to the effect of harmful chemicals released from factory. He was not always like that as Ma Franci tells him: "Such a beautiful little boy you were, when you were three, four, years. Huge eyes you had, black like the Upper Lake at midnight plus a whopping head of curls. How you used to grin. [. . .] your smile would break a mother's heart" (1). And now he dreads the mirror! His plight can be compared to that of the people of Hiroshima and Nagasaki, who were maimed for life due to bombing by America.

Here in Ayemenem, Velutha is the god of small things. He is a man in harmony with the habitat, so he earns his living by making small things from wood and other natural materials. Roy describes him as making "tiny wind mills, rattle, minute jewels boxes out of dried palm reeds; he could carve perfect boats out of tapioca stems and figurines on cashew nuts" (74). When he is driven out of his house by his mother, he takes refuge in the lap of nature near the bank of the river. He catches fish from the river and cooks it in open fire and he sleeps on the bank of the river reminding us of the heroine of Margaret Atwood's *Surfacing*. His thirteen night physical relationship with Ammu starts and progresses near the bank of the river. Nature is the witness of their relationship.

Nature does have impact on the way people conduct their lives. It is raw nature that is at work in brother-sister liaison in *The God of Small Things*. The two transgress the barriers raised by society and respond to the natural urge. Does the writer approve of this kind of relationship? This is left unanswered as no fallout from this link ensues and no character comments on it.

Amitav Ghosh's *The Hungry Tide* (2004) is a perfect piece of eco-fiction. Not only does it highlight the ecology of a unique natural region, the lifestyle of the people and animals, etc., but also deals with important questions that have a bearing on ecology and the human population that is umbilically attached to it. Long back, the economist T.R. Malthus had pointed out that "the power of population is indefinitely greater than the power in the earth to produce subsistence for man" (73). How, in search of subsistence, the dispossessed tend earth to bear fruit for them is graphically portrayed in *The Hungry Tide*. Also the novel discusses the politics of multinationals that results in a horrible episode in which thousands of people are killed. In addition, there is a tender love theme that progresses through the warp and woof of the novel but which transcends the barriers of language, class and culture.

The reader comes across the protagonists Kanai Dutt and Piyali (or Piya) Roy early on in the novel. While the former is a Delhi based businessman running a translation agency, the latter is a Bengali-American scientist from the US. Kanai, in his forties, is on his way to an aunt, who runs a charity hospital on one of the islands—Lusibari, and has invited her nephew to come and take charge of a bundle of papers of her deceased husband, who was also an intellectual activist. Piya is in her twenties and is in India to study the behaviour of dolphins.

According to the environmentalist Jonathan Bate, the dilemma of Green reading is that "it must, yet it cannot, separate ecopoetics from ecopolitics" (266). The MNCs, for example, tinkering with the genes of seeds and flowers for their exploitative innovations must be at loggerheads with the ecologists. The central political issue in Ghosh's novel is the infamous 1979 Morichjhapi massacre of Hindu migrants from the then East Pakistan. Around 30000 migrants had settled in the Sundarbans despite its inhospitable terrain with a large number of small islands which got submerged with frequent waves rushing in from the sea. These islands had mangrove forests and dangerous creatures like tigers. The West Bengal government which was in collusion with the business house known as Sahara Pariwar had earlier evicted around 10000 people from Jambudwip Island in 2002 because the corporate wanted to set up a tourist resort. On the face of it, the idea of a beautifully maintained natural habitat to be touted to the tourists seems to favour ecological maintenance, but the reality is different.

But we are not concerned as much with this story as with the backdrop of Sundarbans spread over parts of India and Bangladesh, where nature always challenges man. The refugees were able to live in a symbiotic relationship with nature—deriving their sustenance while at the same time minding the conservation part. They had the dream of resettling in the Sundarbans which they considered as part of their motherland. (165). They rapidly established Morichjhapi as one of the best developed islands of the Sundarbans. Within a few months, a thriving localized economy without any government support was built in the region. However, the negative fallout was that the left front government of West Bengal felt slighted at the successful resettlement of refugees in Morichjhapi and accused them of having violated the forest acts and caused serious ecological imbalance. (Mohanty 176).

The novel throws in bold relief the novelist's understanding and espousal of the cause of nature. According to Ghosh, nature is all that "included everything not formed by human intention." (142) and it is self-sustaining, as for example, the fish "scrape off the diatoms and other edible matter attached to each grain of sand" (142). The writer also examines various myths, legends, anecdotes and beliefs that circulate in the layman's domain. At the same time, he has taken up various historical facts and scientific theories which form the intellectual discourse of nature and habitation.

Ghosh has gathered large data on the way man has ravaged nature. For example, during the Khmer Rouge insurgency in Laos, the rebel forces killed dolphins to extract oil for running their vehicles (305). He has also explored history, as he clarifies in the epilogue to the novel, and found out that Money S' Daniel wanted a new society set up here where there would be no exploitation. Ghosh has tried to unearth the history of different environmentalists who helped the cause of nature. They include people like Mr. Paddington who disfavoured setting up of a port at Matla but Lord Canning did not heed his warning. The result was that a powerful gale washed away the port in 1871. (286-87).

Through the character of Piya or Piyoli Roy, Ghosh has crafted a character who has devoted her life to the study and preservation of nature. A woman, it is ironically believed by the eco-feminists in our times, is a better custodian of nature than man. "Women have been associated with nature, the material, the emotional, and the particular, while men have been associated with culture, the nonmaterial, the rational, and the abstract" (Davion 9). The support for this stand is found in early human societies. "Eco-feminists have claimed that archaeological research reveals that such early societies were ecological, equal and matriarchal" (Gimbutas in Derek 21). There is also the supporting concept of 'gaia'—the earth goddess of Greek mythology, which has been dug out to fit in with the ecological view of earth as a self-supporting organism. This is not unknown in India where the first morning Puranic mantra to be chanted after rising from bed refers to the earth goddess[2]. Therefore, Derek is right in concluding that "The concept of an Earth goddess is nearly universal and certainly ancient. Egyptian, Greek, Indian and Jewish traditions, to name but a few, provide us with female Earth deities" (74).

We find an interesting dialogue between Kanai and Piya on the issue of preservation of dangerous animals like tigers. While Kanai is a leftist who blames the Western 'patrons' who disregarding human cost that goes into protecting wildlife with the aid of Indian accomplices like him even as they themselves keep a large number of animals in captivity, Piya is in favour of keeping the animals in their natural habitat. She says that it was intended so by nature:

> Just suppose we crossed that imaginary line that presents us from deciding that no other species matters except ourselves. What'll be left then? Aren't we alone enough in the universe? And do you think it'll stop at that? Once we decide we can kill off other species, it'll be people next—exactly the kind of people you're thinking of people who're poor and unnoticed. (301)

This conjecture is in sync with the postcolonial paradigm shift from the exploitation wreaked by colonizers, to the exploitation perpetrated on the downtrodden in indigenously governed societies. About the difficulties of undertaking projects to study and preserve nature, she herself tells Kanai: "Easy?' There was a parched weariness in Piya's voice now. 'Kanai, tell me, do you see anything easy about what I do? Look at me: I have no home, no money and no prospects. My friends are thousands of kilometers away and I get to see them maybe once a year, if I'm lucky. And that's the least of it. On top of that is the knowledge that what I'm doing is more or less futile" (302).

One has to add to this scenario the official apathy and corruption are the major factors responsible for the degradation of eco-system. When Piya applies for the permission to scour the Sundarbans rivers for her research project, she is forced to have an official guard as escort. Ironically, it is the guard who, in cahoots with the boatman whom she is again forced to hire much against her wishes, fleeces her and even steals her camera at the end of the work-day. They could have done her physical harm too as was apparent from their behaviour, but Fokir's entry at the right time averted it.

The philosophical guru of 'deep ecology' Arne Naess puts forth some key observations which must find mention here before we turn to the crucial problem faced by the denizens of the Sundarbans. According to Naess, the well-being and flourishing of human and non-human life on the planet earth has value in itself and secondly, this value is independent of the usefulness of the nonhuman world for human purposes. But the flourishing of human life and cultures is compatible with a substantially smaller human population. (Naess in Sessions: 68). Now, this observation at once pits the human interest against the interest of the non-human world, for what we see is the depletion of non-human population and a rise in the human population. This human/non-human hierarchy in inter-species rationality is linked to other such binaries like civilization/savagery or culture/nature and is indeed intractable.

While the ecologists have their point of view regarding preservation of nature, the migrants demand their right to life. The government's stand is this: "This island has to be saved for its trees, it has to be saved for its animals, it is a part of a reserve forest, it belongs to a project to save tigers, which is paid for by people from all around the world."

The postcolonialists point out that when the colonizers annexed lands of the artless and simple humans living in close proximity with nature as in the settler colonies of America and Australia, they considered the native people as little better than animals. Therefore, when these colonizers of yore come forward to protect the animals, there are bound to be misgivings. Quoting Robert Cribb on the issue of the Dutch colonizers' legislation in Australia, critics Huggan and Tiffin point out: "The creation of national parks and the protection of endangered species have both excluded indigenous peoples from regions they have occupied and managed for centuries and have hampered them from using natural resources as an economic base from which to seek modernity'—a modernity into which European incursion had already propelled them" (Huggan and Tiffin 187).

Here, in the context of the Sundarbans, the migrants' response to the 'project tiger' is articulated before Nirmal by Kusum, which also takes on the delicate issue of notional right of the animal world to exist vis-à-vis needs of human existence:

> "Everyday, sitting here, with hunger gnawing at our bellies, we would listen to these words, over and over again. Who are these people, I wondered, who love animals so much that they are willing to kill us for them? Do they know what is being done in their names? Where do they live, these people, do they have children, do they have mothers, fathers? As I thought of these things it seemed to me that this whole world has become a place of animals, and our fault, our crime was that we were just human beings, trying to live as human beings always have, from the water and the soil" (261-2)

Even though Ghosh examines the different theories propounded by J. Feurer regarding how the tigers turned into maneaters (240), for the landless people the tiger becomes a symbol of the state which seeks to discipline them in the name of the tiger.

Towards the end of the novel, when Piya finds the carcass of a dolphin, the circumstantial evidence and Fokir's testimony suggest that the careless official guards were responsible for its death: "it was probably some kind of official boat, used by uniformed personnel—maybe from the coastguard or the police or even the Forest Department. It had one speeding down the channel, earlier in the day, and the inexperienced calf had been slow to move out of its way" (346).

A powerful note is sounded with the nature overruling the human division of society on the basis of class and leading to the union of Piya and Fokir at a time when a powerful cyclone strikes the area. Both of them have to take shelter on the branch of a sturdy tree. She hugs the tree and Fokir sitting at her back too hugs her and both of them are tied to the tree with the help of

Moyna's old sari. "She could feel the bones of his cheeks as if they had been superimposed upon her own; it was as if the storm had given them what life could not; it had fused them together and made them one" (390). On the whole, Ghosh gives a balanced treatment to various issues involved in maintaining the ecological balance.

Another great novelist and Booker winner Kiran Desai's focus in her novel *The Inheritance of Loss* (2006) on the geographical nature, apart from being an aesthetic embellishment, also forms an allied motif of home. If the consciousness of home lies at the deeper level in the novel, that of the habitat is felt at the surface level, at the level of allied motif. The idyllic description in the vein of pastoral representation of the hill station shows Desai's ecological leanings, which she has inherited from her mother Anita Desai, the well-known novelist. If Nanda Kaul merges with the atmosphere in *Fire on the Mountain*, in *The Inheritance of Loss*, it is the house that merges with the landscape: 'When she looked back, the house was gone; when she climbed the steps back to the veranda, the garden vanished. [. . .] The gray had permeated inside, as well, settling on the silverware, nosing the corners, turning the mirror in the passageway to cloud' (2).

Exotic details of nature—of flora and fauna and lush vegetation—at the foot of the Kanchenjunga present a veritable feast for the nature lovers. Even the solitude of the inhabitants of Cho Oyu has been described in terms of the giant squid spotted there on rare occasions: "No human had ever seen an adult giant squid alive, and though they had eyes as big as apples to scope the dark of the ocean, theirs was a solitude so profound they might never encounter another of their tribe" (2). The symbolic significance of the animal world is, of course, found in countless narratives produced in all times and climes. What stands out is the coexistence of the human and the animal world in that section of the Cho Oyu that is governed by the rustic cook and other servants. A saucer of milk and a pile of sweets is placed by the cook to pacify a pair of black cobras living in a hole. The archetypal cook, as his namelessness suggests, lives in harmony with nature believing that "The natural world exists in its own right and other beings have a will, a way of their own and their own stories" (Drengson 20).

However, as in *The Hungry Tide*, we find conflict in this novel also. The ethnic Nepalese Gurkha people are fighting for Gurkhaland, their homeland to be carved out of West Bengal, and Gyan, a Gurkha, gets drawn to the movement. The environmental problems like paucity of housing and agricultural land have a colonial origin. It is well known that in the middle of nineteenth century, the British colonizers created big plantations for the commercial production of tea. Tea bushes grew in wild fashion in Assam. According to Colleen Taylor Sen, the British encouraged it to break the Chinese monopoly. Later, it slowly grew into a popular drink in India too (26). Assam and Darjeeling are the popular brand names in tea now. But with the development of tea plantations came the ecological and demographic changes. The local workforce was not preferred by the British; instead they went in for indentured Adivasi labour brought in from central and eastern India. Besides, there were small proportions of Nepalese and Oriya labourers too. (Anantnarayanan) This has, over the years, turned into a situation where there is frequent tension, not infrequently, violent over possession of land and means of livelihood between the migrant labour and the native people. There is the question of environmental justice and it "gives these positions a clear affinity with environmental justice movements that protest the common association of acute environmental degradation and pollution with poverty" (Gerard 20).

Sai gets emotionally involved with Gyan, her teacher of Nepalese origin, who lives in the poverty-stricken Bong Busti. Transcending the cultural barriers, nature brings them together as it did Ammu and Velutha in Arundhati Roy's *The God of Small Things*. Against the scenic backdrop of the Delo lake or by the shores of the Teesta river, they tell each other tales of themselves and their families. While nature brings them together thus, the cultural politics creates a gulf between the two lovers. The growing discontent among the Indian Nepalese takes the form of Gorkhaland agitation. Gyan joins this movement and is brainwashed so that he distances himself from Sai and even uses harsh words for her. There is a nasty quarrel between the two. Gyan, like a true postcolonial, places his geo-ethnic identity above everything else. He berates his beloved and mocks at the 'fake English accent' and 'powdered faces' of 'that fussy pair' at Cho Oyu. He now looks down upon them as encroachers on his homeland. However, nature does not make any living creature her permanent guest. "Even if a group has been here for several generations, the fact remains that it is true so far as the recorded history goes. One cannot make history a ground for claiming a piece of land in these postmodern times when any identity, leave aside the one based on settlement, is fluid and changeable" (Batra 170).

Suravi Sharma Kumar's *Voices in the Valley* (2012) is a novel that is suffused with ecological overtones as it highlights the topography, climate, flora and fauna of Assam in a big way. Besides, there is a sharp focus on local customs, food and dress habits, taboos, etc. of the community living in harmony with nature. The writer's narrative, at least in the early part of the novel, is marked by beautiful pen-pictures:

> Millie would observe the kingfisher sitting still on twigs in order to snap up a tiny fish or a tadpole camouflaged in sheets of algae. Dazzling white, the egrets would wade all over the paddy beds with their necks moving back and forth. At a distance from Borkuiiagaon, the Burha Luit [Bramhaputra] flowed in melodic ripples sounding like the clinking of bangles ona bride's heavily ornamented wrists. (42)

Here is a specimen in which the writer reads the language of fish in the leaves: "Some trees were covered by vines, some stood bare, some bore leaves pointed like a singi fish, some spindle-shaped like the kuhi fish, some tiny like the puna fish" (68). The struggle in nature is noted at the minutest level: "Red weaver ants stitched up the leaves of a guava sapling in a corner into enclosures for homes. Drones and bees attacked a thick wasp, that had intruded into their hive, engulfing it in a ball of bees, exterminating it for its audacity" (71).

Some of the images are indeed fresh, as for example, "The reddened river at a distance flowed trembling with the boats and ferries sailing on it butterflied to their reflections" (116) or ". . .yards away from the highway lounged a green pond with thick lining of moss and with turtles who looked like upturned saucers floating on the water" (38). However, this focus on ecological aspect is not retained throughout the narrative. After some eighty pages, the description takes the form of journalistic report and the issues covered are also of socio-political interest rather than of ecological interest.

The protagonist of the novel is Millie, a young girl, who lives in an Assam village with her joint family that includes three brothers and their wives and many children. This is a family of priests whose duty is to foster respect for religion, rituals and traditions. But not all children toe their line. As they grow up, the young birds crave for freedom and experiment with their lives in different ways. Millie's sister Leonny is selected by the visiting parents of an eligible boy. It is Millie's lot to study, be a part of student politics and then rise to be a member of parliament. In the backdrop we find references to sundry events like Bangladeshi influx and the consequent ethnic strife, rise of militancy followed by the formation of state government by young student leaders, police repression, rigged elections, etc. Very recently, on Dec. 23, 2014 to be precise, some 70 Adviasis were butchered by the Bodos of Assam. The pressure on land due to the Bangladeshi influx and earlier by the plantation industry is responsible for this sorry state of affairs. In this context, historian Rajib Hadique states: "The colonial experience in Assam was very traumatic as it entailed huge changes in the ecology and demography of the province. The traditional rights of the indigenous people over the forests were taken away and British imperial interests led to large-scale alienation of land for setting up tea plantations. This loss of land that was once considered common property by tribes like the Bodos created huge problems" (Bora 12).

Some other novels may briefly be considered here for their ecological interest. Aruni Kashyap has come out with an Assam-specific novel *The House with the Thousand Stories* (2013) which is focussed on the issue of insurgency in Assam. It has nature description in plenty but it is still a backdrop. She talks of the scent of the earth, the river Bramhaputra, the animals, the insects, etc. essentially to present a pen picture to the reader. True to its name, the novel *Adrift: A Story of Survival at Sea* by V. Sudarshan relates a gripping account of a tourist couple marooned at sea in the company of the crew. The backdrop is the Andaman and Nicobar islands with their pristine beauty. The novel *Frozen Waves* by S.S. Kumar takes up the Sundarbans region as the backdrop of the thriller that this novel is.

Nature is thus increasingly being focussed upon in postcolonial Indian fiction in English. However, this focus is mostly in the form of a backdrop. Even as Kiran Desai, Suravi Sharma Kumar et al refer to land issues in their narratives, they do not go deep into the machinations of colonial masters the way Amitav Ghosh has done in his novel *The Hungry Tide*. As a postcolonial and postmodern mode of textual representation, literature has to contribute to the construction of both nature and culture in an equalized manner. The challenge is to accept the existence of nature in its own right, "of physical environment (both natural and human built) shaping in some measure the cultures that in some measure continually refashion it" (Buell 2001: 6).In the interest of human survival, there has to be a via media whereby the conflicting demands on both sides can be met. Wall Derek suggests the remedy:

> Economic systems should be infinitely sustainable, cyclical in nature and able to recycle energy and resource inputs. Rather than being based on quantitative measures of gross national product, their goals should be ecologically centred and qualitative. Above all, preservation of, and interaction with, nature are vital. The reduction of human wants and the abolition of degrading, alienating work are also sought. Social justice and the creation of a sense of community are equally important; the end goal of a sustainable economy may in a sense be the abolition of economics as a category separate from other areas of life" (Derek 118).

We must not forget the belated realization by a section of the ecologists that economic transformation alone is not adequate and that instead of consumerism, we should be following a kind of 'Green spirituality' (Derek 182). This has, indeed, been the mantra held aloft by ancient Indian culture. But to lead the way in our times, not only the scientists, the politicians or the literary scholars, but mankind at large also has to wake up to thwart the catastrophe knocking at our door.

NOTES

1. Om Dyau Shanti, Antariksha Gwam Shanti, Prithvi Shanti, Rapah Shanti, Oshadhayah Shanti, Vanas Patayah Shanti, Vishwed Devah Shanti, Brahma Sarvagwam Shanti, Shanti Reva Shanti, Sa Ma Shanti Redhi. Om Shanti Shanti Shanti Om!

   This 'Shantipath' is recited at the end of all types of formal prayers and worship. This Vedic sloka invokes peace on all natural elements and spheres, viz., space, sky, earth, water, herbs, vegetation, all gods looking after various functions of nature, the creator lord Bramha, and every celestial being and worldly object, so as to lead to the realization of peace by us, human beings. What is to be marked here is that the term 'peace' denotes perfect balance and harmony. If the sky, land and water are in natural harmony, then the human beings too would enjoy peace. Thus, it underlines the link between natural elements and human beings. This is perhaps the best wish and prayer for mankind.

2. "*Samudravasanedevi, parvatstanmandale; Vishnupatninamastubhyampaadsparshakshmasva me!*" (O goddess, with the attire of oceans and breasts of mountains; wife of the god Vishnu, my feet will touch you for which I seek thy forgiveness!)

Works Cited

Anantnarayanan, Sriram. "Long disenfranchised, and struggling for ST status" India Together. 5 May, 2008. Web 3 Dec., 2014. < http://indiatogether.org/assamadi-society>

Bate, Jonathan. *The Song of the Earth*. London: Picador, 2000.

Batra, Jagdish. *Form and Style in Indian English Fiction*. New Delhi: Prestige, 2011.

Bora, Bijay Sankar. "The Killing fields of Assam" *The Sunday Tribune* 28 Dec., 2014. Chandigarh ed.: 12.

Buell, Lawrence. *Writing for an Endangered World: Literature, Culture, and Environment in the U.S. and Beyond.* London: Belknap Press, 2001.

___. *Future of Environmental Criticism: Environmental Crisis and Literary Imagination*. Oxford: Blackwell, 2005.

Davion, V. "Is ecofeminism feminist?"*Ecological Feminism*, Ed. K. Warren. London: Routledge, 1994.

Derek, Wall. *Green History: A Reader in Environmental Literature, Philosophy and Politics*. New York: Routledge, 1994, ed. 2004.

Desai, Kiran. *The Inheritance of Loss*. New Delhi: Penguin, 2006.

Drengson, Alan. 'Novels, Philosophical Studies and Ecocriticism.' *Indian Journal of Ecocriticism*. Osle India, Aug. 2009.

Garrard, Greg. *Ecocriticism*. Oxfordshire: Routledge, 2004.

Ghosh, Amitav. *The Hungry Tide*. NOIDA: Harper Collins, 2013.

Huggan, Graham and Helen Tiffin. *Postcolonial Ecocriticism: Literature, Animals, Environment*. Oxon: Routledge, 2010.

Malthus, T.R. *An Essay on the Principle of Population*. London: St. Paul, 1798, Electronic Scholarly Publishing Project, 1998. <www.esp.org>

Mohanty, Bharat Bhushan. "The Dichotomy of Human Survival and the Destruction of the Ecosystem in the Sundarbans Archipelago: A Study of Amitav Ghosh's *The Hungry Tide," The Indian Journal of English Studies*, Vol. XLIX (2012), pp. 174-83.

Roy, Arundhati. *The God of Small Things*. New Delhi: Penguin .1997.

Sen, Colleen Taylor. *Food Culture in India*. Westport, USA: Greenwood, 2004.

Sessions, George, ed. *Deep Ecology for the 21st Century. 1995: Readings on the Philosophy and Practice of the New Environmentalism*, London: Shambhala, 1995.

Sinha, Indra. *Animal's People*. London: Simon & Shuster, 2007.

The Idea of Indianness in Indian English Literature

D.P. DIGOLE

The monolithic character of Indian literature has been a much debated phenomenon due to its intricate matrices of literary productions in Indian vernaculars. As India is a confluence of varying streams of cultures, religions, languages and ideologies, the Indian literary landscape presents a kaleidoscopic panorama replete with distinctiveness of culture and heritage. The multiplicity and heterogeneity emanating from the bewildering diversities of races, religions, castes, cultures, and languages have proved sometimes a prop and sometimes a hindrance, too, in the process of literary homogenization of India. Such an heirloom of multiple heritage brimming with linguistic plurality and cultural diversity naturally seeks accommodation, negotiation or mediation and a very tolerant understanding of each other with due respect for differences. The inevitable exchange between cultures and languages leading to a kind of natural and instinctive receptivity can be easily observed in Indian homes the way people constantly practice translation in everyday interaction. Concurrently, India's diverse literary manifestations in different regional languages reflected her collective consciousness and ethos, socio-cultural mélange and the Indian world-view or to use Suniti Kumar Chatterjee's famous expression *Bharat-Dharma* i.e. Indianans. This sustenance of a unique socio-cultural fabric based on firmness of trust, spiritual grace and unfathomable unity is instrumental in binding India's manifold expressions together, irrespective of her glaring diversities of all sorts.

This artistic expression of India's rich multi-cultural heritage and socio-cultural milieu provided a common basis and deep sense of cultural unity thereby fostering the spirit of mutability and reciprocity among the various regional literatures of India. As a result, the diverse ethnicities, languages and pluralistic traditions got harmoniously blended and synthesized due to certain permanent values of Indian culture and nationality like common cultural ambience, secular character of the Indian Constitution, shared sensibility and fundamental unity of outlook on life based on religious and spiritual consciousness. All these factors enabled the Indian scholar-critics to adopt a holistic perspective for looking at the various Indian language-literatures as a single entity unified by one living and continuous tradition. Just as India's composite culture made up of regionally individualistic components is *one*, despite the geographical peculiarities and linguistic barriers, the vernacular literatures in India have an invisible undercurrent of basic unity beneath the seemingly diverse literary cultures.

India's National Academy of Letters, popularly known as the Sahitya Akademi, has been propagating the idea of "oneness" of India's manifold literary expressions since its inception in 1954 by using Dr. S. Radhakrishnan's assertion "Indian literature is one, though written in many languages" as its motto. It has also been instrumental in popularizing the nomenclature *Indian literature* (in the singular) as the most comprehensive and suitable appellation for denoting the vast corpus of literature produced in all Indian languages, through its journals and manifold activities. This umbrella designation has been established as a common denominator, a national entity or totality with an organically integrated approach rather than a combination of fragmented fixtures. The uniform treatment and acceptance of the omnibus term has provided 'a wide base and healthy orientation to the study of various literary activities in India in its totality on the basis of close inter-relations and common links between the diverse literary traditions cutting across regions, languages and sub-cultures. The broad and firm foundations of Indian culture accommodative of varied religious, cultural and literary practices along with the complexities of multilingualism in India have contributed substantially to synthesizing the diversity of group cultures as well as vernacular literatures on the ground of common bonds and indelible unity of outlook on life. Thriving on the ingrained spirit of religious tolerance and fundamental unity in the midst of diversity demanding a deeper conceptual understanding, the oneness of Indian literary and cultural tradition plays a very significant role in promoting the cause of national integration and transforming India into an enviable epitome of everlasting brotherhood, tolerance and humanity. One is tempted to quote S. Abid Hussain's affirmation: "India's cultural history of several thousand years shows that the subtle but strong thread of unity which runs through the infinite multiplicity of her life, was not woven by stress or pressure of power groups but the vision of seers, the vigil of saints, the speculation of philosophers and the imagination of poets and artists, and that these are the only means which can be used to make this national unity wider, stronger and more lasting' (12).

This hypothesis based on cultural unity and pan-Indian traits has been challenged by many scholar-critics, like Nihar Ranjan Ray, who questioned the very contention of Sahitya Akademi in a vehement and explicit manner, thus: the contention cannot be sustained in its fullest sense. Literature is absolutely language-based and language, being a cultural phenomenon, it is all but wholly conditioned by its locale and the socio-historical forces that are in operation through the ages in that particular locale. If that be so, one may reasonably argue that the literature of a given language will have its own specific character of form and style, images and symbols, nuances and associations, etc. Even themes and contents are more likely than not, have their specific nature and character (Poddar 6).

What the learned critic seems to assert here is nothing but the cultural base of language and the significant role played by the socio-historical forces in conditioning the linguistic resources. He, thus, points to the fact that every Indian language has its own independent literature and, therefore, the very conception of the entire literary corpus of all Indian languages as one unified whole is totally invalid and not feasible. However, the cultural base and social conditioning of literature cannot be denied by over-emphasizing the close interconnection between language and culture. Even the images, symbols and metaphors, etc. do not spring from the language itself but from the life lived by the speakers of the language which may also be shared by neighbouring regions.

Swapan Majumdar also disagrees with the uniform approach of treating the varied Indian literatures as one integrated unit silencing the individual identifications and attributes. He adopts a systematic approach where Indian literature is neither 'a simple unity' as hegemonists of nation-state persuasion regards it, nor 'a simple diversity' as assumed by relativists or poststructuralists. He thus suggests that Indian literature in neither "one" nor "many," but rather a systemic whole where many sub-systems interact towards one in a continuous and never-ending dialectic. This perspective considers all Indian literatures together, age by age, and studies it in the context of unity and diversity in a dialectical interliterary condition and process. Some others have rejected the idea of Indian literature as such by contending that "As long as, we can't cook up a language called Indian, how can there be an Indian literature?" This view can be answered by explaining the fact that 'literature rapports with culture and not by any geographical boundaries or linguistic areas. Based on the generous concept of *vasudhaivakutumbkam* (The whole world is our family) Indian culture-*Sanskriti* has much wider scope and accommodativeness to merge the diversities of all sorts in an organic whole. The constant interaction and togetherness of diverse cultures, languages and religions in India have postulated the characteristic ethos of 'unity in diversity' and 'diversity in unity' as the basic, cardinal principle-the *Elan vital* i.e. the life force of Indian society, culture and literature as well.

Though the languages of India do not belong to the same stock, their literary inheritance is, by and large, common as all Indian writers derive the basic inspiration from the great works like *the Ramayana*, *the Mahabharata*, the *Bhagwad Gita*, *the Puranas*, *the Upnishadas*, and *the Smritis*. The classical Sanskrit literature i.e. the works of Kalidasa, Bhavabhuti, Bana, Jayadeva and Bharatmuni, and the Buddhist and Jain literature in Pali, Prakrita and Apabhramsa have also proved to be the perennial sources of inspiration to them. Relying on such vastly rich heritage and unique cultural essence, Indian literature, no matter in any language or form, leads to the discovery of new strands of unity in India's diverse literary traditions. All these works have immensely influenced the thought-content of all Indian literatures together directly or indirectly and contributed to the unity of India's varied literary cultures. While referring to India's multilingual context, Jawaharlal Nehru, the first Prime-Minister of India and the founder-President of the Sahitya Akademi has observed: "Their root and inspiration have been much the same and the mental climate in which they have grown up has been similar. All of them have also faced the same type of impact from western thought and influence" (Sen v). Such a sharing of diverse experiences and creative expressions deepen our understanding of each other and enhance interliterary exchange. Therefore, we refer to the same entity by using the singular (Indian literature) and the plural (Indian literatures) without much differentiation or hesitation as both are considered acceptable. Again, if any Marathi, Bengali, Hindi, Telugu,

Punjabi, Kashmiri, Kannadiga, Malyalee person can be called an Indian, then why should we not call our multilingual literature as Indian literature?

K.M. George, an authority on Indian literature, opines in the *Preface* to his encyclopedic work *Comparative Indian Literature* that a survey of the regional language literatures like Bengali, Marathi, Hindi, Punjabi, Tamil, Kannada and Malayalam substantiates the possibility "to recognize some common characteristics which reveal their Indianans, some threads which hold them together despite their distinctive flavour and diverse associations" (x). Though language, region, religion, customs and costumes, food and drink do differ, even then the man, his sensibility his soul is essentially Indian. There is full accordance in their faith, beliefs, superstitions, ideas, imagination, anxiety, and so on. Dr. S. Radhakrishnan's observation from his *Foreword* to Sahitya Akademi's publication *Contemporary Indian Literature* (1957) is highly pertinent and summative in this regard: "There is a unity of outlook as the writers in different languages derive their inspiration from a common source and face more or less the same kind of experience, emotional and intellectual." This inherent unity of outlook and experience in spite of a vast multiplicity of religious ideologies and modes of living has been instrumental in uniting the various Indian literatures as a whole and single entity. The like-mindedness of the different writers in India evident in the use of images, symbols, etc. points towards the thought-currents and forces emanating from a common religious, political and socio-cultural background.

There is no doubt that we have a multiplicity of languages, literatures and cultures, but at the same time, it is also true that literature in different Indian languages creates visions that transcend the barriers of diversities. K.M. George's two analogies given in the preface to *Comparative Indian Literature* explain the close relationship between language and literature and thus emphasize the essential unity of Indian literature. How can 22 plants (languages recognized by the Sahitya Akademi) produce one flower? But that is the fact, although a miraculous one, like the concept of God—there are many incarnations, but one God. There are several varieties of roses each with a different hue, fragrance, shape and size, but they belong to the one species of flower called "rose." Can we not view India's different literatures as belonging to the same species, though with different colours and aromas? The second analogy is that of a traditional brass lamp with several wicks jutting out to be lit. The lamp and the oil is the same, but it is the wicks that determine the brightness of light. The light from various wicks merge imperceptibly and produce a brightness which is the totality of many segregated lights. Just as many wicks produce one light, India's many languages can produce one literature. In spite of their limitations, these analogies help us understand the oneness of Indian literature amidst the great vernacular diversity. Dr. Sukumar Azchicode's comment about India's linguistic plurality is quite supportive here: "The Indian Goddess of Wisdom, Saraswathy does not favour any one language, even Sanskrit, but consecrates and blesses all the languages impartially and with equal affection. She is reputed as *Sarva Bhasha Saraswathy*" (George xiv).

The vernacular literatures of India, called *bhasha literatures* by G.N. Devy, thus abound with several pan-Indian characteristics easily discernible from common themes/concerns, deeper socio-cultural bonds, shared history, stoical tolerance and hospitality, high reverence for elders, an unmistakable sense of unity and other parallel developments. These pan-Indian traits which are the major identifiers of Indianans have homogenized the grand symphony of Indian literature and thus contributed towards the emergence of a variegated but integrated Indian cultural tradition. What M. K. Naik and Shyamala A. Narayan have remarked while justifying Indian English literature as an inseparably integral part of Indian literature is relevant here:

> One must, indeed, deplore strongly the pernicious notion that Indian English literature and the regional literatures of India are aliens, or rivals or enemies fighting desperately for space. It is time they realized that they are actually blood brothers, born of the same mother. Indian literature is a vast ocean into which several mighty rivers merge. Among these are the Ganga of Hindi, the Hooghly of Bengali, the Krishna of Maharashtra, the Godavari of Andhra, the Tungabhadra of Karnataka and the Kaveri of Tamilnadu, and so on (Naik and Narayan 252-53).

This highly pertinent observation points to the growing need of cohesion and reciprocity between the *bhasha literatures* and Indian English literature, whether original or translated, and nurturing further the ideals of unity in diversity, cultural synthesis and pan-Indian character of India's literary labyrinth. In the end, one is inclined to agree, with Sukrita Paul Kumar's opinion regarding the interdependence of cultural diversity and linguistic plurality and literary traditions in India:

> India offers just a glimpse of the multicultural complexity that finds its creative expression in different languages at different points of time in Indian history . . . since language and literary traditions emerge from specific historical and political points of reference, they have to be studied from within their constantly changing cultural frames, and not in isolation. The boundaries drawn between various disciplines in academia then have to shed their rigidity to make space for a relatively more comprehensive view of lived reality (Kumar 1).

The institutions like the Sahitya Akademi, the National Book Trust, the All India Radio and a few regional agencies have played a significant role in knitting together India's varied literary treasures reflecting the many-sided bases of Indian culture and sense of integration through their multifarious activities. The sustained efforts of these organizations have proved fruitfully productive, to a great extent, in providing an overall glimpse of Indian literature and thus promoting the inter-literary traffic i.e. Adaan-Pradaan (Cultural Exchange) among the sister languages of India.

‘The Nativist Debate within *Subaltern Studies*: Locating Partha Chatterjee’s *Nationalist Thought and the Colonial World: A Derivative Discourse?*’

RAHUL JAYARAM

The Nationalist[1] school of Indian historiography predicates the Indian freedom movement upon the mobilizing activity and nationalist initiative of the educated bourgeoisie in late nineteenth and early twentieth century India. This bourgeoisie comprises of individuals from rural and urban backgrounds unevenly. As the movement expands, so do its constituents, regardless of internal Indian ethnic issues like caste, language or religion, among others. These personalities share common interests, come under an umbrella organization like the Indian National Congress (Congress Party), and mount the anti-colonial challenge. The Congress Party itself passes through spasmodic phases of intensity in its confrontation with British rule. It comes into existence a few decades after the 1857 Mutiny: the last “pan-Indian,” avowedly violent attempt to overthrow British colonialism. The Mutiny results in the dissolution of the East India Company and initiates a more consensual approach to ruling India, with greater indigenous input. Formed by a Briton, A.O. Hume, the early Congress Party comprises of nationalists like D.N. Naoroji (later a Member of the British Parliament) and G.K. Gokhale: both leaders of a ‘moderate’ hue in critiquing colonialism.[2] But with the onset of future leaders like Lokmanya Tilak, later Mahatma Gandhi, Jawaharlal Nehru and learned lower-caste leaders B.R. Ambedkar in the first half of the twentieth century, an 'extremist' variant within the Congress gains precedence. It is largely the politics of this form of nationalism that maps the Indian independence struggle, and is the object of our foci.[3]

The Nationalist historians are of the view that the Congress and its leading lights were responsible for the freedom struggle and in the shaping of "modern" India. It implies that the Congress was the one outfit constitutive of visionary individuals expansive enough to influence and rope in inhabitants of rural India despite their own privileges: aspects they were willing to utilize and/or forego for the nationalist cause. Working through a quasi-Gramscian framework, historians like Bipan Chandra are major proponents of this view.[4] They further this by giving reasons like "economic nationalism" and "secularism" as fundamental unifiers, which helped the nationalists to build base outside of urban India, while consolidating it within.[5] A phenomenon that they think signifies outstanding leadership, commitment and vision. So an urban, western-influenced but indigenously-rooted populace consolidates cohesively with the rural one. It undermines a past history of exploitation, ethnic conflict and casteism, to collect under a shared platform of anti-colonialism.

The Cambridge/Imperial 'school' disparages this view. Like the Nationalist school, there are internal variations to this historical perspective, as it originates during the Enlightenment. Initial ideologues like William Jones depict India in terms that would now be read as orientalist.[6] Future proponents like James and John Stuart Mill hold a more discriminating, but still patronizing view. The frame of reference shifts from culture to political economy: the Mills view India in blanket utilitarian terms. During a parliamentary session in the House of Lords, the younger Mill infamously calls India a "milch cow": to be exploited to the hilt for purposes of British imperialism and empire.[7] In general, the Cambridge school reads forms of anti-colonial Indian activity with deep suspicion. But even if the most recent developments, (i.e. ones relevant to us), are not as crudely condescending or deny the consolidation of colonialism, they are not short on vitriol. They project a thesis that suggests that India could not have been ruled, colonized or exploited—after the 1857 Mutiny—without Indian "collaboration." The nature of British colonialism had switched to a form of "consensual" hegemony. An infamous pragmatist like Thomas Babington Macaulay, figures the "creation of an Indian class . . . that was Indian by race and colour . . . but British in taste and thinking" to be the common goal for British and Indian interests.[8] It is out of this development that Indians in the latter half of the nineteenth century gain a stronger grasp of relating to the West, and English as a language. So, for the Cambridge group, Indian 'empowerment' as expressed by Indian nationalists was a British creation. Historians of this persuasion like Anil Seal, underline Indian participation in British colonialism.[9] What kept the "collaboration" going in the later nineteenth century was also "competition" amongst the evolving Indian elites, for colonial "favour." Their take on the Indian freedom struggle is controversial. Analysts like Judith Brown see the early freedom movement as a hoax: the elite, urban, educated, and privileged class selectively utilizes and manipulates rural and urban Indians in order to serve its own needs. In an extremely controversial account, Brown calls Gandhi a "subcontractor" for the Congress: specifically his attempts to rope in the lower castes and generically impoverished non-Hindus into the freedom movement.[101] The group extend their theses by explaining that India did not win independence just on its own, but it was the gradual weakening of the colonial state in the first half of the twentieth century (due to World Wars I & II, and related tensions), that led to British withdrawal. In such circumstances, the unifying ideas of the Congress like "secularism," its ideological spread, only come to serve specific purposes for the elites within the party.

The Marxist group posits that "modern India" was definitely built up by mass movements like nationalism, but there were also contradictions within it to create the kind of misgivings that the Cambridge group alleges. Of course, this does not mean that the Marxists side with the Cambridge group. Indeed, the Marxist contention is that an idea like nationalism did play a substantial role, but not to the extent the nationalists and Nationalist historians imagine. There were other factors contributing to the Indian freedom movement as well. The Marxist complaint is that the Nationalist understanding of Indian nationalism assumes a form that is all-explanatory for the various strands within the freedom movement. They are keen to recognize that there were dissonant stresses within the movement too—aspects that differed and did not align with Congress ideology. Some peasant and working-class struggles indeed consciously differentiated themselves from the Congress.[11] The Marxists attempt to gradually shift the focus towards class-relations, and comparable ethnic Indian social indicators like caste and religion. In their view, it is the complex internal interaction within Indian social categories and indices like the rural and urban working-class, the peasants and nationalists vis-à-vis colonialism, which asymmetrically overlap to form the ideological texture of the movement.[12]

Somewhat like the later *Subaltern Studies* group, the Marxists underline the influence of these elements on the independence movement. If the Nationalist group's approach of the relationship between nationalists and the rest of India is primarily a 'top-down' one, for the Marxists it is *also* the opposite. Therefore, the impetus now is on agrarian and industrial movements in India impacting upon the freedom struggle, as much as the other way round. The Marxists feel there is an ongoing dialectic here: an attempt to give equal attention to elites and non-elites alike, which is not as evident in Nationalist historiographical accounts and evident in Cambridge ones by and large, only to serve their stances. Major Marxist historians like Sumit Sarkar have tried to read some of these movements as evidences for a "history from below," suggesting even of "autonomous" and "subaltern" tendencies generating their power.[13] They also think these developments can be placed outside the domain of nationalist ideological dissemination, as the latter tended to get intermittently warped in elite bourgeois concerns.

It is this last point—the nationalist bourgeoisie's tilted perspective of the masses—that the *Subaltern Studies* group picks up and extends. They are of the view that *all* previous historiographies of modern India have been prejudiced in one form or another, playing up the powers of their respective predispositions to an extent that they lose sight of some basic issues at hand: one of the most crucial of these being the voice of the colonized subject, i.e. the "subaltern."[14] Moreover, these social histories come to envisage more a form of elite rhetoric, which renders the "subaltern" silent. *Subaltern Studies* appropriate analytical methods from post-modernism and post-structuralism, for these purposes.[15] They attempt to uncover histories "suppressed" by "nationalism" and try to show that agrarian and industrial groups manifest a tendency for "individual agency" of an extremely sophisticated kind that has not been acknowledged or addressed by "mainstream" historiographies. For example, in an essay like "Gandhi as Mahatma," historian Shahid Amin portrays peasant behaviour in Gorakhpur (on the now Indo-Nepal border), as registered through a series of Hindi newspaper clippings. Despite their exploitation and illiteracy, these peasants are astute enough to utilize the image of Gandhi to suit their own advantage. Once they realize that this addition has a set of problems which would harm their interests, they retreat from their initial positions which run counter to Nationalist historiographical portrayals of the same.[16] In similar ways, the group stake the claim for "individual" histories which have been muted by past narratives. Herein, the peasant, worker or tribe, assumes special significance, and the Nationalist view of them put on the crucible. As is evident, the *Subaltern* group's tricky theoretical positioning is not entirely off the Marxist axis, and offers space for radical investigation. Distinguished Marxist historians like Sumit Sarkar were part of the earlier volumes. The early researches roughly deployed Said-like, Foucauldian parameters of power- and discourse-analysis as evident in *Orientalism*, which elicited aspects of peasant and working-class behaviour projecting personal, even non-nationalist concerns. In due course though, the group's emphasis on "subaltern agency" expressed itself in the form of "micro histories" which appeared devoid of larger, connected concerns.[17]

Sumit Sarkar parted ways with the group in the late 1980s. In a contentious essay titled "Decline of the Subaltern in *Subaltern Studies*" he brought out the collective's flexibilities and limitations, but was specifically critical of post-modern influences that morphed the subaltern subject into a self-enclosed entity, a "fragment."[18] There was further controversy in store though. Even as the later volumes appeared to venerate the colonized (and post-colonial) subaltern as a "fragment," they smacked of religious (primarily Hindu) revivalist and nativist tendencies. In an argument that was not entirely original, the subaltern, the *Subaltern* group argued, did not cease to exist after British colonialism. The new enemy happened to be the post-colonial Indian state itself, peopled as it was with bourgeois Congress elites. The Congress-led freedom movement's defining mantras like "secularism" appeared to exacerbate a lot of the social divisions that remained. This found a reaction in several ways for several segments: through religious revivalism for upper-caste Hindus; through radical Marxism for some lower-caste Hindu groups; through Muslim fundamentalism for certain Islamic sections; and minority lobbying for other Indian ethnic groups—all of whom had personal squabbles of their own in relation to one another, but found a shared enemy in the Congress.[19]

It is imperative to underline these facts as they help to exactly historically place *Subaltern Studies*, and aid us in grasping their real concerns: the problematic, continuing and *transforming* presence of subalterns in independent India. In a way, the collective also endeavoured to trace the dense genealogy of the Indian subaltern to the present, but as the historical contexts shifted, so did their analytical lenses. In the Marxist eyes of Sumit Sarkar, the later features of the (colonial and post-colonial) subaltern, exhibit the politically unwieldy aspects of appropriating post-modernism: what he reads as meshing politically aware social history into an apolitical cultural studies realm.[20] Drawing upon the arguments of Aijaz Ahmad,[21] Fredric Jameso[22] and ArifDirlik,[23] a critique like "Postmodernism and the Writing of History" echoed the dangers of the newer volumes, their culturally uncritical[24] (and so legitimating) estimation of present, self-absorbed subaltern politics.

Subaltern Studies social scientists retorted that in a globalizing India, already part of the process of multi-national capitalism, previous theoretical fundamentals—like the concept of the nation-state, nationalism etc. for instance: all mantras that characterized the Enlightenment-obsessed Congress, Gandhian and Nehruvian vision—did not play as much a role. It is indeed against their waning value that the current cultural, "revivalist" flux emerges; a decline which is not specific to India. If these subalterns of contemporary India (ironically including upper-caste Hindus: the majority community in India) behave in a conservative, sectarian way, it is not because of the post-modernism of the *Subaltern Studies* group. It is the post-modernism provoked by the Indian/Third World present.[25]

This paper will try to uncover the intricacies of nativism and nationalism at their roots in the colonial period, through the influential writings of a primary *Subaltern Studies* member: Partha Chatterjee.

I

> Elitist historiography is of course not without its uses. It helps us to know more of the structure of the colonial state, the operation of its various organs in certain historical circumstances, the nature of the alignment of classes which sustained it; of some aspects of the ideology of the elite as the dominant ideology of the period; of the contradictions between the two elites and the complexities of their mutual oppositions and coalitions; of the role of the some of the more important British and Indian personalities and elite organizations. Above all it helps us understand the *ideological character of historiography itself*. [Emphasis added].
>
> What, however, historical writing of this kind cannot do is to explain Indian nationalism for us. For it fails to acknowledge, far less interpret, the contribution made by the people *on their own*, that is *independently of the elite* to the making and development of this nationalism.[26]

And, in this fashion, runs *Subaltern Studies* editor, Ranajit Guha's famous manifesto against the existing historiography of colonial, modern India. It points out limitations, complexes, contradictions in present Indian history writing, and disparages all these viewpoints as necessarily "elitist." While acknowledging the orchestrated nature of historical narratives (including its own), the argument sets the base for its real aim: recovering the voice of the colonized Indian peasant or worker. But however raucously it defines itself against other historical strains, it leaves its exact theoretical stance unexplained.[27]

This is brought out fundamentally in the collective's understanding of notions of modern Indian "nationalism." Diverse essays in the first three volumes of *Subaltern Studies* dealt with the nature and specifics of peasant, industrial and working-class consciousness, and their linkages with Indian nationalism. These amply tried to prove peasant and working-class initiative in terms that did not fit, or arbitrarily *chose* not to fit with the nationalist framework during and outside key phases of the freedom struggle, while still utilizing the discursive powers and reach of this force.[28] However, these issues too had to be explained—through and against—problematic conceptions like nationalism, its offshoots and discourses. Even at their most independent, individualistic, "autonomous" moments, the subalterns' agency had to be grasped in terms of established (though supple) historical paradigms. So, evidences of independent subaltern action contrary to prevailing perspectives were still screened through nationalist lenses to gain any qualified meaning. The problem thus, was not of the proof of subaltern initiative (which lay scattered), but of evolving modes of its reception and interpretation. Nationalism as a prism in its present form did not serve this purpose; indeed, it undermined it and produced the types of history these critics were fuming against. The idea of nationalism had to be reread in an Indian/Third World situation, *theoretically*. This undertaking meant a deeper, different questioning of Marxist frames that characterized Indian historiography. It also involved an investigation into the dense lineage of paradigmatic ideas like the Indian nation, civil society, Gandhi, Gandhian ideology, religion, caste, women, Islam, culture etc. all of which complicatedly influenced moments of subaltern activity or emerged during its numerous processes. Either way, the *Subaltern Studies* project had to become as much a theoretical one, as it was of germane evidence accumulation. The project had to thus intervene within the history of ideas of the historiography of modern India. The idea of nationalism was at the heart of this matter.

II

First published in 1986, Partha Chatterjee's *Nationalist Thought and the Colonial World: A Derivative Discourse?* attempted to come to grips with this issue.[29] Chatterjee launches a spirited attack on the validity of 'nationalism' as a category for understanding colonial and post-colonial Third World societies. Besides a range of critiques on the current state-of-play in western academe regarding the status of nationalism,[30] Chatterjee's elaborations try to extract from the colonized, elite, bourgeoisie's behaviour—especially in their unwieldy absorption and application of Enlightenment ideas like Science, Reason etc.—evidence of an intellectual anxiety that has not been identified as so. He considers nationalism and its modern referents viz. the nation-state, civil society, et al "as a problem" innate within Indian historiography, the larger domain of post-colonial studies and western academe themselves. Summarily put—especially through Chatterjee's main focus on colonization in India—the current condition of nationalism appears inherently flawed, or a frame with internal rigidities, ambivalences and silences. The situation gets pronounced in the case of liberal Marxist accounts, which form the mainstream historiography of Third World societies like India:

> More often than not they [liberal Marxists] have adopted the same methods as those of the liberals—either a resort to *sociologism*, i.e. fitting nationalism to certain universal and inescapable sociological constraints of the modern age, or alternatively, reducing the two contending trends within nationalism, one traditional and conservative and the other rational and progressive, to their sociological determinants, or invoking *functionalism*, i.e. taking up an appropriate attitude towards a specific nationalism by reference to its consequences for universal history.[31]

Thus mainstream, nationalist and Marxist Indian historiography exhibit all the elements of a "liberal dilemma," but with few exceptions, never recognize them likewise. The differences between Marxism and nationalism as distinct historiographical implements too, collapse. Correspondingly, the bulk of current Indian historiography utilizes this "either/or approach," with a preference for the former, "*sociologism*": i.e. decolonization by and large, as an "eventual . . . indigenous . . . bourgeois-led" movement bearing (alleged) representative claims with agrarian and working-class interests. In Chatterjee's view, the dense relationship between these inveterate Indian entities and their offshoots/subdivisions in the context of colonialism, is the site of a sociological interplay that blanket terms like "nationalism" or "class-struggle" sand their variants, cannot sufficiently explain.[32]

For example, with notable exceptions (like Gandhi), most major colonial intellectual Indian thought of the later nineteenth and early twentieth centuries, dissented against British colonization only through key areas of difference. These were grounds where basic interests clashed: a claim seconded by nationalist and Marxist historiography. Ideas like "economic nationalism" expounded by them as a prime reason for the movement coming under the Indian National Congress, gained currency, even while not accounting for agrarian and working-class initiative, autonomy or dissent.[33] The representative claims of this force thus became questionable. In all fairness, Chatterjee also locates sundry arguments and monographs within these historiographies that did identify the shortcomings of Marxist praxis in an Indian locale. But these few, somewhat differing narratives still aligned with existing historiographies: they did not question nationalism essentially, when related events themselves did.[34] At the same time, Chatterjee does not serve a concrete, working alternative to well-entrenched academic praxis. Most of his arguments only offer interesting or controversial readings of the various shades of the "liberal dilemma" in colonial Indian intellectual thought, the distortions produced in aligning them, even while working through expansive lenses of nationalism.

This issue of the "liberal dilemma" is specifically brought to light in his analysis of the evolution and character of colonial India's bourgeoisie. The process whereby western social structures were grafted onto Indian contexts and moulded to its demands—like English education—provided the very platform for the development of an urban, westernized Indian bourgeoisie in the nineteenth and twentieth centuries that led the anti-colonial struggle. The struggle's unifying ideas were concepts and slogans like sovereignty, and ideals like Reason and Independence. Obviously, the struggle did not end with a replication of British rule with an Indian one alone, while co-opting the structures put in place by colonialism. Ousting the British was just the starting point; a long drawn-out one at that. The long haul meant the logical conclusion of this process: establishing post-colonial, independent India as a rational, enlightened nation-state that dealt with the world (i.e. the West), and on an equal footing; a never-ending task.[35]

The ideological entrapment of the colonized elite through Enlightenment discourses like nationalism appears complete at this point. On the one hand, it is nationalism that gets them to decolonize, but also imposes upon them seemingly unattainable targets on the other. Independent India, with its several legacies and pasts, could not afford to mimic the West entirely either. It had to partially indigenize it; reconcile the West with her progressive indigenous traits. Thus nationalism within the history of this thought, morphs from a colonial issue into a "civilizational" one. Few, like Gandhi, have the foresight to argue it always was. This makes leaders like him reject the scientific, technological, materialistic "modern" European society entirely, while trying to not come across as anti-bourgeois. Evidently, this phrasing is pregnant with tension, contingent upon the struggle's local and national particularities, and hence never binding. Such articulations run the risk of assuming indigenous (read 'nativist') terms during various phases, causing much dismay to popular, pro-Western, socialistic nationalists like Nehru.[36]

Chatterjee identifies the complex intellectual fashioning of a "modern" Indian society attempting to reconcile the spirit of the East with the structures of the West, as a central uncertainty within the "liberal dilemma." It is an undertaking marked by confusion and "shot through with tension." Even if Indian historiography recognized these multiple ambivalences during key or stray moments, it weaved them into the framework of nationalism as a highlight: i.e. basically, the celebration of a home-grown intelligentsia that challenged colonial supremacy *on its own terms* and *despite internal differences*: an interpretation rife with irony.

For Chatterjee, outlining this relationship between the "elites" and the "masses" in the colonial context signally proves the complications in utilizing western models. With the exception of Gandhi, the manner of the anti-colonial challenge mounted by the nationalist intelligentsia was still predicated upon terms appropriated from the West *through* colonialism. This assimilation was not a straightforward one-to-one correspondence, but involved an intricate set of negotiations. The idea of nationalism in Indian circumstances meant something radically different from European ones. To contrast roughly, Indian nationalist thought had to factor in indigenous identity and cultural indices that could well-nigh undermine the very definition of nationalism in its western sense. In the western experience these matters did not appear to impact, take over or sabotage their nationalist projects so fundamentally. Nationalist thought in post-Enlightenment West had a singularity of its own, unique to imperializing Western Europe: it was an "autonomous discourse." On the contrary, "for the non-European world . . . nationalist thought [did] not constitute an autonomous discourse."[37] Such ideas needed to coalesce, continuing (and transforming) pre-colonial issues, new bourgeois interests, as well as inveterate inter-cultural markers (casteism, untouchability, sati for instance). The conception of the nation in non-Western colonial ethos was inherently bound to be a relativist one. So, nationalist thought in the colonial world, emerged as more circumscribed than liberating vis-à-vis its antecedents in Western Europe. The discourse of this bourgeois intellectual thought, with few exceptions, was a "derivative" one in comparison to its "autonomous" western counterparts.

Strangely, while trumpeting the autonomy of Indian subalterns in his other work for *Subaltern Studies* and its correlates, the Indian bourgeoisie's own autonomy vis-à-vis colonialism, is a likelihood Chatterjee does not fully consider. This near-tautology—individual/communitarian agency as intrinsic givens defining 'elitist' groups—seems a curious slippage in his argument. Further, the relationship of the Enlightenment, its impact on Indian nationalism via colonialism, appears to evolve into a strange a-historical vacuum. It runs the risk of homogenizing and ossifying all three categories involved. The absorption of the Enlightenment was an eclectic one, with various elements either imbibed or weeded out; choices made or discarded. An example none better illustrated than in Chatterjee's own explication of Gramsci's definition of "passive revolution" as applicable to Indian ethos:

> The nationalist leadership in such [colonial] situations cannot resort to a 'war of movement'; a 'war of position' becomes necessary . . . Will the 'war of position' be one in which a 'modernization' of these cultural institutions precedes the phase of independent capitalist development and formation of the nation-state, or is the replacement of the colonial state by a national one itself the precondition for capitalist development and 'modernization' . . . The characteristic form of 'passive revolution' in colonial countries follows the second path. That is to say, the 'war of position' implies a political-ideological programme by which the largest possible national alliance is built up against the political rule of the colonial power.[38]

The development of this stance—especially after the Indian Mutiny of 1857—was a well-nigh consensual conclusion for most of India's bourgeoisie. It did not demand a systemic upheaval of colonialism, but sought a "non-dramatic," dialogic transposition within its power apparatuses. This is a basic and striking example of agency and appropriation, even if it smacks somewhat of bourgeois complacency or collaboration.[39] The lack of comparable, related assumptions, considerations and other contextual details colour Chatterjee's canvas, producing telling effects, positions and paradoxes.

III

The 1857 Mutiny and its aftermath are watersheds in Indian history.[40] They also present crucial phases of nationalist thought's continuing confrontation with colonialism in the middle of the nineteenth century. In his illuminating readings of Bengali litterateur Bankimchandra Chattopadhyay (1838-94), famously known as Bankim,[41] Chatterjee identifies some of the central (if not completely new) tensions that marked this period. It is ostensibly, a starting-point of another trajectory within Indian nationalist thought:

> Let us begin with the question of power: why has India been a subject nation for such a long time? Bankim considers one obvious answer to this question: because Indians lack physical strength and courage; because as the Europeans always allege, the 'Hindoos' are 'effeminate.' Yet this answer is obviously false . . . the first is that Indians lack a natural desire for liberty. Some Indians probably nurse a vague feeling that independence is better than subjection, but never has this feeling become a compelling desire; never have a majority of Indians fought for their liberty:
>
>> For more than three thousand years, Aryans have fought Aryans, or Aryans against non-Aryans, or non-Aryans against non-Aryans—Magadh has fought Kanauj, Kanauj has fought Delhi, Delhi has fought Lahore, Hindus have battled against Pathans, Pathans against Mughals, Mughals against the English—all of these people have fought against one another and continually stoked the fires of war in this country. But all of these were battles against kings; the bulk of Hindu society has never fought for or against anyone. Hindu kings or the rulers of Hindustan have been repeatedly conquered by alien people, but it cannot be said that the bulk of Hindu society has never

> been vanquished in battle, *because the bulk of Hindu society has never gone to war*. [Italics added]
>
> And this led to the second great reason for the subjection of India: the lack of solidarity in Hindu society.[42]

The reference of this citation from Bankim to the recent (post-Mutiny) Indian/Bengali past is revealing. It echoes much of the doubts; ethnic (anti-Muslim) prejudice; noted stereotypes of "physical weakness"; complacency and fatalism that wrought Hindu self-perception. But beneath these attacks and asides, is Bankim's aim to rectify these cultural frailties *in a new social situation*: a factor Chatterjee does not quite qualify.

It is this recognition of a new social situation, which informs Bankim's current ideas of "Hindu society" now understood in nationalistic, near-autonomous terms. It also is one of the first instances within this discourse, wherein Hindu society (here synonymous with Indian society) gets explicitly explained through western categories like the nation. (Bankim's imagination was as much a product of English education, the Enlightenment, and was part of what is known in Indian historiography, as the nineteenth century "Bengal Renaissance."[43]) It was thus the classic colonial conundrum: an inchoate attempt to forge a nationality that matched up to images of western progress put out by colonialism. Chatterjee though, rightly locates in Bankim's work, one of the first steps of the entrapment of nationalist thought within Enlightenment discourse. Instead of critiquing western Reason and Progress fundamentally—i.e. their role as proponents of colonialism, economic exploitation and the recent Mutiny—they are instead held as gospel: an ideological basis for this bourgeoisie. However, the manner of achieving this idea of the nation was fraught with contradictions and anxieties. One of its first tasks was to establish that India's past (and by implication her present and future)[44] were/would be glorious, possessing the potential to equal and outdo the West *on its own premises*.

Bankim's construction of the nation with or without its several pasts, faiths and traditions, adds on cultural dimensions, but becomes a civilizational issue. For India, in his eyes, has been a subject nation not for the last fifty or hundred years, but for the last "seven hundred years."[45]

It is this social context of nationalist thought, wherein voices like Bankim view British rule in India as beneficial for Indian society. There are several areas where Bankim naively acknowledges British rule as entirely salutary: policies like laissez-faire; some highly exploitative taxation measures in Bengal; and Britain's handling of Mughal India, Muslims and Islam.[46] But regardless of these developments, Bankim's main attack is against Hinduism *per se*. He unequivocally reads the failure of Hinduism—especially some of its dominant internal strands stressing 'retrogressive' aspects like 'other-worldliness'[47]—in bestowing meaning, order, direction and structure to civil life—as the root-cause for India's current stagnation. The "rationalizing" account of Hinduism also becomes one producing relativist and nativist complexes:

> 'Knowledge is power: that is the slogan of Western civilization. 'Knowledge is salvation' that is the slogan of Hindu civilization' . . . the westerners have found power. Have we found salvation?[48]

Even as these and other elements work themselves out in his hypotheses, the reinvention of Hinduism appears to have its cul-de-sacs. Obviously, 'rationalizing' Hinduism has its limitations and grey areas. But these differences are tided over in a contemporary reading of ancient Hindu epics like *Mahabharata*, where a figure like Krishna is portrayed as 'spiritual' and 'modern' at the same time.[49] Remarkably, Bankim also tries to prove concepts like the Hindu Holy Trinity through modern science: Brahma (Life-Creator), Vishnu (Life-Preserver) and Shiva (Life-Destroyer) as rationally consistent spiritual conceptions.[50] Perhaps the most interesting aspect within this cultural fusion is of

Bankim's resolution that a construction of 'modern Hindu religion' rendered the East 'spiritually superior': a cultural trait that was harmonious with ideals of Progress and Reason, and elements that were missing in the current western zeitgeist.[51] These elaborate intellectual initiatives lend legitimacy for an informed cultural revival.[52] In the process, Bankim's argument prepares the ground for an even stronger assertion: the indigenous pursuit of power i.e. 'dharma' (duty). The reinterpreted figure of Krishna from *Mahabharata* embodies the "traditional" and the "modern" with the kind of definitive machismo required for these times. There are areas in Bankim's arguments wherein violence becomes ethically justifiable, quite in contrast to western orientalist perceptions of India (which he decries):

> Krishna too had little taste for war. But war was often justified in religion. In cases of *just war* Krishna would engage in it. When he engaged in war, he was invincible . . . Krishna is the true ideal for man. The Hindu ideal is superior to the Christian ideal [i.e. Jesus] . . . . Krishna himself was householder, diplomat, warrior, law-giver, saint and preacher; as such he represents a complete human ideal for all these kinds of people.[53] [Italics added]

Nationalism thereby is construed and constructed in cultural terms, with moral and ethical bases. Chatterjee underlines the sheer intensity of justification imbuing Bankim's revivalist aims, through the latter's idea of a modernized, 'pure' Hinduism. But a deeper tension masking this intensity for 'purity' is also one of inter-cultural and economic anxiety. Bankim's initiatives are essentially elitist, reaching out to the upper middle-class of Bengalis which form his audience (regardless of his frequent jibes at them). This hypothesis also leaves Islam out of the Indian question, and considers education a privilege of the upper classes. But Chatterjee places these crucial aspects within nationalist thought separately in his critique, when there is sound reason to read them together: upper-class Hinduism and its antipathy each towards Islam, the lower castes, and lower classes, were inveterate Indian historical traits. Broadly speaking, relationships between culture and economy in this Indian context have proved to be two sides of the same coin; an analytical mode that does not reduce personal nuances of either of these respective categories. The problem is, Chatterjee's threading out of these elements individually, do not add anything new to what we know.

Furthermore, a figure like Bankim is a clear embarrassment to the later "secular nationalism" of the Indian National Congress and nationalist historiography: a case in point for *Subaltern Studies*. But the issue is both these facts (Hindu elitism on the one hand, the constitution of the Congress on the other) run against each other. They do not evenly lend themselves for appropriation by *Subaltern Studies* discourse even if they apparently appear to. Bankim becomes effective for Chatterjee in pointing out (not altogether originally) cracks and holes gaping within early nationalist thought, and critically, within the issues arising out of utilizing western nationalism in an Indian milieu. But does that make Bankim's thought and this nationalism—as Chatterjee would have it—essentially "derivative"?

Chatterjee highlights Bankim as a "moment of departure," but falls short of acknowledging individual autonomy at work. Notwithstanding how derived the beginnings of this "patriotic consciousness" might appear it is identifiable intellectual agency yet:

> This is the characteristic form of nationalist thought in its moment of departure. It is born out of the encounter of a patriotic consciousness with the framework of knowledge imposed upon it by colonialism. It leads inevitably to an elitism of the intelligentsia, rooted in the vision of a radical regeneration of national culture. In Bankim's time, the heyday of colonial rule, this vision could not find any viable political means to actualize itself. Instead, it became a dream: a utopian political community in which the nation was the Mother, once resplendent in wealth and beauty, now in tatters. Relentlessly, she exhorts a small band of her sons, those of

> them who are brave and enlightened, to vanquish the enemy and win back her honour. Imprisoned within the rationalist framework of his theoretical discourse and *powerless to reject its dominating implications*, Bankim lived out his dreams of liberation in his later novels.[54] [Italics added]

It is indeed paradoxical that Chatterjee's own depiction of Bankim contrasting Krishna and Christ a few pages earlier, clearly reveals Bankim excoriating orientalist perceptions of Hinduism while imbibing other influences from Europe.[55] It is ample proof for nationalist thought's capacity to reject colonialism's "dominating implications."

Another interesting facet emerging from Chatterjee's inferences is his hesitation to identify within Bankim's formulations, the roots of nativism and connected impulses inside nationalist thought. Locating these developments now becomes useful, as it surfaces spasmodically during the Gandhian phase of nationalism that follows. Chatterjee's critique constantly refers to mythic ideas like "Mother India," the related repertory of symbolisms that exemplify Indian political and cultural ideological dissemination. In his characterization of Bankim's thought as an embodiment of irreconcilable ambivalences between a "forward-looking rationality . . . and archaic emotionalism," Chatterjee underlines the deep difference that defines "*all* nationalist thought." An aspect wherein the "*modern* and the *national* . . . are part of the same discourse . . . yet distinct and opposed."[56] In his view, it is this "unresolved contradiction" between paradigmatic co-relates, which basically admits for disparate, even diametrically opposed worldviews to take root under the broad ambit of an incipient colonial nationalism, while contouring this nationalism severally. The unwieldy tapestry formed by these plural conceptions of nationalism, pattern elite discourse. But most critically, this discourse has to be rendered compatible to a largely agrarian society forming the bulk of the Indian populace: a case in point for subaltern and *Subaltern Studies*' politics.[57] It is in carrying out the process of this ideological, communicative alignment—which we would see in Gandhi later—that nativist/near-nativist factors within nationalist thought spring up. Subaltern idioms too, get phrased, generated or appropriated out of these processes. They form some of the significant material of the *Subaltern Studies* oeuvre.

Given all of this, these are developments that beg the following historical/sociological questions: does not the later nativism (or a type of "romanticism" as Chatterjee calls it) have its own—albeit complicated—provenance here itself? If it is the simultaneous (but ambiguous), convergence and divergence, of the "modern" and the "national" that primarily shapes internally nuanced nationalist thought—readily identifiable within Bankim—does it not call for a recognition of related impulses at this intersection itself? Tracing the origins of this nativism becomes germane, because the "multiple messaging"—the unique communicative mode through which Gandhi tried to reach out and reconcile distinct, discrete, even opposed segments within Indian society—was fraught with internal complexes, and evidently, not a novelty. Bankim attempted likewise, on a smaller, though elite, scale. Do not the context-specific variations of nativist/near-nativist tensions that emanate from Bankim's elaborations and ambivalences, become an observable trait worthy of individual, germane analysis *per se*?

It is questions such as these that come up in different forms in Chatterjee's critique of Gandhi, but the connections to Bankim's thought, quizzically, remain to be made. Chatterjee's characterization of Bankim as a "moment of departure" wherein the basic contradiction between the "modern" and the "national" defines early nationalist discourse, and Gandhi as the "moment of manoeuvre" whereby this contradiction is shrewdly utilized for political mobilization and peasant inclusion, leaves an unexplained gap between these two phases, yet. A yawning grey area—the roots of nativism within nationalist thought—is left unexplored, and its dynamic, unresolved.

IV

In the case of Mahatma Gandhi,[58] Chatterjee identifies a couple of issues that are of immediate import. One of these corresponds to Bankim directly, but it is a point Gandhi takes up and extends: the nature of British colonialism and the manner of mounting the anti-colonial challenge.

In Chatterjee's observation of Gandhi, we can connect with an acumen that refuses to succumb to colonialism's "dominating implications," contrary to the way that Bankim's thinking does. This escape seems to come about via Gandhi's elementary contestation of Enlightenment frameworks. Gandhi excoriates their *global* impact: the economic drain on the colonies; and the socio-psychological impact of "modernity" on both colonies *and* metropolitan countries. Gandhi appears to recognize the warps and traps within western influences, and refuses to be bound by their relativist chains. Instead we see a formulation—in *his* historical situation—in the shape of a critique of western "modern civilization" assuming conspicuous ethical shades. It is a trait that has a veneer of resemblance to Bankim's absorption of these categories too, but the similarity ends no sooner:

> On the surface it is indeed a critique of modern civilization, 'a civilization only in name.' And the argument proceeds, as in many other nationalist writers, from a consideration of the question: Why is India a subject nation? To start with Gandhi's answer too seems to run along the same lines. He too is concerned with locating the sources of Indian weakness than putting the blame on British avarice and deceit. But the emphasis is not so much on the elements of culture. Gandhi points much more forcefully to the moral failure:
>
> > The English have not taken India; we have given it to them. They are not in India because of their strength, but because we keep them . . . Recall the Company Bahadur. Who

> made it Bahadur? They had not the slightest intention at the time of establishing a kingdom. Who assisted the Company's officers? Who was tempted at the sight of their silver? Who bought their goods? History testifies that we did all this . . . When our Princes fought among themselves they sought the assistance of the Company Bahadur. That corporation was versed alike in commerce and war. It was unhampered by questions of morality . . . Is it not then useless to blame the English for what we did at the time? . . . It is truer to say that we gave India to the English than that India was lost.
>
> It was a moral failure on the part of Indians that led to the conquest of India.[59]

The idea of Gandhi's "moral" critique though, is far more complicated than it might appear. It is intricately embedded with the role and purpose of civil society in order to bring about positive social change; resist or transcend the deleterious impact of forces like colonialism. But it differs from Bankim's somewhat comparable analyses, as Gandhi establishes positions that are understandable in various *new* ways:

> One, that India's current subjection is due to a lack of moral responsibility; two, the way out of this subjection lay in identifying that the problem is not of imitating and attempting to get even with the West, specially vis-à-vis its material advancements, but in severely contesting these trappings of "modern civilization" India has fallen prey to; and three, therefore to devise means through which contemporary civil society can develop ways to handle these issues, beginning with the cognizance of India's personal responsibility/voluntary error, in ushering in colonization. Therefore, an *existential* reinterpretation of the function of contemporary Indian civil society precedes the ouster of colonialism. This implied that British rule was not at fault intrinsically, and as Gandhi famously continues, India would still have had "English rule without the Englishman."[60]

The difference with Bankim becomes clear. For Gandhi, the issue of "modern civilization" is the heart of the matter; but in a strangely "ethical" way, it is a problem as much for the colonizers as it is for the colonized. From a specifically Indian perspective, regardless of her subjection, Gandhi argues that India still possesses the agency and potential to emerge from her current morass. The acknowledgment of the material, "consumerist" nature of contemporary "modernity" as a universal issue and not just a colonial one, transpires as a very qualified and significant first step in consciously stepping off any of the booby-traps slipped in by western discourses. It aims to provide a strong rationale for the nationalist bourgeoisie in India to shy away from materialist temptations, while simultaneously focussing on vital indigenous issues. The centrality of morality as a critical weapon imbues Gandhi's continuing formulations, emitting striking effects.

In a veiled sense, Gandhi's take on current industrialization in India by British colonialism opens up a range of connected concerns and complexes. It situates modernity's emphasis on materiality as the root-cause for the collapse of internal, indigenous, rural forms of subsistence in India. Gandhi underscores that while this phenomenon is primarily due to colonial economic exploitation, this line of thought only restates the obvious, while obscuring its other dimensions, significant for Indians *per se*. Industrialization is at the heart of the evil of modern civilization because it puts in a system—which despite achieving and surpassing its original, apparently egalitarian designs—also succeeds in generating contagious side effects. As Chatterjee rightly observes, in this system:

> productive capacities of human labour are multiplied several times, creating increased wealth and happiness. Gandhi argues that far from achieving these objectives, modern civilization makes man a prisoner of his craving for luxury and self-indulgence, releases the forces of unbridled competition and thereby brings upon society the evils of poverty, disease, war and suffering. It is precisely because modern civilization looks at man as a limitless consumer.[61]

And Gandhi himself later on:

> When I read Mr. Dutt's *Economic History of India*, I wept; and as I think of it again my heart sickens. It is machinery that has impoverished India. It is difficult to measure the harm that Manchester has done to us. It is due to Manchester that *Indian handicraft has all but disappeared.*[62] [Italics added]

In a scenario like this, it is the resurgence of Indian "handicraft," India's indigenous proxies and correlates; in short, her overall internal, *pre-colonial potential*, which has to collectively counter the material ills of present modernity. Gandhi famously takes up the case for developing *khadi* (homespun textiles), as the substitute for cloth finished and processed in Britain.

The appropriating act is rife with complex symbolism, pregnant with the dense "multiple messaging" which would become a hallmark of Gandhi's public communication and ideological dissemination. It also provides scope for the symbolic reconciliations between the "modern" and the "national" divergence that Chatterjee identified in Bankim previously. Moreover, Gandhi's attempt here tries to align elite nationalist discourse with basic peasant and lower working-class needs. The attempt to bend this nationalism for such objectives, appears as anti-industrial, anti-modern, (even anti-elite nationalist[63]) in its rhetoric. But Gandhi's line of reasoning could still curiously pass off as modern. Ironically, it is Gandhi's rationale for anti-modernity, which unconsciously renders him as modern.

Chatterjee observes that Gandhi constantly tried to "emphasize the strict economic argument against heavy industrialization in a large agrarian economy with an abundance of under-employed labour."[64] For all of Gandhi's indigenous nationalist impulses, the reasoning for the feasibility of *khadi* could also be read through purely economic bases of social production:

> khadi is the only true economic proposition in terms of the millions of villagers until such time, if ever, when a better system of sup-

> plying work and adequate wages for every able-bodied person above the age of sixteen, male or female, is found for his field, cottage or even factory in every one of the villages of India . . . khadi must hold for any length of time we can think of.[65]

Gandhi's assertion again compares with Bankim, but his rationalizing frame departs markedly, by further modulation. It is one of the few instances where nationalism, morality and nativism within nationalist thought appear to converge, but escapes Chatterjee's attention:

> I am always reminded of one thing which the well-known British economist Adam Smith has said in his famous treatise *The Wealth of Nations*. In it he has described some economic laws as universal and absolute. Then he has described certain situations which may be an obstacle to the operation of these laws. These disturbing factors are the human nature, the human temperament or altruism inherent in it. *Now, the economics of khadi is just the opposite of it. Benevolence which is inherent in human nature is the very foundation of the economics of* khadi. What Adam Smith has described as pure economic activity based merely on the calculations of profit and loss is a selfish attitude and it is an obstacle to the development of khadi; and *it is the function of a champion of khadi to counteract this tendency.*[66] [Italics added]

As is evident, explaining away solely the uses and economic practicality of *khadi* as such, do not suffice. Mundane acts like weaving cloth and spinning the wheel, quite literally, need more 'spin' if they are to have popular resonance and mobilizing power. Unsurprisingly, it is characterizing this activity as morally superior vis-à-vis western colonial practice that renders it popular and doable for the masses. Simultaneously, the practical premise behind it disarms the nationalist bourgeoisie from criticizing it, as this idea is not conceptually anti-modern altogether: indeed, it represents a unique merger.

In the process to achieve this though, Gandhi has to resort to a type of ethical rhetoric that produces impulses and expressions like "khadi's . . . inherent benevolence": nativism, for short, which Chatterjee fails to identify likewise. Furthermore, *khadi* also becomes a clear instance, wherein Chatterjee's idea of the unsettled paradox between the modern and the national within nationalist thought finds a resolution. It appears to align both sections, but again, the manner of arriving at this reconciliation seems to need, and ends up evoking, nativist proclivities. Funnily, the generation of this type of an idiom with multiple messages (and recognized nativist tendencies) embedded, is a noted trait within subaltern initiatives. In the context of Gandhi—i.e. his relationship vis-à-vis Indian peasant consciousness, and the latter's registration of his plural, manoeuvrable powers—the issue of nativism (even while remaining intangible) becomes particularly tense. Its complex presence in various field researches and writings of *Subaltern Studies*' different volumes is distinguishing.[67] Considering this situation, it becomes all the more intriguing to find Chatterjee missing this angle (given the skein of thought he disaggregates) altogether.

On another related aspect, the location of nativism at this intersection within nationalist thought appears to produce even more interesting, and contentious developments. One of the defining issues inside Gandhi's thought is the establishment of the post-colonial, independent Indian state. Interestingly, Gandhi's formulations right at the outset come down heavily on the institutions and structures of the contemporary western nation-state. Notwithstanding their collective representative claims, western societal apparatuses (like the British Parliament for example[68]) in truth become bodies that serve elite, individual, class or other interest-specific aims. Their behaviour stands in total opposition to the larger humanitarian and social concerns that define their *raison d'être*. This explanation becomes another illustration of Gandhi's ethicality and morality pervading readings of contemporary western society, and the problems of transplanting its structures onto Indian soil. This in turn allows him to compare and contrast India's incipient society vis-à-vis the West (i.e. India's several internal, continuing and transforming constituents bracing themselves for the future) again, without falling into a relativist trap. Gandhi's surgical analyses of these combine critiquing the West while offering a specific Indian perspective as well: another instance of a multiple message. The ethical tone of his articulation succeeds in placing these issues of institutional and structural purpose, on a universal plane. Although his messages are specific to the matters at hand, Gandhi appears to communicate to a global audience.[69] The task of disentangling *to whom* these messages are addressed becomes increasingly unwieldy (for us) as the audiences themselves appear to fuse in his thinking. At these *global* levels too, nativist or near-nativist paradoxes and proclivities subtly surface:

> The power to control national life through national representatives is called political power. Representatives will become unnecessary if the national life becomes so perfect as to be self-controlled. It will then be a state of *enlightened anarchy* in which each person will become his own ruler. He will conduct himself in such a way that his behaviour will not hamper the well-being of his neighbours. In an ideal State there will be no political institution and therefore no political power.[70] [Italics added]

The thought of "enlightened anarchy" clearly proves Gandhi's astute handling of disparate discourses, while escaping or transcending their built-in checks and balances. The idea of this utopia applies equally to the West as it does to the East. While becoming an eclectic moral merger of both, however, it involves more intricate detailing. For Gandhi, this assertion provides the space to further filter in indigenous ideas, for contemporary cultural and political initiation.

One of the effective ways of concretizing ideas produced from the East-West merger, like "enlightened anarchy," is through digging up comparable elements within India's rich pasts. Gandhi's depiction of this new country, and its civil society, is in terms of a "*Ramarajya*": the golden era of Lord Ram.[71] As Chatterjee quickly observes, it is yet again, the ethical basis, the rectitude of Lord Ram and morality of *Ramarajya* "a patriarchy in which the ruler, *by his moral quality and habitual adherence to the truth, always expresses the collective will*"[72] [italics mine] that holds a central attention. Despite such transparent evidence, Chatterjee fails to read the strange and striking bases for Gandhi's morality. The fruition of this utopian society is premised upon a particular exceptional "individual" who is capable of expressing the collective consciousness: a point that could be inferred severally. Does this imply that Gandhi is creating space for a distinction between the rulers and the ruled within the new society? Does this mean the egalitarian society would also have a ruling class of 'morally superior' individuals, capable of articulating the "collective will"? Does this imply that the rest of this society will remain powerless on account of an apparent moral deficiency? Given his concerns and interests, these are some vital (and concrete) questions one might have assumed Chatterjee would have jumped to explain. They clearly possess some interesting entry-points, investigative leads and show discrepancies within this moment of nationalist thought, apart from suggesting nativist presences: the raw material for *Subaltern Studies* analysts.

Moreover, for all of the *Ramayana*'s generic resonance, like most ancient Hindu epics it remains a deeply controversial account running several plural narratives for generations through the Indian vernacular terrain, densely cadenced through caste, class, gender and numerous other Indian indices. It poses a fundamentally problem-ridden premise to base the future of Indian society upon. Curiously, Bankim's acknowledgment of this problem of plural narratives within indigenous (Hindu) Indian epics, and the troubles in appropriation for the nationalist cause, is a point that Chatterjee dwells on at good length.[73] Bankim's efforts in establishing and clarifying the specific version (s) of the *Mahabharata* and depiction (s) of Lord Krishna which he claims to be the 'macho' (but indigenously sensitive) counter to the material prowess of the contemporary West, clearly compares with Gandhi's formulation of *Ramarajya*: another connection Chatterjee fails to make; a clear continuity within nationalist thought, with visible individual qualifications. While Bankim's formulation appears to fall into the relativist trap of fighting fire-with-fire with the West, Gandhi's moral conceptualization links ancient India's idea of *Ramarajya* as the blueprint for the future ideal society that now wrestles its way out of colonialism. In so doing, Gandhi effectively transcends barriers of geography (East or West), but leaves the internal dynamics of this *Ramarajya* nebulous. On some passing occasions, like the previous one, his rendition echoes and tempts one into reading them as *his* validation of conservative, pre-colonial, local Indian power structures.[74] The judgment on evidences like these is open yet; but the fact that such a formulation in Gandhi's thought bristling as it does with these types of tension, goes unnoticed by Chatterjee (given his foci), is simply surprising.

But evoking ancient Indian epics and scriptures (as Bankim discovered earlier) is not a straightforward business; even if Gandhi exhorts their feasibility in a tone that does not try to play the East off the West. Gandhi's formulations carefully eschew the somewhat naïve, even confrontationist mode that Bankim adopts. Even so, there are further internal complications in store. Working along somewhat similar lines to Bankim, Gandhi proceeds to assess other vital indices that have generically impacted upon Indian civil society. The importance and role of caste and women come out as cases in point here:

> Caste has nothing to do with religion. It is a custom whose origin I do not know and do not need to know for the satisfaction of my spiritual hunger. But I do know that it is harmful both to spiritual and national growth.

When his critics argued that caste practices were quite explicitly sanctioned by the *sastra*, his emphatic reply was; 'Nothing in the Shastras which is manifestly contrary to universal truths and morals can stand.' So also on the question of the social status of women as described in the canonical *smriti* texts:

> It is sad to think that the *Smritis* contain texts which can command no respect from men who cherish the liberty of woman as their own and who regard her as the mother of the race; . . . The question arises as to what to do with the *Smritis* that contain texts . . . that are repugnant to the moral sense. I have already suggested . . . that all that is printed in the name scriptures need not be taken as the word of God or the inspired word.
>
> Gandhi's position then is that the true principles of religion or morality are unchanging . . . 'The true dharma is unchanging, while traditions may change with time. If we were to follow some of the tenets of the *Manusmriti*, there would be moral anarchy. We have quietly discarded them altogether.'[75]

In this case too, Chatterjee's outlining of Gandhi's argument, throws up more paradoxical inferences. Gandhi's almost regular escaping from the East-West 'either/or' relativist "prison-house," comes about through an elaborate dialogue between the defining characteristics of both of these categories. Gandhi's trenchant criticism of the presence and alleged validity of female suppression and casteism in Hindu scriptures becomes one more manifestation of Chatterjee's formulation of the ambivalence between the modern and the national getting nearly resolved. The disparagement of these aspects colours Gandhi in a modernizing hue, while the assertion of real dharma as constant and "unchanging" imposes upon him a nativist garb. So, the ancient scriptures, be they eastern or western (for all of Gandhi's adulation for them) are only to be taken up to a point. Unquestionably, his aim of revitalizing tradition also renders him as someone who accords a fraction of currency to contemporary notions of "modernity." At the same time, Gandhi's take on this assertion would be, that just because he decries some obviously regressive elements in Indian (or other) traditions, it does not immediately mark him out as rational in the western sense. Indeed, an embedded point in his civilizational project is to challenge notions of rationality or modernity as ideas patented or owned solely by the contemporary west.

Gandhi appears to hit two birds with one stone here. The idea of disparaging areas of one's own traditions that might be unambiguously unjust towards some human beings (like women or the lower castes), do not need the implements of western rationality or "modernity," to be condemned likewise. And even if these insights were understood primarily as evolving from western reason through colonialism in India, it did not offer anything new or constructive about the Indian condition. Regardless of these intrinsic tensions and limitations, Gandhi's positions on caste and women in Indian society, help locate this vital trajectory of his thought: an aspect that could be accurately described as his anti-rational modernity.[76] But yet again, and as we will further see, Chatterjee fails to discern within the Gandhian evidence he cites, discernable elements of nativism that characterize such forms of anti-rational modernity. The explanation of tradition as "unchanging" begs to be further explored and qualified, as it appears to have tangible resonances later. Anti-rational modernity—as located at the intersection between the modern and the national in this discourse—is also imbued with nativist traces. Rationality and modernity, of course, become extremely loaded words hereafter, if they have not been so already.

In an infamous row with the Nobel Laureate, distinguished man of letters and ardent Indian nationalist Rabindranath Tagore, Gandhi assigns 'ethical' reasons to natural disasters like the recent earthquake that hit the north Indian state of Bihar in 1934. The carnage in Gandhi's eyes is a 'divine chastisement,' but he shrewdly circumscribes this insight as originating from morality and not superstition.[77] As Chatterjee explains:

> In any case he felt there are very few things which we understand well enough to be able to prove by the use of reason. And 'where reason cannot function, it is faith that works.' Some physical phenomena are intricately related to our ways of living, and since we have only an 'infinitesimal' knowledge of the rational working of physical laws, the proper attitude is not to remain content with this partial knowledge but to take a unified moral view of those relations:
>
> > Rain is a physical phenomenon; it is no doubt related to human happiness and unhappiness; if so how could it fail to be related to his good and bad deeds? We know of no period in human history when countless people have not related events like earthquakes to sinful deeds of man. Even today religious-minded people everywhere believe in such a relationship.
>
> Such faith was based on firm principles of morality. It was not therefore superstitious.[78]

As observed earlier, Gandhi puts spin on issues like caste and women without giving into rationality or modernity; here he moulds the idea of morality likewise. By extension, this phenomenon of articulating hitherto inexplicable phenomena like natural disasters, etches another complex dimension into Gandhi's expanding framework for nationalist discourse. The previously identified anti-rational modernity, impacts upon prevailing notions of morality in this situation. The presence and power of natural, cosmic phenomenon becomes another site for ideological evolution and development. The former anti-rational modernity, transforms into anti-rational *morality* now. Chatterjee infers that for Gandhi:

> truth did not lie in history, nor did science have any privileged access to it. Truth was moral: unified, unchanging, transcendental. It was not an object of rational inquiry or philosophical speculation. It could only be found in the experience of one's life, by the unflinching practice of moral living.[79]

Gandhi's definition of "truth" is a significant, new development which Chatterjee introduces, but leaves quizzically half-explained. Gandhi's idea embodies and illuminates the greater meaning behind his earlier assertion about physical phenomena being related to human life, activity and deed. One of the striking messages emerging from this elaboration is the link Gandhi establishes with indigenous modes of thought without referring to them directly. In Indian contexts particularly, such inexplicable phenomena also allow Gandhi a unique excuse and opportunity: to plant onto them reasons that would help uproot prevailing injustices to generically deprived sections of the Indian populace. Tactically too, it is a comparatively safe connection to make, while consolidating large sections of the Indian populace under the ambit of the Congress. Simply put, this Gandhian characterization is also open to analysis as pragmatic politics with barely-concealed nativist or near-nativist leanings: a fairly valid *moral* association which—despite the circumstances—Chatterjee is oblivious of. Therefore, Chatterjee's interpretations of Gandhi's interpretation of Indian natural disasters help identify the liaison between morality and truth, but obscure the all-important fact that this happens within a context of nationalism: the propelling force behind the bulk of Gandhian thought; and a matter Chatterjee himself takes such pains to sharpen otherwise. He concludes that for Gandhi:

> [Truth] . . . could never be correctly expressed within the terms of the rational theoretical discourse; *its only true expression was lyrical and poetic* . . . From this evidence it is tempting to characterize Gandhi as yet another example of that typical reaction of the intelligentsia in many parts of the world to the social and moral depredations of advancing capitalism: *romanticism.*[80] [Italics added]

However qualified Chatterjee's extraction of a "romantic" content, his reading of Gandhi's idea still runs the risk of freezing and ossifying it into an abstraction. Quite contrarily, Chatterjee later acknowledges that the mobilizing, intellectual, "interventionist" potential defining this formation of truth is implicit and tangible in nationalist discourse, especially with reference to Indian peasantry: i.e., it obviously was never meant to reside on the *theoretical* plane alone.[81] Thereby, his current inference that Gandhi formulates truth as "moral, unified, unchanging, transcendental," does not quite harmonize with his personal assertion that this was its "only true expression." The idea's abstract qualities were not to be read literally, even if it tempted and compelled such an evaluation: an aspect Chatterjee is himself cognizant of, yet falls victim to. The "lyrical and poetic" elements of Gandhi's truth lie open to alternative analyses. In other words, as nativist or near-nativist slants engendered by the complex interaction of nationalism, morality and truth, inside Gandhi's thought. And this thought seems understandable specifically in a nativist vein, as it is a primary implement in ideological mobilization and spread. The inherent fluidity (or abstraction as Chatterjee might see it) of "Gandhi's truth," is precisely what lends it a *concretely* inclusive character; permitting compatibility with agrarian and other 'subaltern' Indian social realities.

Ironically enough, on the specific matter of theory alone, Chatterjee's comparative assessment of Gandhi's overall formulations comes very close in ascribing to him nativist inclinations. He continues from the citation we left above:

> Gandhi's descriptions of the ideal moral order and the standpoint of his moral critique of civil society suggest strong similarities with that aspect of Russian *narodnichestvo* which Lenin called 'economic romanticism.' In Gandhi too there seems to be the vision of a utopia—'a backward looking petty-bourgeois utopia'—and an idealization of pre-capitalist economic and social relations. One could of course concede to Gandhi, as Lenin did to the Populists, that despite the backwardness of his solution to the fundamental problems of a society in the throes of capitalist penetration, he nevertheless took 'a big step forward' by posing, comprehensively,

> and in all its economic, political and moral aspects, the democratic demand of the small producers, chiefly the peasants. But in the *theoretical* sense Gandhian ideology would still be 'reactionary,' since, as Lenin pointed out in the case of the Russian Populists, not only is there a romantic longing for a return to an idealized medieval world of security and contentment, there is also 'the attempt to measure the new society with the old patriarchal yardstick, the desire to find a model in the old order and traditions, which are totally unsuited to the changed economic institutions.' In spite of conceding the 'democratic points' in Gandhi's thought therefore the Leninist would have to pronounce that it is based on false, indeed reactionary theory of the world-historical process, or else that it refuses to acknowledge a theory of history at all. In either case it would be a variant of romanticism.[82]

But once when it (inevitably) comes to the practicability of this idea, Chatterjee is keen to establish its historical location and specificity. The "romanticism" departs, and with it, unconsciously embedded insinuations of nativism. Here is Chatterjee contrasting western Enlightenment influences (in this case, Ruskin) on Gandhi:

> The critique of civil society which appears on the pages of *Hind Swaraj* does not emerge out of a consideration of the historical contradictions of civil society *as perceived from within it*. . . . His [Gandhi's] idealization of a peaceful, non-competitive, just and happy Indian society of the past could not have been a 'romantic longing for the lost harmony of the archaic world,' because unlike romanticism Gandhi's problem is not conceived at all within the thematic bounds post-Enlightenment thought.[83]

Surely, the two conclusive assertions appear to counter one another: "in either case it would be a variant of romanticism," and "his idealization . . . could not have been a 'romantic longing for the lost harmony of the archaic world.'" Chatterjee's approach on Gandhi's truth, morphs in his analysis from its theoretical situation to its practical application. At one level, it appears a qualified romanticism, and on the other does not bear the remotest resemblance to Enlightenment discourse. Chatterjee's attempts at mapping Gandhi's formulations as originating outside of contemporary frames of reference might appear convincing; but these however, are not outside of Gandhi's own vision of nationalism. As stressed a bit earlier, the reason it is imperative to assign even theoretical, ostensibly abstract-appearing formulations of Gandhi's thought within the *concrete* context of nationalism and never cast off those lenses, is simply because of Gandhi's single-minded "nationalist" ideological and mobilizing purposes, notwithstanding apparent inflections of "elitism" within his thought. Namely, this issue fundamentally questions any critical-nationalist, historiographical, misgivings that insinuate Gandhi's "elitism" in relation to the organization of subaltern classes: understandably, a problem for *Subaltern Studies* practitioners.

The complex process of achieving this "elite-bourgeois intervention," in order to make it compatible for the "appropriation of the subaltern classes," becomes possible by implements which were as much a product of the complex interaction of the previously mentioned (nativist/near-nativist) elements inside Gandhian thought. What we observe now is the "unresolved contradiction" between the "modern" and the "national" (that Chatterjee previously elaborated upon) growing into a concrete, fertile grey area for nationalist discourse. Its innate amorphousness underscores its inclusive organizational potential, producing an ability to account for subaltern classes as much as the elite bourgeoisie, without necessarily bringing these two entities in contradiction with each other: another example of Gandhi's famed "multiple messages" and unusual reconcilability. Chatterjee illustrates and locates the case of two highly distinguishing Gandhian ideas which combined these elements with a surprising minimum of paradox (which albeit, had other difficulties of their own): *Satyagraha* (passive resistance) and *Ahimsa* (non-violence). These ideas though, still needed validation by—and were predicated upon—India's internal, ancient history. Compare some of the following perceptions patterning the evolution of Gandhi's thinking in this context of 'passive' political action:

> It is said that it is a very difficult, if not an altogether impossible, task to educate ignorant peasants in satyagraha and that is full of perils, for it is a very arduous business to transform unlettered ignorant people from one condition into another. Both the arguments are just silly. The people of India are perfectly fit to receive the training of satyagraha. India has knowledge of dharma, and where there is knowledge of dharma, satyagraha is very simple matter . . . some have a fear that once people get involved in satyagraha, they may at a later stage take arms. This fear is illusory. From a path of satyagraha, a transition to the path of *a-satyagraha*, is impossible. It is possible of course that some people who believe in armed activity may mislead the satyagrahis by infiltrating into their ranks and later making them to take arms. This is possible in all enterprises. But as compared to other activities, it is less likely to happen in satyagraha, for their motives soon get exposed and when the people are not ready to take up arms, it becomes almost impossible to lead them on to that terrible path.[84]

The overwhelming belief in the success and applicability of *satyagraha* is thus established in no uncertain terms. What remains in doubt though, is the ability of the masses to be convinced of this medium and accept its terms unconditionally; especially when under pressure from other voices that offer alternatives to these (read the Left/Right-Wing forces, through different, indeed contrasting, modes of armed and ideological struggle). Other vital questions too, remain to be answered: who will impart this training in *satyagraha*? How do you "make people ready . . . to not take up arms"? Gandhi leaves the answer to this question open, without referring to any social segment in particular. He continues:

> People in general always follow in the footsteps of the noble.
> There is no doubt that it is difficult to produce a satyagrahi leader.

> Our experience is that a satyagrahi leader needs many more virtues like self-control, fearlessness, etc. than are requisite for one who believes in armed action . . . The birth of such a man can bring about the salvation of India in no time. Not only India but the whole world awaits the advent of such man. We may in the meantime prepare the ground as much as we can through satyagraha.
>
> It was the faith in the relatively spontaneous strength of popular resistance to injustice that lay behind the call to the nation to join in the agitations in 1919 against the Rowlatt Bill. There was little concern yet about the distinction between leader and satyagraha or the satyagraha and the masses, or about the precise degree of maturity before the masses could be asked to join a satyagraha, or about the organizational and normative safeguards against the inherent unpredictability of a *negative consciousness* playing itself out in the political battleground.[85] [Emphasis added]

Both these prompts from Gandhi, as Chatterjee correctly assigns, display a remarkable amount of confidence in the masses, on the question of the "relatively spontaneous strength of popular resistance to injustice." As Chatterjee rightly identifies again, the deeper internal concerns and nuances of how these had to organizationally take place were left open early on (which quickly became a problem). But the reading of peasant mindset blanketed as "negative consciousness"[86]—the fact that Gandhi had to make modes of nationalist mobilization either compatible with, or transcend or overcome these marks of peasant behaviour while reconciling the interests of all parties involved—would surely seem to emit a dense set of impulses, with anticipatable nativist, near-nativist complications. On the one hand, Gandhi's elaboration indeed brings forth several strands that might suggest such tendencies while attempting to create space for elite-bourgeois initiation and leadership: declarations like people generally "always follow the footsteps of the noble"; and more crucially, that it is not only India waiting for a genuine *satyagrahi* genius but the "whole world"—thus making India's liberation a global issue and a blueprint for the future. While on the other hand, Chatterjee seems to imply (without fully explaining), that non-violence might be a useful tool for mobilization in a largely agrarian locale, because of its basic correlation with these people, its noted presence as an implement for resistance through their collective agrarian, and individual communitarian histories. His contention that after the Rowlatt Bill fiasco (i.e. when masses did turn violent and Gandhi had to call off the movement in 1919) Gandhi had to fundamentally reconsider the organization (both practically and theoretically) of the non-violent movement surely makes sense, but already misses out important factors impacting on this moment in Indian history as just outlined above.

Gandhi's argument after the Rowlatt debacle of 1919, now advances from an acknowledgement that the concept of *satyagraha* as it currently stood was not effective enough; the masses had to be trained, individuals/groups had to be chosen for this specific purpose. Put simply, mounting the anti-colonial challenge through non-violence and passive resistance, needed further concretization while maintaining a resolution that would hold different sections (indeed keep them united) for the long haul. But the vital inflection in this process, as Chatterjee argues, was that the movement had to be achieved through a consciously chosen non-confrontationist mode of protest vis-à-vis the colonial state. As Gandhi continues, "he only is able and attains the right to offer civil disobedience who has known how to offer voluntary and deliberate obedience to the laws of the State in which he is living."[87] That is, for *satyagraha* to succeed, a certain form of adherence to contemporary structures of colonial organization and rule had to be conceded. Modern Indian historians of varying hues have read into this assertion evidence of colonial 'comprador' class "collaboration."[88] But the Gandhian rationale behind this appears to provoke both elitist and nativist tensions. Anticlimactically, Gandhi's purpose behind this is because his perception of the masses too (at least, at this moment in time of his life), is somewhat stereotypically, that of a "mob":

> In my opinion, the thing was organized, but there it stands. There was no question as to whether it was a deep-laid conspiracy through the length and breadth of India or a deep-rooted organization of which this was apart. The organization was hastily constructed; the organization was not in the sense in which we understand the word organization . . . If I confined that word to Ahmedabad alone, to masses of absolutely unlettered men, who would be able to make no fine distinctions—then you have got the idea of what that organization is . . . . There were those poor deluded labourers whose one business was to see me and Anasuyabai released. That it was a wicked rumour released by somebody I have not the slightest doubt. As soon as these things happened, the people thought there should be something behind it. Then there were the half-educated raw youths. This is the work of these, I am grieved to have to say. These youths possessed themselves with false ideas gathered from shows, such as the cinematograph shows that they have seen, gathered from silly novels and from the political literature of Europe . . . . it was an organization of this character.
>
> The direct physical form in which the masses appeared in the political arena was always that of a mob. It had no mind of its own. Its behaviour was determined by the way it was led.[89]

And so, in this vein, Gandhi's approach too codifies mass behaviour while opening it up for the nationalist leadership's appropriation. This characterization of the masses unambiguously portrays the masses through nativist/near-nativist shades reminiscent of and not unlike indigenous Indian depictions of their behaviour: a form of detailing missing in Chatterjee's critique. But tactically and practically speaking too, such a depiction allows Gandhi the space for a concrete form of mobilization and organization to evolve through nationalist discourse. Thus emerges the rationale (and the idea) which brings the masses under the leadership of the nationalists, and weaves them into a cohesive unit: *ahimsa*. As Chatterjee shrewdly locates and identifies:

> Ahimsa was the necessary complement to the concept of satyagraha which both limited, and, at the same time, made it something more than 'purely and simply civil disobedience.' Ahimsa was the rule for concretizing the 'truth' of satyagraha. 'Truth is a positive value, while non-violence is a negative value. Truth affirms. Non-violence forbids something which is real enough.' Ahimsa, indeed, was the concept—both ethical and epistemological because it was defined within a moral and epistemic practice that was wholly 'experimental'—which supplied Gandhism with a theory of politics, enabling it to become the ideology of a national movement. It was the organizing principle for a 'science' of politics—a science wholly different from all current conceptions of politics which had only succeeded in producing the 'sciences of violence,' but a science nevertheless—the 'science of non-violence,' the 'science of love.' It was the moral framework for solving every practical problem of the organized political movement.[90]

But this unique concept also carries with it a sharp almost 'western' streak of pragmatism, *realpolitik* too. Here is Gandhi's own perception:

> Ahimsa with me is a creed, the breath of life. But it is never as a creed that I placed it before India or, for that matter before anyone except in casual or informal talks. I placed it before the Congress as a political weapon to be employed for the solution of practical problems.[91]

Chatterjee continues to show how a concept like ahimsa, forms the complex tapestry of Gandhian methods of ideological mobilization, fusing elements from the West and East without apparently getting trapped within either of their discursive warps entirely: a concretization and resolution of the contradiction between the "modern" and the "national" as identified in Bankim. This first step in the actualization of nationalist discourse extends with the fruition of concepts that emit great symbolic power through the dense Indian terrain. But this very process now seems to have come full circle. Now consider Gandhi's contrasting perspective on the spinning-wheel (khadi) vis-à-vis his position earlier on:

> I have never tried to make anyone regard the spinning-wheel as his *kamadhenu* or universal provider; . . . When in 1908 . . . I declared my faith in the spinning-wheel in the pages of the Hind Swaraj, I stood absolutely alone . . . I do regard the spinning-wheel as a gateway to *my* spiritual salvation, but I recommend it to others only as a powerful weapon for the attainment of swaraj and the amelioration of the economic condition of the country.[92]

Moving quickly, connecting one aspect with another, Chatterjee's construction appears to possess a roundedness and sense of completion in characterizing Gandhi as a "moment of manoeuvre." This process of concretizing nationalist discourse, further extends to areas like the appropriation and uplift of the lower castes within Hindu society, while combining it with the increasing power, mobilizing and organizational sophistication of the evolving satyagrahi. Considering all these complexities Chatterjee arrives at a range of conclusions that appear to flip-flop constantly on the Gandhian contribution, or mirror the latter's paradoxes and grey areas. Sample this declaration that might read contrarily to Chatterjee's own Gandhian evidence-analyses hitherto:

> Gandhism finally reconciled the contradictions between the utopian and the practical aspects of its political ideology by surrendering to the absolute truthfulness and supreme self-sacrifice of the satyagrahi. It had gained its strength from an intensely powerful moral critique of the existing state of politics. *In the end it saved its Truth by escaping from politics* . . . And yet as Gandhi himself put it, 'politics encircle us today like the coil of a snake.' The historical impact of the Gandhian ideology on the evolution of Indian politics was of monumental significance.[93] [Italics added]

Or, the uneven, qualified participation (and individual presence) of the peasantry in the nationalist movement:

> While it was the Gandhian intervention in elite-nationalist politics in India which established for the first time that an authentic nationalist movement could only be built upon the organized support of the whole of the peasantry, the working out of the politics of non-violence also made it abundantly clear that the object of the political mobilization of the peasantry was not at all what Gandhi claimed on its behalf, 'to train the masses in self-consciousness and attainment of power.' Rather the peasantry was meant to become a willing participant in a struggle wholly conceived and directed by others.[94]

And despite these evident paradoxes and complications in the relationship between peasants and nationalism—which Chatterjee himself identifies—there is a temptation to become judgmental yet. Indeed a concrete, *Subaltern Studies* reinterpretation of nationalism:

> And so we get within the ideological unity of Gandhism as a whole the conception of a national framework of politics in which the peasants are mobilized but do not participate, of a nation of which they are a part but a national state from which they are forever distanced . . . It is not surprising therefore that in the unresolved class struggles within the social formation of contemporary India, oppositional movements can still claim their moral legitimacy from the message of the Mahatma.[95]

As we see, Chatterjee's own conclusions appear to mirror the contradictions, complexities, ambivalences and ambiguities within Gandhian thought. Clearly, from what we gather (both the Gandhian evidence and Chatterjee's analyses of these), a lack of further precise clarification, perhaps an absence of identifying nativist/near-nativist sentiments inherent within Gandhian thought as an essential characteristic of bourgeois nationalist discourse, pose analytical problems aplenty.

In the first conclusive instance above, Chatterjee's characterization of Gandhian ideology as a type of escapist politics immediately follows with his submission that Gandhian politics was a "monumental achievement." The second inference identifies Gandhi's distancing of the peasants from the imminent nation-state, while obscuring indigenous peasant politics impacting upon nationalist discourse: i.e. that the peasant appropriation into nationalism was a *dialectic* involving uneven agency for *both parties involved*. The third elaborates how Gandhi becomes exposed to, and open for, adoption by all and sundry within the Indian context: a conclusion that does not necessarily shed new light into this debate, while still falling into some of the competing perspectives and patterns of Indian historiography.[96] Indeed, the very plurality of Gandhi makes it possible for multiple and competing perceptions of him possible. Overall, Chatterjee's intervention comes close in reading a new idea—the presence of "romanticism"—with near-nativist tinges, but fails to detail it with further precision. It only really becomes noteworthy given the terms of his analysis, foci and historiographical standpoint. His conclusions thus, while theoretically re-evaluating the category of nationalism through early nationalist thinking—for all its sympathies towards peasants, workers and other subaltern classes—would still be read as a variant of Marxist/quasi-Marxist accounts, if not read in consonance with *Subaltern Studies* volumes and specific field researches that have detailed the impact of Gandhi. For want of further qualification and clarification of nationalism, only the bourgeois aspect of *early* Third World leadership (like Bankim) appears to raise fundamental doubts in this arena, with obvious difficulties of their own.

Chatterjee's portrayal of the resolution between the modern and the national continues to the post-colonial Indian state. He puts Nehru under the crucible, identifies his era as a "moment of arrival" whereby Indian/Third World nationalist discourse comes to terms with its internal tussles and self-perception vis-à-vis western discourse and Enlightenment influence, to culminate in a celebration of the modern nation-state.[97] However, as the Third World nation-state comes more into its own as an independent polity, a lot of the colonial structures and the classes to whom these structures benefited, assume a form of high-handedness towards still marginalized sections in the rural (and sometimes urban) hinterland like tribes, lower castes, non-Hindus etc.: in short, the continuing problem of subaltern oppression in post-colonial India, which according to Chatterjee and his faction lies in the very conception of the contemporary structure. Gandhian ideology still remains a strong presence, but it does not appear to be as relevant now. For deep internal Indian reasons that need not be detailed here for our current purposes, the continuing decades of India's experience bring some leading ideas of nationalism (like indigenized Indian versions of western "secularism") under severe attack. By the 1980s and 1990s the debate on the Nehruvian legacy is constantly disparaged by various quarters (including some Congressmen) and acquires an extremely mordant outlook. The resolution of the modern and the national as put into effect in post-colonial India is screened through a variety of lenses, fundamentally including post-modernist ones. The earlier Gandhian contribution now gets phrased through the terms of *this* debate, opening up hitherto relatively unavailable spaces for conservative, even rightwing perspectives.[98]

V

Predictably, criticisms railed against Chatterjee and *Nationalist Thought in the Colonial World*, have come from the usual Marxist, Nationalist and critical Marxist-cum-Nationalist quarters of Indian historiography.[99] These critiques have been predicated upon known issues of bourgeois and peasant "agency" in the making of Indian nationalism 'Indian' as such: elements and limitations we have noticed in Chatterjee's argument before. But in a daring critique, former *Subaltern Studies* member and Marxist historian Sumit Sarkar has understood both the *Subaltern Studies* project and *Nationalist Thought* to embody the problematic influence and application of currently fashionable post-colonial and/or postmodern paradigms—like the impact of Edward Said's *Orientalism*—on an Indian context, having pernicious effects.[100] Indeed, Sarkar views Said's formulation itself as inherently flawed in the discourses and contexts it outlines, achieving at times, the exact opposite of what it intends:

> If Orientalism essentialized and homogenized the Oriental 'Other,' critics from James Clifford in 1980, down to Aijaz Ahmad have regularly found Said guilty of an identical charge. The critique of Orientalism and colonial power-knowledge does often use terms like 'Enlightenment rationality,' 'colonial discourse,' 'Third World culture,' as well as of course 'Orientalism' itself, in the grossest of homogenizing ways. The pattern of rejections intermingled with complicities actually extends further, into many other varieties of post-modernisms too . . . The argument sometimes offered—that such complicity is bound to be there—as it is impossible today to go totally beyond post-Enlightenment discursive patterns, sound suspiciously like an attempt to have the best of both worlds: critiquing others for essentialism, teleology, and other related sins, while claiming a special immunity from doing the same oneself.[101]

Sarkar continues to demonstrate on the theoretical plane how Said's argument's collapsing tendencies have contoured patterns of thought and analyses in realms of post-colonial and/or postmodern studies within and beyond South Asia. The idea and the conception of "power," Sarkar observes, continues to have very vague associations, in sharp contrast to the very precise and differentiated meanings Foucault (by and large, Said and *Subaltern Studies*' collective but unprofessed inspiration) attaches in his oeuvre. Its application in the colonial Indian situation adds newer problems to existing ones:

> The homogenizations to which the Saidian framework seem particularly prone are related, I feel, to major problems in its concep-

> tion of power. There is first the tendency . . . to ascribe virtually unlimited domination to ruling forms of power-knowledge . . . . Assumptions of total domination foreclose investigation of elements of resistance or partial autonomy, and rob subordinate groups of agency. The colonial middle class in particular, has been found capable of only 'derivative discourses' in one, extremely influential version. Such assumptions also tend to grossly simplify and homogenize power-relationships. In the Saidian framework, for example, the focus remains relentlessly on colonial domination alone. *The indigenous and pre-colonial roots of many forms of caste, gender or class domination are generally ignored*, for the dominant assumption is of a kind of total rupture or tabula rasa, with colonialism completely remoulding such indigenous structures, making them dependent or derivative. The possibility of these *helping to mediate colonial authority in vital ways, and even functioning autonomously at times*—and there is ample evidence for both—is simply ignored. A parallel homogenization occurs at the other end of the power-equation. Colonial domination gets robbed of all complexities and variations, and so Macaulay's notorious Minute is thought to be a sufficient description of more than a century of British cultural policy in India.[102] [Italics added]

We see that Sarkar criticizes *Subaltern Studies*, and Chatterjee's argument, for lack of cognizing prospects and possibilities that had, ironically, gone on to become the group's calling-card: the idea of "autonomy." Obviously, as mentioned earlier in this essay, if autonomy was possible for peasants and subalterns, it is truly paradoxical, even absurd, that the colonial middle class is found wanting on this count. But with Sarkar too, the criticism of this argument rests simply with drumming the import of issues like the internal, indigenous Indian involvement in colonial processes that produced a variety of effects and developments. Therefore, the precise nature and contribution of these factors—even in this general assessment of Said's impact on contemporary pan-Asian studies—begs to be further detailed: a further qualification and clarification of related ideas and categories.

What exactly are the "indigenous" or the "pre-colonial"? What does discrimination through "gender" and "caste" precisely mean? How are we to read them? Are these indices in a context of colonial nationalism nuanced by nativist slants and/or retrogressive dashes? These are some of the questions worth considering for purposes of greater clarity.

Sarkar proceeds to address points that Chatterjee outlines in his critique of some of the important ideologues of nationalist discourse, like Bankim, Gandhi and Nehru. Before doing so, he intelligently locates (without greater detailing though) the impact of a book like Ashis Nandy's *The Intimate Enemy* as a type of precursor to the theoretical elaborations that *Subaltern Studies* social scientists look up to, if not entirely appropriate. To put it summarily, Nandy's refreshing and highly controversial socio-psychological approach addresses the complexity of Gandhi's ideological contribution to nationalist thought by eliciting indigenous elements as vital in its mobilizing processes—with clear nativist intonations that Nandy finds as a salve for current ills of Indian version of "secularism."[103] Sarkar sees this argument as the one that opened up the space for "radical" critiques on Gandhi and colonial nationalism in India, but with built-in dangers as well as positives: an issue not cognized by the likes of Chatterjee and his ilk.

To maintain our focus for the present purpose just on Chatterjee though, Sarkar's primary criticism against him emerges in the very structure of Chatterjee's parameters that appear to freeze internal variations within Enlightenment discourse vis-à-vis its impact on colonialism and nationalist thought. For instance, the possibility (and fact) that not all of nineteenth century Europe was in unison pro-laissez faire or pro-imperialist, questions Chatterjee's assumption of Bankim's almost wholesale embrace of these, which in the process makes Enlightenment discourse come out as monolithic.

Conversely, the fact that Gandhi was indeed influenced by more thinkers from the Enlightenment different and contrary to the ones mentioned by Chatterjee, undermines Chatterjee's formulation that Gandhi was one of the few intellects to have escaped/transcended or successfully merged Enlightenment's nationalist-cum-rationalist frames, without falling into its relativist traps.[104] Moreover, on the question of Chatterjee's handling of Gandhi, his singular depiction of the Enlightenment as an influence within the colonial nationalist context and Gandhi's near-successful handling of it, makes Sarkar wonder whether the Enlightenment was such a powerful influence at its point of origin in Europe itself. If it could have been so (relatively) easily transcended by Gandhi, how powerful was it globally in the first place?

But Sarkar's biggest criticism comes against Chatterjee's ideation of the "romanticism" that we identified in the latter's outlining of the resolution between the modern and the national at the Gandhian intersection of nationalist discourse. Here is Sarkar's take on this area:

> Critiques of modern Western power-knowledge cast in the Saidian mould, I have argued, have often tended to evoke a romanticized 'pre-modern,' or 'pre-colonial,' and Chatterjee too, often gestures vaguely towards 'community-consciousness' as valorized counterpoint. *The discussion of such consciousness, both here as well as in other writings of Chatterjee, is kept at a level abstract enough to avoid, on the whole, a slide towards overtly conservative conclusions.* But that such a possibility remains in the structure of his argument . . . [can be seen] in . . . Gandhi's standpoint.[105] [Italics added]

So, in Sarkar's case too, the argument against Chatterjee rests largely with a criticism on issues of homogenizing essential factors and processes. He goes on to detail, ways in which Chatterjee and some other members of the *Subaltern Studies* collective in their other writings have come up with similar validating evidences and analyses for the 'pre-modern'/'pre-colonial.'[106] But the matter for Marxist critics like Sarkar ends with just asserting the dangers of such orthodox positions in these writings. The "conservative" and/or "romanticized" angle in these writings is the closest they come in identifying the centrality of nativism in these writings. Its presence as a telling force in the *Subaltern Studies* oeuvre, indeed, an idea that well-nigh merits isolated, independent, focussed investigation at theoretical and practical historical levels, is a prospect that goes missing entirely.

Finally, it also becomes an issue that crops up in the subsequent controversy and debate generated by Chatterjee and other members of the *Subaltern* group's work in South Asian and post-colonial academia. By this time though, the debate flows over and beyond just *Nationalist Thought*: it goes back and forth from the *Subaltern* historians to Marxists like Sarkar. Primarily fuelled by Sarkar's this very essay the debate expands to analyze the larger impact of western trends like post-modernism and post-structuralism in the specific context of South Asian history writing, which *Subaltern Studies* appears to represent along with other individual accounts from some of the other Indian historiographical dispensations. The concentration on nationalism, nativism and related ideas becomes more and more blurred in relatively new historical situations which present their own different challenges.[107] The terms of analysis now shift to more contemporaneous theoretical work about a post-colonial, independent India caught on the threshold of economic liberalization and subsequent globalization on the one hand, paralleled by the upsurge of a Hindu rightwing political dispensation emerging as an alternative to three decades of 'secular,' 'centrist,' Congress rule on the other: sentiments echoed within Chatterjee's subsequent *The Nation and its Fragments*—as much a product of *Nationalist Thought* and the controversies that followed in the late 1980s and early 1990s .[108] In establishing the connections between the colonial and the post-colonial, the continuing resolution of the modern and the national in contemporary South Asian academic and intellectual discourse, considerable tensions of the nativist type crop up: an idea like 'secularism,' and its impact through Nehru on the Indian condition, becomes the heart of the matter in this debate, which aspires to find alternatives. This paper, in different ways thus, tried to locate its origins in the theoretical work and negotiation of nationalism by *Subaltern Studies* historians in the different contexts of an evolving contemporary India.

NOTES

1. This essay will use the term 'Nationalist' with a capital 'N' to denote this historiographical dispensation in Indian history and differentiate it from the more general meaning of the word 'nationalist.'
2. An example of 'moderate' nationalism: Naoroji wrote a famous book called *Poverty and un-British Rule in India* in 1901. In the book he argues for British exploitation of India as inherently "un-British," and that India should be meted better treatment. In contrast, the writings of Tilak, Gandhi and Nehru are more strident in their anti-colonial stances. See, Bipan Chandra, *The Rise and Growth of Economic Nationalism in India* (New Delhi: People's Publishing House, 1966).
3. See Bipan Chandra, *Nationalism and Colonialism in Modern India* (New Delhi: Orient Longman, 1981) for useful, lucid snapshots of all of these. Also note Chandra's famous elucidation of 'economic nationalism' in later work, especially *Essays in Colonialism* 3rd ed. (New Delhi: Orient Longman, 1999).
4. I specifically mean Gramsci's reading of the role of the "intelligentsia" vis-à-vis the "intellectuals." As we will later see, the appropriation of Gramsci is eclectic at various stages from other strands in Indian historiography as well. See Antonio Gramsci, *Selections From Prison Notebooks* ed. & trans. Q. Hoare and Geoffrey Nowell-Smith (London: Lawrence &Wishart, 1971).
5. Bipan Chandra et al., eds., *India's Struggle for Independence: 1857-1947* (New Delhi: Viking, 1988). Also look at Chandra's *Essays in Colonialism* for greater elaborations on all of these.

6. See William Jones, *A History of India*. (3 Vols.),
7. See Bruce Mazlish, *James and John Stuart Mill: Father and Son in the Nineteenth Century* (London: Hutchinson, 1975) for an illuminating account of the differences and transitions in perceptions about colonialism through a comparative biographical assessment.
8. See G.M. Young, ed. *Speeches by Lord Macaulay with his Minute on Indian Education* (London: Oxford University Press, 1935) for a perceptive introduction to Macaulay and thinking about India in the British imagination. Macaulay's standpoint on the English language and education as implements of power and rule is rather complex, alluding even to ways in which indigenous Indians could use this to their own advantages.
9. Anil Seal, *The Emergence of Indian Nationalism: Competition and Collaboration in the Later Nineteenth Century* 2nd ed. (Cambridge: Cambridge University Press, 1971).
10. Judith Brown, *Gandhi's Rise to Power: Indian Politics 1915-22* (Cambridge: Cambridge University Press, 1972).
11. See D.N. Dhanagare, *Peasant Movements in India: 1920-1950* (Delhi, Oxford University Press, 1983) which gives a critical *Nationalist* account of some peasant movements, but from an out-and-out *Marxist* standpoint. Also see, A R Desai, ed., *Peasant Struggles in India* (Bombay: Oxford University Press, 1979): an outstanding and challenging collection that incorporated essays on the subject from a lot of contesting historiographical perspectives. For a lucid, comprehensive account on the experience of the industrial rural/urban working-class and its relationship with Indian nationalism see V B Karnik, *Strikes in India* (Bombay: Manaktalas, 1967). But for a far more challenging reading of the idea and category of the working-class in an Indian context, from a radical Marxist, *Subaltern Studies* viewpoint, see Dipesh Chakrabarty, *Rethinking Working Class History: Bengal 1890-1940* (Princeton, Princeton University Press, 1989).
12. See Sumit Sarkar, *Modern India: 1885-1947* (Delhi: Macmillan, 1983) for a pretty comprehensive narration of the Indian national movement deploying expansive frames of social history writing as embodied by someone like E P Thompson.
13. See Sumit Sarkar, *Writing Social History* (Delhi: Oxford Universi-

ty Press, 1998) and *Beyond Nationalist Frames: Postmodernism, Hindu Fundamentalism, History* (Bloomington: Indiana University Press, 2002) for lucid, versatile and controversial essays on the theoretical and practical debates surrounding contemporary Indian historical study, some of which attempt to locate the problematic links between Marxism, post-modernism and *Subaltern Studies*. For an entire history of *Subaltern Studies*, from its origins in (radical) Marxism to its imbibing of post-modernist and post-structuralist thought, to its wider impact on Third World studies, see Vinayak Chaturvedi ed. & intro. *Mapping the Subaltern and the Post-Colonial* (London: Verso/New Left Review, 2000). Also, to understand its theoretical location purely, refer Gayatri Chakravorty Spivak, "Subaltern Studies: Deconstructing Historiography" in *Selected Subaltern Studies* ed. Ranajit Guha & Gayatri Chakravorty Spivak, intro. Edward Said (New York; Oxford: Oxford University Press, 1988), 3-32.

14. See Ranajit Guha, "On Some Aspects of the Historiography of Colonial India" in *Selected Subaltern Studies*, 37-44, and his "The Prose of Counter-Insurgency" ibid. 45-86, for the historiographical and the theoretical locations of the Indian "subaltern" respectively. To put it very roughly, the term "subaltern" is constantly inflected upon in the *Subaltern Studies* volumes, departing and adding on definitions outlined by Gramsci. On the one hand it can mean the most exploited of individuals within a social system; on other occasions, the colonized subject plain and simple, who runs the risk of being misrepresented or not fully understood by prevailing paradigms. In general, the "subaltern" in these volumes constitutes peasants, tribes, agrarian and industrial workers, lower castes, women and their social co-ordinates that constitute the populace and workforce in rural and urban India.
15. For a further elaboration on the exact theoretical positioning of *Subaltern Studies* look at Sumit Sarkar, "Post-Modernism and the Writing of History" in *Beyond Nationalist Frames*, 154-94.
16. See Shahid Amin, "Gandhi as Mahatma: Gorakhpur District, Eastern UP, 1921-22" in Ranajit Guha ed. *Subaltern Studies: Vol. III*, (Delhi: Oxford University Press, 1986) 1-61. Amin's interpretation along with Gyanendra Pandey, "Peasant Revolt and Indian Natio-

nalism: The Peasant Movement in Awadh 1918-22" in *Selected Subaltern Studies*, 233-84, provide a strong contrast to the Nationalist viewpoint on roughly related events, a sharp account of which is provided by Majid Siddiqi, *Agrarian Unrest in North India: The United Provinces 1918-1922* (New Delhi: Vikas, 1978).

17. Another linked area of debate had been the problematic influence of Edward Said, and East-West relations in the context of contemporary history-writing in the Third World. A later *Subaltern Studies* member like Gyan Prakash argues for a critical appropriation—not blind imitation—and even transcendence of the *Orientalism* paradigm. See "Writing Post-Orientalist Histories of the Third World: Perspectives from Indian Historiography" in *Mapping Subaltern Studies and the Post-Colonial*, 163-90. This invited a sharp and qualified counter from Cambridge school historians Rosalind O'Hanlon and David Washbrook in "After Orientalism: Culture, Criticism and Politics in the Third World," ibid., 190-219, who argued for greater caution in handling processes of colonialism and the colonial subject without collapsing them into isolated fragments. Prakash replied with accusing Washbrook and O'Hanlon as much of post-modern and post-structuralist appropriations. See "Can the 'Subaltern' Ride? A Reply to Washbrook& O'Hanlon," ibid., 220-38. A slightly different critique comes from Sumit Sarkar, which we look at in greater detail later. See "Orientalism Revisited: Saidian Frameworks in the Writing of Modern Indian History," *Oxford Literary Review*, XVI, 1-2, 1994: 205-224.
18. Sumit Sarkar, "Decline of the Subaltern in *Subaltern Studies*" rep. in *Mapping the Subaltern and the Post-Colonial*, 300-23.
19. See, Rajeev Bhargava ed. *Secularism and its Critics* (New Delhi: Oxford University Press, 1998), for a simultaneously comparative and deeply specific discussions of the idea of "secularism" and its problems in Indian and western situations.
20. Sumit Sarkar, "Postmodernism and the Writing of History," 164-69.
21. Aijaz Ahmad, *In Theory: Classes, Nations, Literatures* (London: Verso, 1992); and "The Politics of Literary Postcoloniality" rpt. in *Contemporary Post-Colonial Theory: a Reader* ed. & intro. Padmini Mongia 3rd ed. (New Delhi: Oxford University Press, 2000),

276-93.

22. Fredric Jameson, "Postmodernism: Or the Cultural Logic of Late Capitalism" rpt. in *Postmodernism: A Reader* ed. & intro. Thomas Docherty (New York; London: Harvester Wheatsheaf, 1993), 62-92.
23. Arif Dirlik, "The Post-Colonial Aura: Third World Criticism in the Age of Global Capitalism" rpt. in Padmini Mongia *Contemporary Post-Colonial Theory*, 294-320.
24. 'Uncritical' in the Marxist sense.
25. See Dipesh Chakrabarty, *Habitations of Modernity: Essays in the Wake of Subaltern Studies* (New Delhi: Permanent Black, 2002), for a rejoinder to Sarkar, and a validation of the newer emphases in the later volumes of *Subaltern Studies*. Moreover, Chakrabarty views these developments in South Asian social sciences as entirely salutary, a further creation of space for the decolonizing process of Third World (here South Asian) intellect; indeed, an escape/transcendence of Enlightenment indices as embodied by other historiographical perspectives like Marxism. In fact, these positions have now opened the arena for restoring the *global* balance in history writing. Such formulations embody his idea of "provincializing Europe." For further details see, *Provincializing Europe: Post-Colonial Thought, Historical Difference* (New Delhi, Oxford University Press, 2001).
26. Ranajit Guha, "On Some Aspects of the Historiography of Colonial India" in *Selected Subaltern Studies*, 38-39.
27. As noted earlier, Ranajit Guha does detail the theoretical position of the group in terms of defining notions of the "subaltern," while critically appropriating it from Gramsci (see fn. 14). But a different type of argument is required, as the problem lies equally with preceding paradigms that characterized this historiography, which Partha Chatterjee, an important member of the collective, later attempts to explain.
28. To cite some examples, see Shahid Amin, "Gandhi as Mahatma: Gorakhpur District, Eastern UP, 1921-2" and David Hardiman "Adivasi Assertion in South Gujarat: The Devi Movement of 1922-3" both in *Subaltern Studies Volume III: Writings on South Asian Society and History*, ed. Ranajit Guha (Delhi: Oxford Uni-

versity Press, 1984), 1-62 and 196-230 respectively. For a particularly enlightening example of such a shrewd nationalist requisition by peasants while escaping its framework see Gyanendra Pandey, "Peasant Revolt and Indian Nationalism: The United Provinces 1921-2" in *Selected Subaltern Studies*, 233-88. In many ways, it offers a counter to, and also delivers, a powerful critique of a nationalist historical account of the same event.

29. Partha Chatterjee, *Nationalist Thought and the Colonial World: A Derivative Discourse?* 2nd ed. (Minneapolis: University of Minnesota Press, 1993).
30. Ibid., 1-22
31. Ibid., 22.
32. Ibid., 19-22. Chatterjee's particularly sharp in his attacks against theories of nationalism expounded by Ernest Gellner and Benedict Anderson.
33. See Bipan Chandra, *Nationalism and Colonialism in Modern India*, for economic nationalist explanations. Also see fn. 3.
34. For instance, see Majid Hayat Siddiqi, *Agrarian Unrest in North India: United Provinces 1918-22* (New Delhi: Vikas, 1978). A nationalist account that is later critiqued by *Subaltern Studies* member Gyanendra Pandey, also see fn. 3.
35. For a clearer picture, see Chatterjee's handling of Jawaharlal Nehru, "The Moment of Arrival: Nehru and the Passive Revolution," 131-67.
36. Ibid., 85-87.
37. Ibid., 8.
38. Ibid., 48-49.
39. Anil Seal, *Emergence of Indian Nationalism: Competition and Collaboration in the later Nineteenth Century* (Cambridge: Cambridge University Press, 1971).
40. See Bipan Chandra et al., eds., *India's Struggle for Independence: 1857-1947* (New Delhi: Viking, 1988) for a lucid, detailed discussion of the event, bearing a Marxist-Nationalist emphasis.
41. See Chatterjee, 54, for a brief snapshot about the man, his life and work. The surname 'Chattopadhyay' is also referred to as 'Chatterjee'; the switch was made in the course of British-Bengali colonial interaction.

42. Ibid. 55, also Ibid. 82 fn. 2. Chatterjee quotes a celebrated essay from Bankim that suggests the establishment of a militant, Hindu nationalism.
43. The monographs on this topic are voluminous. But our focus here is on elite, colonial, Bengali viewpoints of the West in the nineteenth century. For starters, see Tapan Raychaudhuri, *Europe Reconsidered: Perceptions of the West in Nineteenth-century Bengal* (Delhi: Oxford University Press, 1988).
44. Ibid. 56-7
45. Ibid. 56
46. Ibid. 60-4
47. Ibid. 56-7, see Bankim's discussion of the relationship between Sanchay philosophy and Hinduism and its deleterious effects.
48. Ibid., 57.
49. Ibid., 59.
50. Ibid., 68, Bankim utilizes utilitarian and biological theories from Mill and Darwin respectively, to prove his point!
51. Ibid., 68-9.
52. Ibid., 66.
53. Ibid., 70.
54. Ibid., 79.
55. Ibid., 70.
56. Ibid., 80-1.
57. Ibid., 81.
58. Partha Chatterjee, "Gandhi and the Critique of Civil Society" in Ranajit Guha, ed. *Subaltern Studies III: Writings on South Asian Society and History* (New Delhi: Oxford University Press, 1984), 153-95. The same essay is reproduced with very minor changes as "The Moment of Manoeuvre: Gandhi and the Critique of Civil Society" in *Nationalist Thought*, 85-130. This essay will cite from the former.
59. Ibid., 156-57, the word *Bahadur* means "brave."
60. Ibid., 157
61. Ibid., 158
62. Ibid., 158
63. Ibid., 160: anti-nationalist, meaning, Nehru's difference with Gandhi on the question of industrialization

64. Ibid., 161.
65. Ibid., 161.
66. Ibid., 162.
67. For a single example of such a Gandhi-specific instance of registration in peasant consciousness, see Shahid Amin, "Gandhi as Mahatma" in *Subaltern Studies Volume III: Writings on South Asian History and Society*, (New Delhi: Oxford University Press, 1984), 1-62. Amin follows this up with the slightly spatially differentiated "Approver's Testimony, Judicial Discourse: The Case of Chaurichaura" in *Subaltern Studies Volume V*, (New Delhi, Oxford University Press, 1987), 164-202. But his most comprehensive account that encapsulates these tensions at this moment in Indian nationalism is *Event, Metaphor, Memory: Chaurichaura 1922-1992*, (Berkeley, California: University of California Press, 1995). It ties up and goes beyond the earlier researches.
68. Chatterjee, "Gandhi & Civil Society," 163.
69. Ibid. 166: "What appears as a critique of western civilization is therefore a total moral critique of the fundamental aspects of civil society . . . the West has forgotten the true teachings of the Christian faith . . . his [Gandhi's] solution is meant to be universal, applicable as much to the countries of the West as to nations such as India."
70. Ibid., 164-65.
71. Ibid., 165: the utopian rule of Lord Ram ensuing the demolition of the Sri Lankan demon-king Ravana in the *Ramayana*, is a Hindu mythological equivalent of the Augustine era of the Roman Empire.
72. Ibid., 165.
73. "The Moment of Departure," 59: "The fact was, of course, that the texts on the life of Krishna as handed down to the present day contained numerous additions, abridgements and recensions on the 'original,' carried out by unknown and unidentifiable editors over a period of many hundreds years. The first task therefore was to select out and brush aside these later alterations and reach the 'original historical account' of the life of Krishna. To do this Bankim devised several criteria, all of them strictly scientific and rational."
74. Ibid. 168: On another tangent (not entirely relevant for us), Chat-

terjee records how Gandhi differentiates between western, rational, 'History' as an inauthentic account of Truth. While, discoursing on the ancient Indian epics Gandhi would characterize the truths of the *Ramayana* and *Mahabharata* as 'poetic truth.' Indeed, he did not even consider them as 'historical narrative': Yet another illustration of Gandhi's sidetracking from any potholes that get him into an "either/or" position while simultaneously critiquing the East and West.

75. Ibid. 169-70. *Shastras* simply mean texts for instruction, governance and other areas of managing civil life according to the Vedas. *Manusmriti* ("The Laws of Manu") is a Vedic treatise about managing women and marriage from an out and out conservative male position. See, *The Laws of Manu* trans., intro., eds. Wendy Doniger& Brian K. Smith (London: Penguin, 1991).
76. Ibid., 171-72.
77. Ibid., 171-72.
78. Ibid., 171-72.
79. Ibid., 172.
80. Ibid., 172-73.
81. Ibid., 176: "For Gandhism, like Russian Populism, was not a direct expression of peasant ideology. It was an ideology conceived as an intervention in the elite-nationalist discourse of the time and was formed and shaped by the experiences of a specifically national movement."
82. Ibid., 173.
83. Ibid., 175.
84. Ibid., 181-82.
85. Ibid., 182 .
86. Chatterjee himself cites the idea of "negative consciousness" as a primary step in the pattern of agrarian peasant subaltern resistance as elaborated by Ranajit Guha in his groundbreaking *Elementary Aspects of Peasant Insurgency in Colonial India* (New Delhi: Oxford University Press; 1983), see Chapter 1, "Negation," 1-45.
87. Chatterjee, "Gandhi &Critique of Civil Society," 183.
88. For an example of a counter interpretation see, Judith M Brown, *Gandhi's Rise to Power: Indian Politics 1915-1922*, is an extremely controversial analysis of early Gandhi's mobilizing motives and

principles.

89. Chatterjee, "Gandhi & Civil Society," 184-85.
90. Ibid., 186.
91. Ibid., 187.
92. Ibid, 187.
93. Ibid., 189.
94. Ibid., 193.
95. Ibid., 194-95.
96. To cite just one instance Majid Siddiqi's *Agrarian Unrest in North India*, as mentioned earlier in this essay, influenced from a critical Nationalist viewpoint had already suggested the expansion of the image of Gandhi in the peasant imagination as far back as 1978, three years before the first volume of *Subaltern Studies* came out.
97. "The Moment of Arrival: Nehru and the Passive Revolution," Chatterjee, *Nationalist Thought*, 131-66.
98. For an equally more controversial extension and elaboration on Nehru and the nature of the post-colonial Indian state as enshrined by the Congress (Gandhi, Nehru et al.) and the current state-of-play, see, Partha Chatterjee, *The Nation and its Fragments: Colonial and Post-Colonial Histories*, (Princeton, New Jersey: Princeton University Press, 1993).
99. See, Vinayak Chaturvedi ed. *Mapping the Subaltern and the Post-Colonial*, (London: Verso in arrangement with New Left Review, 2000), for exhaustive samples of the impact and debate generated by *Subaltern Studies* and analysts like Partha Chatterjee.
100. See Sumit Sarkar, 'Orientalism Revisited: Saidian Frameworks in the Writing of Modern Indian History,' *Oxford LiteraryReview*, XVI, 1-2, 1994, 205-24.
101. Ibid. 206-7, also see, Aijaz Ahmad, *In Theory* and James Clifford, 'Review Essay, *Orientalism* by Edward Said, *History and Theory* 19 (1980).
102. Ibid., 207-8.
103. Ibid., 210: "More than ten years ago, Ashis Nandy had sketched out the parameters of today's counter-orthodoxy in his *The Intimate Enemy*, a work with little overt Saidian influence that sought to justify and defend the *innocence* which confronted modern Western colonialism" [Italics by Sarkar]. Nandy's text particularly

appears to open up the nativist-nationalist intersection. See Ashis Nandy, *The Intimate Enemy: Loss and Recovery of the Self Under Colonialism* (New Delhi, Oxford University Press, 1983).

104. Sumit Sarkar, 'Orientalism Revisited,' 212.

105. Ibid. 213.

106. Ibid., 214.

107. Some of the rejoinders have specifically come from Gyan Prakash and Dipesh Chakrabarty, as detailed in earlier sections of this essay. See fn. 17, 19 & 25 above.

108. Rajeev Bhargava ed., *Secularism and its Critics*, (New Delhi: Oxford University Press, 1998).

Contributors

Akaitab Mukherjee is a Ph.D. Scholar in the Department of Humanities and Social Sciences at Indian School of Mines, Dhanbad (Bihar).

Dahood El-Oqla holds a Ph.D. in English and the Teaching of English from Idaho State University. His dissertation was on modern Arab-African literature, and his article "Postcolonial Identities: The Fragmented Self in Hisham Matar's *In the Country of Men*" appeared in *Journal of Contemporary Thought* 36 (Winter 2012). He is currently a full-time adjunct in the same department.

D.G. Digole teaches English at People's College, Nanded. He has obtained Ph.D. on Indian literature, adopting a comparative framework within regional languages and Indian English literature.

Diane Yerka received her M.A. degree in English from Idaho State University in 2013, completing a final project on Amitav Ghosh. She is currently an adjunct instructor in Idaho State University's English Department.

K. Balraj is a Research Scholar in the Department of Humanities & Social Sciences at JNTUH College of Engg. in Hyderabad

Kelly Meyer holds a Ph.D. in English and the Teaching of English from Idaho State University. She currently lives in Cambridge, Minnesota, and teaches writing and literature full time at Anoka-Ramsey Community College.

Parvathi V. is Associate Professor and Head of the Department of Humanities & Social Sciences at JNTUH College of Engg. in Hyderabad.

Pier Paolo Piciucco, Turin University, Italy, has expertise on Indian English fiction. He has delivered talks and published extensively in this area.

Priyanka Lamba is Associate Professor in the Department of English at Govt. P.G. Girls College in Gurgaon.

Rahul Jayaram is an Assistant Professor at the Jindal School of Liberal Arts & Humanities in Sonepat, Haryana. He holds multiple postgraduate degrees—in History from Jawaharlal Nehru University in New Delhi; Literature from the University of Edinburgh; and Journalism from Columbia University. He was a journalist for a decade and his work has appeared in most of India's major English language publications.

Dr. Rajni Singh is Associate Professor in the Department of Humanities and Social Sciences at Indian School of Mines, Dhanbad (Bihar).

Dr. Santwana Haldar retired from Odisha Govt. Service (OES-1), having performed her duties as Reader and Principal in different undergraduate and postgraduate colleges of Odisha. She has to her credit twelve published books of criticism and about one hundred articles in various national and international journals.

Dr. Sakunthala A.I. is Associate Professor of English at M.P.M.M.S.N.Trusts College, at Shoranur, Palakkad, Kerala. She has published a scholarly book entitled Image of Woman in the Fiction of Anita Desai and Margaret Atwood.

Shraddha Tripathi is an English language instructor at O.P. Jindal Global University, Sonepat (NCR).

Sushil Gupta from P.G.D.A.V. College, University of Delhi, is an eminent critic of fiction. Also, he is a creative writer and his novel *The Fourth Monkey* has been well received in literary circles.